Memories of Madagascar

and Slavery in the

Black Atlantic

Ohio University Research in International Studies

This series of publications on Africa, Latin America, Southeast Asia, and Global and Comparative Studies is designed to present significant research, translation, and opinion to area specialists and to a wide community of persons interested in world affairs. The editors seek manuscripts of quality on any subject and can usually make a decision regarding publication within three months of receipt of the original work. Production methods generally permit a work to appear within one year of acceptance. The editors work closely with authors to produce high-quality books. The series is distributed worldwide. For more information, consult the Ohio University Press website, ohioswallow.com.

Books in the Ohio University Research in International Studies series are published by Ohio University Press in association with the Center for International Studies. The views expressed in individual volumes are those of the authors and should not be considered to represent the policies or beliefs of the Center for International Studies, Ohio University Press, or Ohio University.

Memories of Madagascar and Slavery in the Black Atlantic

Wendy Wilson-Fall

Foreword by Michael A. Gomez

Ohio University Research in International Studies
Global and Comparative Studies Series No. 14
Ohio University Press
Athens

To obtain permission to quote, reprint, or otherwise reproduce or distribute material
from Ohio University Press publications, please contact our rights and permissions
department at (740) 593-1154 or (740) 593-4536 (fax).
www.ohioswallow.com

Printed in the United States of America

The books in the Ohio University Research in International Studies Series
are printed on acid-free paper ∞™

25 24 23 22 21 20 19 18 17 16 15   5 4 3 2 1

Library of Congress Cataloging-in-Publication Data
Wilson-Fall, Wendy, author.
 Memories of Madagascar and slavery in the Black Atlantic / Wendy Wilson-Fall ;
foreword by Michael A. Gomez.
   pages cm. — (Ohio University research in international studies, global and
comparative studies series ; No. 14)
 Includes bibliographical references and index.
 ISBN 978-0-8214-2192-5 (hc : alk. paper) — ISBN 978-0-8214-2193-2 (pb : alk. paper) —
ISBN 978-0-8214-4546-4 (pdf)
 1. Slavery—United States—History. 2. Slavery—Madagascar—History. 3. Slave
trade—United States—History. 4. Slave trade—Madagascar—History. 5. United
States—Relations—Madagascar. 6. Madagascar—Relations—United States. 7. African
diaspora. I. Title.
 E446.W69 2015
 306.3'6209691--dc23
                        2015030042

Contents

CHAPTER FOUR

After the American Revolution

Undocumented Arrivals

CHAPTER FIVE

Free, Undocumented Immigrants

CHAPTER SIX

The Problem of the Metanarrative

APPENDIX

Jeremiah Mahammitt's Malagasy Words

Illustrations

Maps

Foreword

To name a thing is a powerful act, with implications and consequences far reaching in nature, conveying for the named both meaning and purpose. Insofar as it concerns the human condition, it is a transformative event, by which the unknown travels a circuit of discovery, of intelligibility. But such a process also constitutes a beginning, at times in a literal sense, while always in a cognitive one. To name a thing is equally transactional, conveying import for both the one who names and the one who is named. To the degree that the name endures, the former achieves recognition as progenitor, a causal source in at least some sense, while the latter is given visibility. To these aspects of naming must be added its spatial quality, locating the one naming and the one named in mutual social relation. But such pursuit of nomenclature is also directional, as the name bestowed, whatever its meaning, provides a level of orientation. And direction, by its very definition—and notwithstanding its capaciousness—also has boundaries, a certain terminality, situating the one named relative to all and anyone else, delimiting the universe of possible permutations of experience.

Wendy Wilson-Fall's incisive book *Memories of Madagascar and Slavery in the Black Atlantic* is about the social and cultural properties and implications of naming and demonstrates that the more specific the naming, the more powerful and consequential the act. In following the story of the Malagasy in what becomes the United States, she succeeds in continuing to dismantle, piece by piece, the formerly unassailable notion of the improbable, the implausible, and the far-fetched as it relates to the originating experiences of African

Americans. And in advancing our understanding of those origins, she simultaneously underscores their heterogeneity, effectively making the point that the African American community issues from an array of geophysical points of departure.

Memories of Madagascar and Slavery in the Black Atlantic is an arresting example of how black folk collectively remember a past that extends centuries back in time, yet without benefit of written records or other forms of recorded documentation. It is a moving account of how families refuse to allow this special part of them to die, to go unrecognized, to be unnamed. It is an inquiry into insistence, reflecting a quiet, unshakable confidence of verities for which collaboration would be welcome, but in any event it is not to be confused with verification, for which there is no absolute need. The claim of Malagasy descent is a certainty, resting not in the testimony of the learned, nor reliant on the certification of the bureau, but rather very much grounded in an intergenerational transfer of information and family tradition that is self-authenticating. It is assertive in its position, unwavering in its conviction.

Deftly and masterfully employing the skills and insights of the social anthropologist, Wilson-Fall has produced an amazing account of the ways in which the traditions of families claiming such descent indeed interact with and connect to "history," to the written record of transoceanic voyages and enslavement and postemancipatory mercantile activity on an international scale. Carefully collecting and "listening" to multiple family traditions that have as their common thread the report of an ancestor from Madagascar, Wilson-Fall has undertaken the historical work of searching for the imprint of that ancestor in the ledgers of slavers and planters and runaway slave advertisements, and she has found it. The author limits her inquiry to North America, and more specifically the American South, where she has uncovered evidence for the importation of the Malagasy, evidence that comports well with the traditions of those families for whom Madagascar has long been recognized as a place of origin. But in narrowing the aperture, the author simultaneously draws attention to the fact that captives from Madagascar were distributed throughout the Americas by the thousands.

The more precise focus of *Memories of Madagascar and Slavery* is eighteenth-century Virginia, where some 1,450 Malagasy captives arrived between 1719 and 1721. Though sold in small parcels of several individuals upon disembarkation, Wilson-Fall's research indicates the majority remained geographically proximate to each other on farms and plantations along the York and Rappahannock Rivers, suggesting they would have been able to maintain degrees of social commerce, critical in that they were engulfed by African captives from elsewhere. Indeed, in the first twenty-five years of the eighteenth century, nearly thirty-eight thousand Africans are reported to have arrived in Virginia and Maryland, of which slightly over twenty-five hundred hailed from the Swahili coast, Madagascar, and possibly other Indian Ocean islands, representing a little over 6 percent of the Chesapeake's enslaved population. If the importation record for the whole of the eighteenth century is considered, the Malagasy contingent becomes entirely subsumed, representing even less of a fraction (less than 2 percent) of the slightly more than one hundred forty-two thousand Africans brought to the Chesapeake.[1] It is truly a wonder, therefore, that any memory of the Malagasy survives at all, and that it does necessitates explanation.

Part of that explanation lies in Wilson-Fall's skillful discussion of the period following Virginia's 1782 Manumission Act, when a number of freed persons, which would have included descendants of the Malagasy, ventured together into such towns as Petersburg and Hopewell in search of employment, where again they would have maintained social and cultural ties. But the positing of the Malagasy in the corporate recollection was not wholly dependent on constant renewal and replenishing of such ties, as the post-1808 domestic slave trade resulted in their movement to the Lower South, relocations very much embedded in family lore. To these migrants Wilson-Fall would add captives illegally transported into American territory, with many family traditions actually periodizing the arrival of their ancestors, specifying the 1830s and 1840s, circumstances made all the more plausible by the level of detail describing locations, individuals of relevance, and other circumstances.

That most of the Malagasy were women and children raises fascinating questions about how their memory may have been enshrined or otherwise elevated to levels sufficient to facilitate their recollection by descendants as well as others (as contemporaries making no claim to Malagasy ancestry nonetheless also remarked on their having passed this way). Wilson-Fall offers informed suggestions as to how mothers may have negotiated the concept of lineage and descent with, for example, Igbo fathers for whom patriliny may have been the norm. Such insistence on the part of mothers may well explain an ongoing, fervent embrace of Malagasy ancestry, but in any event *Memories of Madagascar and Slavery* attends to matters of gender in ways that provide depth and texture to what can otherwise often be flat and assumptive discussions of social and cultural relations among the enslaved.

But of course, another reason why the memory of the Malagasy would have been preserved concerns the theme of exceptionality, a matter Wilson-Fall addresses unflinchingly, though with acuity and dexterity. The Malagasy were everywhere described as phenotypically distinct from (other) Africans, with hair textures and facial features that garnered attention and commentary. Wilson-Fall is careful to explain that in a context of virulent racism, in which everything about the African was denigrated and disrespected, it is understandable that individuals and families with "atypical" characteristics would experience that difference in ways that brought a bit of relief from unrelenting disparagement. It may have been the case, she suggests, that the interest in Malagasy women living in towns was such that many entered concubinage, bearing children to white males, which further suggests that an ensuing free black population would have disproportionately reflected Malagasy ancestry.

That the Malagasy and their descendants would acknowledge if not embrace differences with the similarly oppressed is hardly surprising and fits well within a trope of exceptionality that can also be observed among African Muslims in the Americas, who were often enough viewed by the slaveholding class as separate from other Africans by virtue of their distinctive physical features as well as their religion.[2] African Muslims did not always internalize such divergence, but in enough cases they did, viewing themselves as a distinct community and separate from other Africans—even though they were all Africans, a construct whose meaning would become increasingly apparent over centuries. In contrast the Malagasy, though in some ways not unlike African Muslims, did intermingle with Africans and their descendants, such that their progeny do not claim Malagasy ancestry to the exclusion of other lines of descent, recognizing their heritage as multiple.

The examples of African Muslims as well as the Malagasy also make the point that the trope of exceptionality was not always or simply a response to racism, though it was performed within the context of New World slavery, but that differentiation often had origins in Old World settings, from where it was transferred to the Americas along with the captives themselves, where it underwent magnification and embellishment as a component of racial discourse. As such, the Hausa-Yoruba would emerge as a leading configuration in early nineteenth-century Bahia, reflecting a dynamic that began on the soils of what would become southwestern Nigeria; while the Kromanti ("Coromantee"), who would earn a reputation as the defiant ones in Jamaica and elsewhere in the Caribbean, issued out of conditions of conflict internal to what is now Ghana and Ivory Coast.

The intensification of differentiation among the enslaved and subsequently oppressed is therefore one of the more unsavory aspects of hierarchies of power organized along grids of racial and ethnic categorization, and it has had lasting effects. Even so, it is a marvel that, as Wilson-Fall reflects, individuals and families transported from one side of the world to the other would remember a specific place-name—Madagascar—without having any firm idea as to where it might be located. The embrace of Malagasy ancestry, in addition to its various social implications, therefore also speaks of a resolve, a determination to preserve human dignity—a human dignity with a face—with a name.

The record of the Malagasy held as slaves in the American South is remarkable enough, but their experience may not have been confined to processes of enslavement and manumission, as Wilson-Fall further reports that they may have also arrived in the first half of the nineteenth century in the United States as merchants and sailors, possibly as indentures. Again, this is based on family histories that maintain Malagasy ancestors were aboard American and British vessels as crew members, a development that could be related to the formation of such arrangements in South Africa, the latter possibility established through the author's research efforts.

By focusing on a particular formation—the Malagasy—*Memories of Madagascar and Slavery* also makes important conceptual and methodological interventions into the study of slavery and its aftermath. As to the former, one of the book's more striking innovations is an expansion on and elaboration of the concept of the shipmate. Heretofore understood to represent the bonding process of the Middle Passage, Wilson-Fall extends the notion to the final sale of persons in small parcels to individual families, after having experienced the transoceanic voyage with a largely homogeneous cohort. This "fourth great fracture," as she labels this final sale, followed the initial capture in Madagascar, embarkation, and disembarkation in Virginia. The effect of reconsidering the shipmate experience and lengthening its gestation is to emphasize an increasing sense of isolation among the Malagasy, countered by an intensification of the bond between those who remained together into the fourth phase, in turn heightening the sense of their uniqueness.

With respect to methodology, the historian can learn much from the author's approach, by which she produces, chapter by chapter, information on various aspects of the Malagasy presence as established or verified through conventional records and written testimony, followed by a discussion of the way in which the evidence maps onto those components of family tradition that relate most closely to the period and experience in question. The order of the process of relation and substantiation is revealing, inverting the customary progression of authentication by suggesting that it is the recorded evidence that is in need of oral tradition's verification, rather than the reverse. But more important, the method reflects the seriousness with which the author treats the family traditions. Standard indices constituting historical verity are provided in collaborative fashion, but familial collective memory is given at least equal weight.

In fact, it is indeed the family traditions that formed the basis, the reason, the impetus for the search for collaborative information. It is the family tradition that is the generative source as well as the connective tissue for the whole of the project, without which we have little save disaggregated, occasional references to a runaway "Madagascar" here and there. Their memorialization by subsequent generations is convincing testimony that they did not run in vain.

The historian typically approaches resolution of a problem through consultation with an archive of some sort, which has often already been organized in a fashion in anticipation of particular lines of inquiry, if not out of an interest in actually shaping that inquiry. As such, it is an artifice as well as an instrument of power, its collections emblematic of social and economic disparities implicit in the very process that determines what is preserved and what is discarded. To be sure, the circumstances and experiences, even the voices of the disenfranchised and marginalized, can be found there, the successful recovery of which is testimony to the expertise and dedication of the researcher so committed, as well as to ever-developing techniques designed to uncover such experiences, making it possible to read against the archive, extracting from it information often thought unobtainable.

In contrast, collective memory represents those persons and places and circumstances for whom and which the archive was not intended, serving as a counterbalance and corrective to what is regarded as official and authoritative. It addresses, in its own inimical way, that which the archive refuses to honor, speaking to the silences and ellipses and vacuities in the standard account. As such, it is inherently oppositional and highly resistant to efforts at policing its content and claims. It necessarily exists in the realm of the recalcitrant; indeed, it must inhabit uninhibited, lawless spaces into which authority is forbidden entry. Rather then a "subjugated knowledge," it is more of a parallel discourse, and as opposed to being policed by outsiders, it serves as its own sentinel over a past that would otherwise be readily denied and conveniently forgotten.

In this way, the realm of the familial recollection is critical to the pursuit of the African American experience. There remain many accounts of forebears both enslaved and free, born in Africa or the Americas or elsewhere, whose inclusion into the aggregate investigation of the past would add considerable detail and shed much needed additional light on the sojourn and travail of black folk in the Americas. However, such stories and information tend to travel only interior circuits of familial exchange. In some instances the exclusivity of the traditions may indeed be with all intentionality, but there are other traditions not so restricted, and simply have not been afforded serious attention. They have no one with whom to share their information, there is no one listening. In the United States alone, given the African American population, such circuitries must range in the thousands, if not even more.

By tapping into these circuitries and taking them seriously, Wendy Wilson-Fall has shown the way to begin accessing such accounts, offering a method by which to bring such parallel discourses into conversation with conventional means of understanding the past. As such, her work may well prove to be a major new avenue through which knowledge of the African American experience can travel. To be sure, reasons for sheltering family lore would include an unwillingness to subject what is precious to the scrutiny of a process that can be indifferent, callous, and even hostile. But there is so much to learn, and so much to gain, as *Memories of Madagascar and Slavery* demonstrates. Wendy Wilson-Fall has produced an exquisite rendering of a process spanning thousands of miles and hundreds of years. We do well to emulate her example.

Michael A. Gomez
November 2014
New York

Acknowledgments

An endeavor such as this volume cannot be achieved without the support, goodwill, and shared knowledge that characterizes a vibrant community of scholars. I would like to begin, therefore, by acknowledging my gratitude toward the scholars of Indian Ocean studies and African diaspora studies who helped me on the journey of this book's realization. The hospitality that these scholars offered me, via suggestions for sources, reading drafts, and countless discussions, reflects the warmth and enthusiasm typical of the scholarly milieu of African studies in our era.

This book would not have been possible without the generous correspondence and suggestions of Dr. Lorena Walsh and others of the Williamsburg Colonial Foundation. In addition to the critical input from Dr. Walsh, I received a fellowship from the Williamsburg Colonial Foundation that allowed me uninterrupted time to do research at the Rockefeller Library and the libraries of the College of William and Mary.

Professor and scholar Sulayman Nyang was perhaps the first to discuss the project with me and to join Sheila Thomas and myself on an early field trip to rural Maryland. Thanks to Professor Nyang, and to Professor Robert Edgar of Howard University for his observations on Cape Town and his facilitation of contact between Malagasy researchers and the Gregory clan. My gratitude is also expressed here to historian Michael Gomez, who commented on my ideas for the research and offered me encouragement in the first stages of the project. Paul Finkelman, from the Albany Law School, was very helpful and made me think harder about the effects of the post-1808 illegal slave trade to the United States. Thanks to Mustafa Toure and Moulaye Keita of Dakar, Senegal, for research assistance, and to Judith Scales Trent, Alice Morton, Sylviane Diouf, Michael Lambek, and Erin Augis for readings of earlier versions. Pier Larson, Richard B. Allen, and James Armstrong were encouraging and generous in their commentaries and guidance to sources. I also thank Joseph Miller and fellow partici- pants for fruitful hours at the National Endowment for the Humanities "Roots" seminar at the University of Virginia in 2007. Special thanks must go to the anonymous reviewers' excellent critiques and sugges- tions, to the editors at Ohio University Press, and to Director Gillian Berchowitz for her faith in this project and her expert advice. I thank Mary Ann French, Jennifer Yanco, and Christine McVay, who kept me working for better ways to say what I sought to share. Thanks also to the Morgan family for the use of their ancestor's image for the book.

This volume was preceded by a monograph that was the result of a memorable and unique scholar-community collaboration that took place in Ashland, Virginia, with the assistance of Professor Reber Dunkel of Randolph-Macon College, local historian Ann Cross, and the Clark, Winston, and Gordon families of Ashland and Hanover, Virginia. Through their efforts we received support from the Virginia Foundation for the Humanities, the Hanover County Black Heritage Society, and the Hanover County Historical Society to put on an excit- ing community event that brought diverse people together who shared a common history and the desire to learn more about the state's ties to Madagascar. Dr. Diedre Badejo assured support from Kent State Uni- versity's Department of Pan-African Studies. At the Library of Con- gress, Joanne Zeller took the initiative to organize our Madagascar ancestor workshop. Likewise, the librarians at the Mariners' Museum in Newport News, Virginia, were of immense help. The Embassy of Madagascar staff, particularly Eulalie Ravelosoa, were consistently interested and supportive collaborators, and provided an invitation to the Gordon, Clark, and Winston descendants to the embassy for meaningful and fraternal evenings of discussion and Malagasy hospi- tality. My gratitude is here expressed to them, as well as to colleagues at the National Archives, and at the University of Antananarivo, in Madagascar, particularly to Dr. Julie Ratsimandrara, chair at the Center for Language Study of the Malagasy Academy.

Among those who have been critical to my understanding of Madagascar, Emmanuel Tehindrazanarivelo, is here sincerely acknowledged for his insightful and challenging discussions, his critical input in field trips in Madagascar and Frederick, Maryland, and his leadership in the Library of Congress sponsored Malagasy Ancestors project. Michael Lambek, Gwyn Campbell, and other colleagues at the Madagascar Workshop at the University of Toronto were very helpful in offering their commentaries and remarks on a working paper on the subject. My thanks also go to my maternal aunt Sheila Thomas, who led the way in the Mahomet family history research, followed by journalist and Columbia University professor and cousin, June Cross. I am indebted to librarians at the Virginia Historical Society, the Albert and Shirley Small Special Collections Library at the University of Virginia and at the Library of Congress, including but not limited to Angel Baptiste and Joanne Zeller. I extend my thanks to members of the Washington, D.C. Genealogical Association, and countless others who shared their stories with me. Finally, the completion of this work would not have been possible without the critical support and stimulating scholarly discussions of Andrea Smith, Ana Luhrs, and other colleagues at Lafayette College, where I have received funds for the completion of the manuscript and, as important, intellectual sustenance. I would like to acknowledge John Clark, data visualization GIS librarian of Skillman Library, for his expertise and discussions about maps, geography, and databases. My thanks go out to all of you, and to all the participants in this project, which has stretched over many years and many miles. I apologize for the unintended omission of any particular person who has helped me along the way.

I am very grateful for the awesome patience of my sons, Aziz, Pap Souleye, and Habib. They encouraged me through all phases of the research and book and gave me the space to think and write even as they engaged me with their own projects. They have been, as always, an inspiration.

Introduction

A Particular Ancestral Place

IN 1796 A WOMAN, reported to be a slave, managed to bring a court case regarding her captivity in Maryland. In the case, *Negro Mary v. The Vestry of William and Mary's Parish* of October 1, 1796, the petitioner claimed to be the daughter of a woman who had been captured in Madagascar a generation before, enslaved in North America on her arrival. It is astounding, from a contemporary point of view, that a woman slave in 1796 would be so well informed regarding British law. Nevertheless, on the basis of the former status of her mother, the enslaved woman in Maryland argued that she should be set free. Madagascar, she said, "was not a place from which slaves [usually] were brought." Her point of view was that Madagascar, and thus Malagasy people, should not be considered as legally imported labor, as in the normal course of the slave trade. It was true that under the New East India Act of 1721, American colonists could no longer legally obtain East India goods unless through Britain, or bring slaves from East India region ports.[1] Unfortunately for Mary, the judge ruled that she could be set free only if she could provide documentation of the original status of her mother. Having thus responded, the judge cleverly avoided the question of whether "out-of-bounds" slavery in Madagascar was a sufficient charge for changing slave status. He knew it would have been exceedingly uncommon for a person such as the enslaved plaintiff to produce papers documenting her claim.[2] Furthermore, the court argued that since it was known that "petty provinces" in Madagascar made war on each other to produce slaves for the European

1

trade, they should normally fall under the same classification as slaves from the African continent.[3]

The case described above gives evidence of the sense of difference that may have been common among Malagasy slaves brought to the English colonies of North America and their compatriots who arrived after independence in the years before the Civil War. The fact that an enslaved woman in Maryland somehow had the wherewithal to take her petition for freedom to the court is remarkable; the fact that she called on her identity as a descendant of a Malagasy goes against most popular assumptions that a first-generation slave in the North American colonies would *not* identify by a parent's pre-capture ethnicity, or "tribal" affiliation. Consequently, exploration of the conditions that would produce such an event can potentially tell us more about the process of creolization that took place on American plantations and more specifically, the experience of descendants of Malagasy slaves in that process.

In the following pages I have taken on the challenge of exploring the conditions that might have created or allowed a "Negro Mary," or any self-identified Malagasy descendant who had slave or free progenitors in what has become the United States of America, to invoke Madagascar as a signifier of difference. This book was therefore written with the intention of contributing to the study of African diaspora communities in the Americas as well as the study of Malagasy diasporas. It presents an example of how Malagasy captives got caught up in the nexus of two major slaving networks of the modern era: the Indian Ocean and transatlantic slave trades. The Indian Ocean island of Madagascar stood at the intersection of these two systems, and the island furnished slaves at various times to the Indian Ocean world as well as to the Americas.

The dispersal of people from Madagascar throughout the Indian Ocean is well known, but little scholarly attention has been directed toward the trade of captives from Madagascar to the Americas.[4] Thousands of slaves from Madagascar were exported to American ports, from Argentina to Canada, and the trade lasted from the seventeenth into the nineteenth century.[5] One of the destinations of Malagasy captives during the eighteenth century was the Commonwealth of Virginia. Later, during the nineteenth century, Malagasy contract laborers, merchants, sailors, and slaves traveled to American ports and eventually became part of black communities.

Though my intent is to open a door on one aspect of the New World slave experience that helps us better understand local histories of African Americans, these stories are also part of a larger history of the relationship of North America to the Indian Ocean. This relationship started during the era of pirates, in the seventeenth century, and peaked much later, in the second half of the nineteenth century, with Yankee traders and the pull of the spice trade, British maritime expansion and control of the "Indies," and the establishment of American diplomatic and commercial representation at Majunga (Mahajanga), in northwestern Madagascar, in the 1820s. Official consulates later served the United States in Antananarivo, in central Madagascar, in the late nineteenth century.

The narratives are discussed in the context of the era of the transatlantic slave trade and shortly thereafter, focusing on the period between 1719 (when large numbers of Malagasy slaves were imported into the Commonwealth of Virginia) and 1850 (when there were still incidents of foreign slave smuggling into mainland America, and indentured servants arriving to the Americas from the Indian Ocean region).[6] After 1850 (and until the mid-twentieth century), most Malagasy people who arrived in the United States or Europe were either Christian refugees traveling under the auspices of church missionary societies or sailors on steamships, and that history is beyond the scope of the present volume. This volume begins with the rash of entrepreneurial forays to the western Indian Ocean carried out by American colonists and ends in the period when Britain was a major maritime power and the War of 1812 was past.

For this story of Malagasy slaves and early immigrants to the Americas, I draw on two kinds of sources: historical documentation and contemporary narratives of remembrance of ancestors from Madagascar. In order to take full advantage of these two compelling but disparate ways of looking at history, the book has a rather unusual approach to treating the historical and ethnographic material gathered in the course of research. In order to make clear which information is drawn from documented historical accounts or from family oral tradition, chapters begin with a review of the available information in the historical record and are followed by a section devoted to family oral traditions and their analysis, presenting ethnographic commentary on the style, content, and uses of these narratives.

The text suggests the possibility that slaves and early free-black immigrants from Madagascar, as well as their descendants in Virginia and a few other places in the American South, remembered, reinvented, and imagined a particular geographic site they held in common. It is also about the pervasive sense of loss that contemporary families express about their separation from an ancestral geography that is symbolized, for them, by a specific ancestor from a specific place. I explore ethnic negotiation and identity formation among Malagasy newcomers to North America and their Afro-Malagasy, creole descendants by drawing on family narratives that are woven from memories and stories passed down by successive generations. With family ideas of a particular ancestral place came an allegiance to a particular history and to an inheritance of stories that describe a sense of difference from other families, and other stories, in the African American community.

My intent is to provide a reflection on the process of creolization that led to African American identity by following one strand: the legacy of slaves and early free immigrants from Madagascar. Whether the legacy I mention above is direct descent or creations of assumed genealogies, it is a received notion deriving from ideas and thoughts of Madagascar. The approach here is not statistical but rather focuses on historical context and memory. It addresses the problem of family historical narratives as received testimonies of a past that has been embroidered and otherwise transformed in narratives stretching over successive generations. The meaning of narratives of Madagascar is explored, therefore, as an example of the complexity of memory work as it affects group identity.

Identity and the Question of Authenticity

It is a difficult, almost impossible enterprise to corroborate the genealogies suggested in the stories collected, because there are few existing
records linking any Malagasy slave or early immigrant with particular African American descendants, although there are many African
Americans who claim Malagasy descent, as "Negro Mary" did. There
is, thus, a dialogue that continues throughout this volume between
ethnographic analysis of the storytellers and their narratives, on one
hand, and historical documentation, on the other. Today's family narratives, as I see them, are not a recent response to public memory
enterprises but, on the contrary, are built on remnants and recon-
structions of much earlier narratives.[7]

Family oral traditions offer a unique way of understanding how
people experience history. The archives, which offer multiple sources of
slave lists, do not reveal the transition that most slaves or early black immigrants experienced between their ethnic identities and their newly ap-
pointed racial identities. For example, while names are by nature meant
to identify (a person, a thing), in the case of slaves they also hid, or even
erased, personal identities. In North America once the slave received a
name—his or her "slave name"—that person's past identity and place
of origin was effectively lost to future generations, because African and
Malagasy names suggested linguistic or ethnic origin. Moreover, origin as
a criterion of reference quickly went into disuse by slave owners (usually
with the first country-born generation). If a document such as a diary
or journal ever recorded the naming of individuals in a group of slaves
from Madagascar, then the descendants of each slave might yet be trace-
able in plantation records. Unfortunately, no such record has yet been
found, and records of this sort are notoriously rare for any slaves in North
America. Moreover, slaves coming to the Americas generally could not
read or write in English and rarely in Arabic[8] and, thus, did not leave
their own written records. This fact seems apparent, but the simplicity of
this problem has often led to its invisibility, particularly for those outside
the academy who want to understand or contribute to African American discourse on identity, such as the descendants of slaves. Nor has the

existence of African American stories of Malagasy ancestors been common knowledge. It is not surprising, then, that this is the first scholarly publication to attempt to situate ancestor stories of Madagascar told by contemporary African Americans in a historical context.

It is always difficult to find material evidence that demonstrates the accuracy of oral histories in the case of illiterate societies, and this is especially true of disempowered communities. How does one corroborate an oral tradition that has been passed down by a repressed minority? In this case, I have chosen to present such narratives chronologically so that historical evidence provides a background, even though there are few documents that directly substantiate Malagasy origins. But family oral-history narrators do seek to tell a chronologically based story, and the purpose of the story is to frame the present in relation to the past, specifically, a shared family past. This chronological feature exposes a desire for coherence and logic—an attempt to order the past, to signal what should be remembered and, hence, to give meaning to the present.

The infamous Middle Passage was not long enough for people to forget who they were: the average time from West Africa across the Atlantic was two and a half to three months, and from the western Indian Ocean about three months more. Over generations, people did forget much about where they came from, and it must be imagined that remembrance was in many ways painful and underlined the powerlessness people felt. Yet if family oral history is any indication, then within the cultural aggregate that has been the African American community, traces of ethnic particularities from diverse sources and very specific experiences remain in perpetually new and ever-changing configurations, for example, as embodied practices, as folk tales, or family historical narratives. The Madagascar example, based on a less known minority population among North American slave imports, provides circumstantial evidence of how ethnic or national clusters from Africa and its islands responded to the imperative to integrate into existing black communities, enslaved or free, in the New World.

My research has shown that authenticity is not a concern of the family oral narrative insomuch as families accept that they are not pure Malagasy, but do argue that they are of Malagasy descent. Their focus, which they clearly admit, is on their identities as people of a mixed heritage that *includes* an ancestor from Madagascar. This is an aspect of the narratives that is approached in various ways throughout the book, as we seek to understand why the "Madagascar" lineage was remembered or otherwise noted, especially in contrast to other less visible or forgotten stories, such as those on continental African descent. This book is thus not a project in search of "lost authenticity" but of offering a context for a particular kind of family oral tradition through exploring the historical record.[9] For understanding the internal significance of the Malagasy lineage and thus the Malagasy story, I turn to ethnography and discussions in anthropology on memory and identity.[10]

In contrast to archival materials, family oral traditions give a sense of the tension and displacement experienced by slave descendants. I find that the practice of the family narrative is intentional; its purpose is to transfer information. However, the family oral narrative depends principally on memory, unlike professionally written histories as we know them today. The problem of understanding the past through family oral histories lies in a gray area between memory, mnemonic behaviors, and available historical evidence.

Recent historical research has pioneered alternative ways of looking at slaves who arrived in the New World, and this volume draws on these new theoretical perspectives and findings.[11] We know that when enslaved captives arrived on American shores, they did not yet see themselves as simply "black" people or Africans. We can take the narrative of Olaudah Equiano, known also as Gustavus Vassa, as an example.[12] There has been considerable debate regarding whether Equiano was indeed born in Africa and transported as a youth on a slave ship, or born in the Caribbean of Ibo parents, or born in South Carolina. Nevertheless, any reading of his history gives evidence of the importance of ethnicity to Equiano's own story of himself. He spoke of himself as a displaced Ibo person and as an African.[13] Paul Lovejoy, for instance, in "Olaudah Equiano or Gustavus Vassa—What's in a Name?" suggests that the methodological issues regarding the Equiano debate relate to how historians engage oral tradition and literary custom with the archival record.[14] This volume addresses issues of the Equiano debate, suggesting there is a reasonable probability that most, if not all, of the family narratives derive from a family history linked to the slave cohort of the eighteenth century or slaves smuggled into the United States in the nineteenth century. It also suggests that contemporary family narratives of free Malagasy immigrants likely stem from accounts of lived experiences. As with Equiano, there are no written sources to lend credibility to a claimed identity that precedes the American experience. However, I am most interested in what importance the narratives have for the people who use and recite them. I am less concerned with proving that they are "true," because the written documentation necessary to make that claim has not been found and perhaps was never written.

In the case of the nascent African American community of the eighteenth century, the racial concept of "black" people in America as a new, homogeneous group was being constructed at the same time that various Europeans acquiesced to new identities of being "white" and American. Later, in the early days of the republic and particularly in the mid-nineteenth century, prior national or ethnic origins were to have little public meaning for those blacks born on American soil. In response to the problems of understanding past black identities, some African American genealogical narratives are presented here as a way to explore how some people today imagine and remember their ancestry beyond being "black" or "mixed" in the United States, where laws governing racial identity have been strictly applied until very recently.

The contradiction implicit in adjusting to a new, despised identity while holding on to an older, more dignified one applies to early immigrants of African and Malagasy descent as well as to slaves. For example, the particular ethnic or national identity of (nonwhite) sailors who "jumped ship" or otherwise opted to remain in America, and of black women who arrived as personal servants to white families (discussed in chapter 4) was rarely registered by customs or immigration offices due to the very nature of their arrival. They were most often registered simply as "black sailor" or "black servant." In the mid-nineteenth century, most whites had very little understanding of

African ethnicities and perceived African difference as tribal, savage, and primitively formed. Such identities were deemed irrelevant, if not an obstacle, to being an American. Blacks rightfully assumed that public discourse on African identities would not suit their cause for citizenship. Within the black community, insistence on difference was not highly appreciated and sometimes perceived as antisocial. Unity was the most important operational theme.

African and Malagasy identities, first and foremost, were shaped by language, custom, and geography, and from Madagascar, as elsewhere, captives arrived with particular language and ethnic affiliations. Their first allegiances were to their lineages, their clans, and their ethnic groups. Among those who came to North America, the most numerous were the Ibo and related groups; the Wolof and other Senegambian ethnicities such as the Bambara, Mande, or Diola; and people from Central Africa, notably the kingdoms of Kongo and Ngola. People from the island of Madagascar, from Mozambique, or from the Yoruba city-states were distinct minorities in North America. Most knowledge of these affiliations did not last into the nineteenth century, yet some slaves held on to family lore that described their origins, even while they were busy becoming creoles.

A black person who arrived in North America in the nineteenth century, whether as a captive or as a free person, had to perform two identities simultaneously: one that acquiesced to the general category of black and one that enlisted various strategies to hold on to an identity that essentially was covert. This basic tension has always been at the heart of the African American experience and is perhaps what led W. E. B. DuBois to his thesis of double consciousness.[15] Narratives from descendants of early free immigrants show that Madagascar receded into a sometimes glorified past and was usually discussed only in the home and among relatives, as people quickly sought to live and possibly even prosper in the segregated black community.

Identity is relational and depends to a great extent on how one is perceived, to what extent cultural norms are shared between self and others, and opportunities to externalize beliefs about one's self, one's community, and even the universe. Without the opportunity to act on personal beliefs and morals, for example, or to speak one's language, many behaviors that were once normal become extravagance in a new setting. Since African and Malagasy societies perceived the individual as an expression of group identity, involuntary separation from one's group in violent circumstances must have presaged an acute identity crisis and an existential conflict, as it would for any person in such events.[16] In looking at the problem of culture, power and place, identities, like the contents of cultures themselves, are historically contingent. Identities are not simply affected by changing schemes of categorization, or discourses of difference, but may be actually constituted or interpolated by them,[17] and thus epistemological differences (and ontological shifts) are a lived experience. The case of a self-ascribed Malagasy identity must be examined in this context.

Oral Traditions and Family Narratives

The practice of the narrative in the twenty-first century is as much a result of a community experience of the eighteenth and nineteenth centuries—including public acknowledgment within the African American community of a "Malagasy," "Madagasco," or "Madacasar" identity—as it is the result of individual proclivities, fashion, or personal design. The numbers of slaves on the ships, the dates and conditions of sale, of transfer by inheritance, and even of escape appear in planters' correspondence, account books, and newspapers. What does not appear so clearly is the human qualities of the slaves, which have been preserved in oral traditions. Similarly, in the case of free arrivals, the circumstances of the alliances they formed or contracts they signed that brought them to America are not referred to in great detail in the narratives. The fact that this information is absent in all the narratives of free immigrants suggests a common theme.

The narrative of the ancestor is a story intended for a lineage, even though that lineage might have been partially fictive. In the threatened black communities of the eighteenth and nineteenth centuries, siblings may have shared one mother and had different fathers or some other variation of household kinship. Repetition over generations signifies nevertheless the oral tradition's importance to family as an important tale to be told. The centrality of the family as the source of, and often the only place to assume, a Malagasy descendant identity gives evidence of a sort of household-level or extended-family project of self-identification. This sort of family identity is layered and complex. Moreover, each narrative suggests a reading of social and symbolic space (where and when narratives are recited and by whom) in relation to continuously reassembled information that has traveled through generations, in the sense in which Pierre Bourdieu talks of symbolic social space, the variability of positionality through time, and cultural capital.[18] This always contemporary performance nevertheless reconstitutes a past sense of urgency for listeners because the information is shared in order that it not be forgotten.

Each ancestor from Madagascar serves a symbolic function as a claim to humanity that predates and survives the calamities of captivity, enslavement, and exile. In this case, the symbolic space to which I refer is not Bourdieu's referent of class but an ethnicity claimed and possibly reified—and certainly sanctified as a special and impermeable quality that each family holds. The ancestor narrative's dynamic quality derives from its function as more unconscious ideology than physicality, more metaphysical than biological, and is part of family cultural repertoire and its cultural capital. This function is addressed in the concluding chapter, which discusses how history is learned through reenactment and stories or lived in traumatically induced and transmitted narratives, and in the moral character of memory.

A neat line from a specific Malagasy village to the early captives who came to America or from those captives to the people who tell their story today cannot be drawn. Most details of slave ancestors' lives before captivity have been lost, if they were ever transmitted, as discussed above. The narratives show an internal struggle and dialogue whose main forum was the slave community or the segregated black community. Though the narratives are told through the aegis of the family, it is also useful to consider the possible meanings of the aggregate of families who share this practice of storytelling to question the metanarrative, the possible overall meaning of the narratives as a collection of stories. The subject of this book is, therefore, not the biography of an individual or individuals, but rather an attempt to describe a disparate group of people with common origins and common practices. It is a sort of ethnographic biography of an experience.

Commenting on Michael Lambek's essay on remembering as moral practice, Maurice Bloch observes that there are instances where "questions of individual memory are developed by means of a public idiom and conversely the memory burdens of individuals contribute to the reproduction of that idiom and its ability to continue to commemorate the past [in Madagascar]."[19] This description could also describe others' cultural practices, such as those whose stories are in this volume. Their family narratives seem to be about, and used by, a network of families and are in fact sustained by such networks. In fact, the stories defy biological logic. They supersede the intricate mathematics of subdivision in genetic histories. If such beliefs are not based on the force of physical proof or on the evidence of an essentialist self-view of purity, what is the logic of their persistence? Do these narratives also have some moral functions? The answer to these questions is the main theme of this book.

Ethnographies and History

The work of memory is not the same as the work of history, for memory follows its own purposes and logic, focusing on selected events and discarding others. Memory exists in a fluctuating personal dialogue between what was and what is. Consciously or unconsciously, a story may be changed according to the narrator's relation to the past or to the present. The work of history, on the other hand, is consciously intentional. It represents a concerted effort to bring together different kinds of material evidence to demonstrate that an event, or series of events, occurred. In writing on the subject of African American family stories about ancestors from Madagascar, I have sought to engage the thorny issue of the oral narrative as memory and as history. As I suggest earlier, this volume is characterized by the tension that exists between the oral historical narrative, on the one hand, and written histories and the archive, on the other. This book necessarily employs an interdisciplinary approach, using history and ethnography, to look at family oral narratives in a historical context.

My intention has not been to write a history of early Malagasy arrivals in the United States but rather to present diverse stories together in historical context and to fashion a picture of the larger story that this assembly creates. The discussion in this volume, thus, is not based on past quotes from written slave narratives and autobiographies (although a few will be included) but on contemporary claims, collected over the last two decades, to Malagasy descent among African American families. Their stories are often frustratingly shallow and lacking in detail and description. Yet, the bare quality of these testimonies is itself a marker of the conditions under which the stories originated and were passed down. The silences speak loudly of the limited social space and time that was available for first-generation descendants to learn about the country of their mothers or fathers.

As the narratives themselves show, their recollection and performance is a practice that continually enhances family solidarity and, thus, individual rootedness. The pronounced interiority of these performances (limited to home and family) underlines their value as a source of joy and wonder that should be protected. The wonder is that the ancestor survived to tell the tale; the joy is that the current generation works at the survival of the tale itself and thereby on the continued commemoration of the ancestor. Their stories serve as both history and entertainment because the story finishes in the present generation, to be later embellished and modified by coming generations. The profane of today becomes the sacred of tomorrow.

Global history is the not the only form suitable for recounting the past in a globalized world, and as Natalie Zemon Davis has stated, "local storytelling" may serve a global program toward decentering the mainstream historical narrative.[20] By tracing a series of local stories about Madagascar and using primary sources, I demonstrate that first-person testimonies and other historical accounts can be employed to expand the view of a local situation to its global causes.[21] In this way the reader's attention can be drawn to the potential that local histories of slaves can bring to understanding early modern global dynamics.[22] These considerations are primary concerns addressed in this volume: how local stories lead to global histories and how ethnography can complement and stimulate new perspectives of and questions regarding the historiographic project.

Historic research has contributed a great deal to furthering our understanding of slave communities in the Americas. Earlier ethnographic overemphasis on "remaining" or "surviving" cultural traits among slave descendants probably led to the failure among earlier scholars to read instances of the dynamic creolization and hybridization processes that took place from the seventeenth through the eighteenth centuries, which entailed various African responses to plantation and urban culture in colonial America.[23] Searches for "Yoruba culture" or "Wolof practices" have in some ways prevented us from seeing the nuances that actually tell a far more succinct story. However limited they may have been, early ethnographic studies of New World African diaspora communities were, however, critical in drawing scholarly attention to the presence of a rich field of inquiry that had previously been obfuscated by racism in and out of the academy.

Early on, sociological and anthropological studies of African American communities in North America argued that discernible evidence of particular "national" cultural traits or ethnic affiliations were no longer in evidence by the time of emancipation. This view was particularly true of the African American sociologist E. Franklin Frazier, who argued that no discernible, particularly African-derived behaviors existed, and that "American Negroes" by and large practiced a culture that was a successful synthesis of African and European cultures, with an overwhelming prevalence of western European culture.[24] The anthropologist Melville Herskovits disagreed and argued that even though no direct evidence of specific African cultures or ethnic groups was present, an aggregate African-derived culture had resulted from the importation of slaves from various parts of the continent, and this aggregate presented what could be considered a New World African cultural dynamic based on African-originated practices in religion, the arts, and family structure.[25] In the 1970s, anthropologists Sidney Mintz and Richard Price introduced a more dynamic model. They stressed the amalgamation of various African influences and the invention of a new Atlantic Afro-American culture, which, by virtue of the conditions of its development in various slave societies, had some discernible African traits that could be identified, but in new forms of expression.[26]

Beyond the African creolization and African hybridized cultural core discussed by Mintz and Price, both respectively and together, lies a territory that is increasingly being explored and illuminated through research in African history and the transatlantic slave trade.[27] The recent burst of intellectual productivity of Africanist and Americanist historians has shown that for any given slave environment a continuum of more or less African continental cultural expression could be found, due to the constant arrival of new slaves, which continued in some places up to the mid-nineteenth century. Scholars have recently demonstrated that chronology, geography, and demographics have everything to do with what cultural syncretizations or borrowings did or did not take place in New World African diaspora communities.[28] The present volume draws on this perspective of ethnic and identity transformation over time as impacted by such factors as geography and settlement patterns.

Specific information on points of embarkation and arrival has allowed new perspectives and greater understanding of the formation of the African diaspora communities of the Atlantic. We now know that trade and credit networks affected who went where and thus had much to do with the sorts of African cultural practice and cultural negotiation that took place in any given American site.[29] Recent scholarly work argues for close attention to the dynamic and synergetic nature of slave identities in the New World.[30] Increased research on New World slave cultures in the eighteenth and nineteenth centuries has revealed that not only regional differences and differences in plantation regime but also differences of management style and local social practices among planters had much to do with the evolving character of slave communities.[31] For example, Robert "King" Carter in colonial Virginia had the tendency to purchase and settle "lots" of slaves led to cultural clusters of slaves from common or proximate cultural origins.[32]

Paying attention to local narrative and slave demographic patterns suggests posing questions concerning what African ethnic differences may have meant in plantation life, and the use of archival materials to evaluate social processes that characterized slave life from the point of view of their cultural lives, rather than the cultural universe of their masters.[33] At the same time, it is important to recognize that there was significant cultural borrowing between black slaves and their masters.[34] My book draws on both concerns, as the settlement of Malagasy slaves was dictated by the labor needs of the white families who owned them, and their cultural experience was dictated by their relationships with those whites and other Africans and creoles that whites owned. These issues were critical to understanding the processes of layering and hybridization that characterized the founding slave communities of the Americas.[35]

It is thus not a question of choosing between the creole (Mintz and Price) versus "pure" African (Herskovits) continuity arguments, but rather of assessing which framework best relates to specific contexts *through time*. My thesis is, then, that if any African, Malagasy, or other specific cultural practices, memories, or material-culture expressions remain in any observable form, they are to be found in the contrast of their specificity to the general creole nature of African American self-definition and practices through time.

The Madagascar example, ironically, is from outside the African continent. Yet this difference in geography provides an important example of self-definition that may tell us more about the processes of rapid and deep change that characterized African American experiences in the eighteenth and nineteenth centuries. The continued arrival of "saltwater" Negroes into already creolized communities and the paucity of archival evidence of specific African responses to the communities they encountered in New World societies make ethnohistoric analysis of this layering and integrative process difficult, if not impossible. It is noteworthy, however, that what is important to the oral narratives of slave descendants is often not what was important to early chroniclers of the American slave experience.

Collection and Analysis of the Stories

This study is more concerned with community experience and less focused on individuals, as my starting point is groups of people who arrived on ships, and the text continues with groups of people and their stories. The individual testimonies are about family groups and communities; they are narratives about the collective. In fact, seldom did any story confine itself to the life of the narrator. The social and cultural currency the narratives represent is to be brought out, admired, and shared among fellow believers and family members.

I have used a wide lens to examine images of capture, slavery, and constraining conditions for free blacks in the early part of the nineteenth century as recounted by families today and as represented in the historical literature. Though some of the stories I collected are little more than anecdotes, their existence is important and merits serious inquiry. Life stories or individual oral histories would have been insufficient to the project of understanding the larger issues of the origins and persistence of practice of these family narratives. This monograph proceeds, therefore, from the viewpoint of a historical ethnography of a group experience. It is a study of how and why some people resisted simply being "negroes" or "blacks," or even to be dominated by other African ethnic groups. I have sought to understand how some families instead fashioned a composite, layered identity of being "negroes" who were also, in some primordial way, children of people from Madagascar.

As a social anthropologist, I have relied on ethnographic method in my interactions with various families and individuals and the Internet to maintain and sometimes sustain communication. As much as possible I have used historical context to weave many disparate threads together. What is to be learned from the emerging tapestry of texts can be gleaned neither solely from the substantive matter of the stories nor from the documented histories of slaves and slaveholders in Virginia. There is a lot to be learned from what was not said, both in the archives and the family stories, the emotional textures of what was remembered with pride or with shame, as well as the ideas that are repeated both within each narrative and among the narratives as a body. At times, I used my own African American identity to dig down to emotions and my own memories of hearing "the old folks talk" in order to extrapolate what the slave experience might have been and how the early immigrants might have felt. My mother's great-grandfather is claimed as a Malagasy ancestor, so I have mined my own childhood experience of hearing that story for a notion of how to behave when listening to others' stories.

The material in the book is drawn from a collection of some thirty family narratives gathered over an extended period of time from face-to-face interviews, e-mails, focus group interviews, and telephone conversations. On a few occasions I learned that I had interviewed two or three people who were actually from the same core family group. The narrators are generally self-selected; they are all people who self-identify as descended from either an enslaved Malagasy person who arrived in the American South or a very early free immigrant from Madagascar. It seems that word of my research quickly spread among online communities, and at least a third of the stories I followed up on came to me via genealogy sites or direct e-mails from people who were interested in my work. The fact that I set up a website on the topic was surely important in helping me gain access to personal stories about "Madagascar ancestors."[36]

I was also aided in my analysis of oral and written narratives by public responses to lectures I gave on my research over the years.[37] Some testimonies are from genealogical sites, where queries about Malagasy ancestors occur with surprising frequency—both on Afro-centered genealogical websites such as *afrigeneas.com* (run from Mississippi State University) and other more widely used search engines and genealogy study communities such as *rootsweb. ancestry.com, ancestry.com,* and *cyndislist.com.* I followed numerous leads based on hearsay, often calling people on the telephone to chat with them, inform them of my research, and ask if they would like to share their own families' stories.[38] Since I began this research, some ten years ago, no six months have passed without a query about my work from people searching for information about ancestors from Madagascar.

In evaluating the nineteenth-century-focused narratives, the presence or absence of descriptions of the experience of slave ancestor arrival were used as rough indicators of the approximate age of slaves and migrants when they arrived, supposing that age impacted the migrating person's ability to situate him- or herself in a new setting and pass on their story of capture. Thus, for my analysis, the more elaborate the story, the more likely it was handed down by an adolescent or adult. For example, some narratives of immigrants explicitly named white patrons, places of origin in Madagascar, or occupational and other social details.

If my supposition is correct, the Malagasy slaves who were imported illegally were children or adolescents when they arrived in the nineteenth century, and they would have understood less of what was happening to them, especially once embarked to the United States. There is, thus, a possible interesting contrast between slavery stories inherited from enslaved adults and stories inherited from, or significantly impacted by, enslaved children.[39]

The Book's Structure

Each chapter contains a section, "Family Oral Traditions," that proceeds with excerpts from oral narratives and ethnographic discussion about the content and style of the narratives individually and collectively. The ethnographic-essay approach focuses on social meaning, the symbolic importance of the narrative as origin story, and the internal logic of the intergenerational repetition of the narrative. The text analyzes the narratives in this context of cultural production. The model of *habitus,* or *disposition,* is thus engaged in the book's discussions of the practices and meanings of the family oral traditions.

Chapter 1 of this volume is devoted to presenting a summary description of Madagascar in a historical context that provides an understanding of how the slave trade of Madagascar's northeastern coast developed. (I have also included a glossary in order to make the information on Madagascar more accessible to nonspecialists.) Chapter 2 introduces the slave cohorts of 1719–21 who ultimately arrived in the Commonwealth of Virginia. It includes a review of available historical documentation of slave arrivals and relevant histories of slave owners meant to aid understanding of the lives of their captive labor force. Chapter 2 also describes the trajectories traveled by captives from Madagascar that finally brought them to various Virginia households, discusses the conditions the slaves encountered upon arrival in Virginia, and gives particular attention to cultural and social issues Malagasy captives probably faced as new arrivals in an already settled but constantly changing slave community.

Chapter 3 extends the story to the era of the children of planters who were the original investors in the Madagascar slave shipments and is drawn from archival as well as secondary research. I have chosen to focus primarily on the case of Robert "King" Carter, one of the primary investors, and his descendants, because there is much more historical documentation available on the Carter family. The chapter also presents a few brief slave descendant stories in counterpoint to the detailed information that the archives provide about the lives of white planter families. The stories gathered from contemporary slave descendants seem to hark back to the time of the children of the eighteenth-century Malagasy captives. Chapter 3 addresses how and why stories of Madagascar may have transited through generations and households in antebellum Virginia and whether the proximity of "shipmates" and the existence of shipmate networks may have contributed to the longevity of the narratives.[40] I discuss the social environments that could have enabled slave descendants to pass information from one generation to the next, and the relationship between geography and kinship networks is explored. What were the social units that supported the creation and transmission of these stories? Were there actually Malagasy slave communities in America? These are the key questions this chapter addresses.

Chapters 4 and 5 look at narratives that appear to have originated during a later era. As in preceding chapters, I begin with a historical discussion. In chapter 4 my focus is on the nature of illegal slave trading in the southern United States and the quality of life of slaves in general at the beginning of the nineteenth century. To illustrate conditions of the period, I turn to social histories written about Virginia, of which there are sufficient number to draw a general understanding of the challenges the black community faced. In the ethnographic section of this chapter, I present stories that point to the probable arrival of a number of illegal transshipments of slaves from Madagascar through Cuba or Brazil to the Lower South of the United States, and also to the arrival of free Malagasy who may or may not have been manumitted somewhere outside the United States before arrival. Here I hope to provide a sense of how archival records can silence alternative histories. Drawing on Michel-Rolph Trouillot's discussions of silence and history, I argue that certain oral traditions remain because they are kept alive as narratives that contradict or supplement the mainstream story, suggesting something different from, or more than, what is written on paper—or does not appear at all—in the official record.[41] The narratives seem to remain as stubborn rejoinders to both a written and unwritten record that denies their existence. The stories suggest to us that descendants of slaves and de-territorialized immigrants have been invisible people who suddenly appear in the twentieth century with cultural and national identities they do not always name as American.

What historical conditions could have encouraged free or recently manumitted Malagasy to travel to America during the period of slavery, and were they aware of the earlier arrivals? What do their family narratives tell us about their integration into the African American community? Did they knowingly marry into families of Malagasy descent whose progenitors were slaves, and why were they willing to do so? These are other questions that I attempt to answer in chapter 5.

In chapter 6, the concluding chapter, I explore how the overlapping effects of geography and history have had ramifications for the survival of all the "Madagascar stories" and the durability of the idea of a Madagascar ancestral homeland among some African American families. The text interrogates the persistence of the idea of Madagascar and the credibility of Malagasy origins *within* the general African American community over time. It also addresses the character of these stories as a metanarrative reflecting one stream in the process of creolization of African and Malagasy slaves. By metanarrative I mean, in this instance, the cumulative effect of all the stories considered as a larger story, perhaps recalling a period when ethnic differences and self-defined historical trajectories were being negotiated and reconfigured in public and private discourse in the African American community, even while precise references to these processes do not appear in the stories.

1

Madagascar

A SUMMARY DESCRIPTION of major events, people, and places in
Madagascar linked to the exportation of slaves in the eighteenth century will be helpful for readers in understanding the events described
in ensuing chapters. What follows here, therefore, is neither a general
history of Madagascar nor a comprehensive explanation of the various ethnic communities on the island. Rather, the chapter presents a
brief discussion of terms, concepts, and events relevant to the trans-
migration of Malagasy people from the western Indian Ocean region
to the Atlantic (see glossary for an explanation of these terms; map
1.1 shows the location of the coastal ports central to the book). The
following questions lead the main themes of this chapter: What were

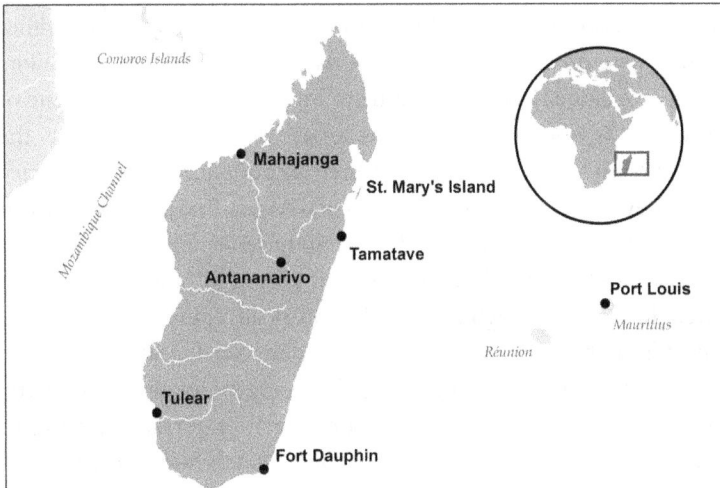

Map 1.1. Madagascar (showing St. Mary's Island, Majunga (Mahajanga), and Fort Dauphin)

the conditions that developed in this island that led to the export of slaves from the Indian Ocean region to the Atlantic seaboard of North America and to the Caribbean?[1] Is there documentation in the archives or quoted in secondary sources that references this movement of human cargo? What were the economic and political conditions that drew Virginia planters into the global network of Indian Ocean and transatlantic networks?

The Historical Record

Geography and Early History of the Island

Madagascar is a large island, almost a thousand miles long and about 350 miles across at its widest point. It is two and a half times the size of Great Britain.[2] The eastern coast of the island faces the Indian Ocean, while the western coast is on the Mozambique Channel. The Malagasy language is an Austronesian language and most closely resembles the languages of central Borneo. Most recent research suggests that the island was first settled by immigrants from the Indonesian archipelago from fifteen hundred to two thousand years ago.[3] Scholarly research also indicates that mixture with Africans took place either somewhere on the eastern coast of Africa, where Indonesian sailors may have landed before migrating to Madagascar, or on the island of Madagascar, shortly after Indonesian arrival there. In any case, the omnipresence of zebu cattle and their importance to Malagasy culture shows an early link with continental Africa. The predominance of early Indonesian and then Arab immigrant settlements in the east can be attributed to the wind patterns of the western Indian Ocean. It is thought that in the eighth or ninth century adventurers may have arrived from the Arab gulf states or from Islamicized areas of Indonesia.

There is fairly strong cultural homogeneity throughout the island, with certain striking features such as terrace farming of rice, reverence of ancestors, and square thatch huts, which reflect historical links with Indonesia. The Malagasy language is spoken throughout the country, with some regional variations. In addition to much Bantu vocabulary of East African origin, there are also Arabic loan words in Malagasy, especially for days of the week and words connected with astrology, arithmetic, and divining.[4] This influence derives from the Anteimoro, Antambahoaka, and Antanosy peoples of the east.[5] Although there is substantial evidence of an Arab presence along the eastern littoral since the eighth century, and Chinese contact before that, Madagascar was not "discovered" by Europeans until 1500, and in the following centuries it became familiar to seamen of western European nations as a staging point on the route to the Indies.[6]

Privateers and various European adventurers used both the western and eastern coasts of Madagascar as important provision points, as they also used the Comoros Islands, to the northwest, both being long known as sources of fresh foodstuffs that were critical to keeping ship crews alive. The Malagasy traded cattle and fresh vegetables in a world where food preservation was rudimentary and fresh daily fare on European ships was meager. Access to fruits, vegetables, and meat was integral in planning a sea voyage of any duration.

The Sixteenth Century

In the late sixteenth century the people of northeastern Madagascar lived in communities whose identity was based on affiliation with maximal lineages and clans. Families within clans shared the same taboos (*fady*).[7] The geography of eastern Madagascar did not favor large political groupings, which may have been constrained by the north-south mountain ranges some miles inland from the coast. One indication of this is the way kingdoms in the coastal southeast developed, such as the Antambahoaka, the Anteimoro, and the Antanosy, noted above.[8] These kingdoms did not expand beyond the mountain ranges leading to the western plateaus. During the late sixteenth century the northern clans of the northeast, living in loosely centralized communities, were repeatedly raided for slaves by Sakalava from the northwest, who sold them in a variety of directions. By the mid-seventeenth century, the people of the eastern coast were themselves involved in exporting slaves, some of whom had been brought across the island by Sakalava traders.

Recent research suggests that the slave trade from Madagascar is probably much older, and of greater volume, than has previously been suspected.

The Seventeenth Century

Archival material and historical studies of Indian Ocean commerce in the seventeenth century show Dutch, British, French, and colonial North American activity. These sources provide some historical context for the claims of today's American slave descendants to Malagasy heritage. By the middle of the seventeenth century both the French and the English were attempting settlements in eastern Madagascar, which included missionaries, adventurers, and pirates. In this context, pirates were seamen whose maritime violence was justified by neither written commission nor unwritten policy and thus considered outside both international and local European law, though many had tacit government support or the support of gentry and merchants who profited from their activities.[9] Sometimes, it must be noted, the same men who were pirates began or ended up as legal privateers or the reverse. Many of the pirates who came to Madagascar were fleeing action by the English government to suppress piracy in the Caribbean.[10]

Some pirates took part in interclan raids and wars either as mercenaries or on their own account in order to obtain slaves to sell to visiting slave ships, although slaving was not the major activity or economic base for pirates in Madagascar. Trade in captives was well established in the seventeenth century, as were networks to the New World (via Portuguese or Dutch trade). Between forty and one hundred fifty thousand slaves or more "were exported during the seventeenth century solely from the northwestern town of Mazalagem Nova alone, over an extended period."[11]

A colonial report, dated 1676, mentions that Barbados already had a population of over thirty-two thousand slaves from Guinea and Madagascar; Malagasy slaves were also exported at that time to Jamaica and the Carolinas, and even to Boston, where there were two hundred African and Malagasy slaves in 1676.[12] Likewise, it has been suggested that as many as "2,000 to 3,000 slaves were exported from Madagascar annually before 1700 by Swahili merchants working out of Lamu and Pate particularly" on the East African coast.[13] It is likely that some of these slaves were shipped in British vessels during the periods that the trade was allowed by the British government; other slaves may have been traded by the Dutch, who had an important port in what is now South Africa, at the Cape of Good Hope (Cape Town), and in New Netherland in the Americas (which became New York State and parts of Delaware and New Jersey). Among what can be learned from the European shipping records, of special interest is the fact that the people of Madagascar were noted separately from Africans. These records tell us that at this time Europeans recorded slaves coming from Madagascar as a particular population.

In the mid-seventeenth century the British Board of Trade, fearing the creation of a pirate state, reported fifteen hundred men, forty to fifty guns, and seventeen ships at the settlement on Saint Mary's alone.[14] Numerous reports which the British Privy Council received from India and America indicated New Amsterdam (New York City) as the home port for many pirates.[15] From the end of the seventeenth century to the beginning of the eighteenth, Madagascar remained an important pirate refuge.[16]

One of the first instances of slave capture and trade as a retaliatory act was when a Huguenot named Pronis sold seventy-three Malagasy to the Dutch in Mauritius.[17] This event in the mid-seventeenth century gives additional evidence that the risk of enslavement was already established when slaves boarded ships for Virginia and Barbados. By 1663 eighty more French settlers had arrived in Madagascar along with a Lazarist missionary priest. During this period a considerable number of Malagasy women had taken French husbands as well, thus creating marriage links and kin networks to nonpirate Europeans.[18] At this time, slaves were also exported from the west of the island. This may be explained to some degree by the military expansion of the Menabe Sakalava, the establishment of the Sakalava Boina kingdom, and the increasing demand for captive labor by the Dutch settlers at the Cape.[19]

The Eighteenth Century

In the early eighteenth century, slave trading was only a corollary activity for European pirates and their Malagasy counterparts, but it was increasing.[20] The presence of pirates in northeastern Madagascar stimulated local trade, contributed to the growth of local power centers, and led to increased access to firearms. By the eighteenth century people of the northeast began to raid for slaves in the more southerly regions along the foot of plateaus that faced the eastern coast.[21] It was ultimately the presence of pirates and other European "antisocials" that drew the attention of Anglo-American colonists who were looking for new ways to get silver and more ways to invest their tobacco income, eventually causing London to look for ways to crush the unruly trade centers of Madagascar.[22]

Pirates not only aided various factions in interregional and interclan wars but also lived in extended webs of Malagasy kinship. The strong pirate presence was ended at Saint Mary's by 1708, and a British squadron was sent to assure this was so twelve years later, in 1720. By then, Malagasy on the eastern coast had entered the transatlantic slave trade as traders and victims. Britain had rescinded the injunction against American direct trade to the Indian Ocean in 1719.[23]

The Betsimisaraka in the Eighteenth Century

As we have seen, the coalescing of the Betsimisaraka federation was preceded by interclan conflicts attended by diverse European parties. The escalation of conflict among the various locally held power centers in the northeast of the big island evolved over time. In 1712, at the same time as pirate influence dwindled, commerce in slaves from Madagascar increased significantly, even though it had been discouraged by British policy just a few years earlier. Because of the growing demand for labor in the Caribbean, which began surpassing even Cape Town, in the early eighteenth century Madagascar and Mozambique became important sources of slaves bound for the New World.

The political origin of the Betsimisaraka people is attributed to the son of a princess named Rahena and a pirate named Tom. Around 1712 their son, Ratsimilaho, came to the forefront as a local leader who marched north and seized control of Tamatave, Foulpointe, and Fenerive during regional conflicts. Ratsimilaho eventually became titular head of the *malata* (mulattoes) and the *zanamalata* (children of the mulattoes), the families that resulted from pirate marriages to local women. In fact, the dynasties between Antongil Bay southward to Foulpointe (Mahavelona), Tamatave (Toamasina), and Mananjary were characterized by occasionally arranged French-Malagasy marriages that also functioned as contracts for exclusive trade rights between Europeans and locals as well as for marital privileges and obligations for both sides.[24] Ratsimilaho was far more closely integrated into the history of the Sakalava monarchy of Boina than has generally been appreciated and was closely affiliated with overseas systems of commerce, as shown in recent research.[25]

Indicating the growth of internal violence that paralleled the growth of the slave trade, Rasimilaho's son and successor was killed in 1767. By 1791 the kingdom had all but collapsed, and the last king was killed in 1803 by his own subjects.[26] The Betsimisaraka have continued as a cultural community to the current era.

North American Slave Trading in Madagascar

The official (or legal) slave trade from Madagascar to the Anglo-American colonies was actually short lived. Official slave trading open to English and colonial vessels began in the 1670s, only to close again in 1698 by an act of Parliament.[27] The legal Madagascar trade reopened to the Americans in 1716 and remained open until 1721, when it was permanently discontinued.[28] American colonist participation in the slave trade with Madagascar created government debate in late-seventeenth- and early-eighteenth-century Britain regarding the interpretation of the Acts of Trade and Navigation, such as the issue of whether Negroes should be classified as merchandise within the meaning of the acts.[29] This issue, much debated at the time, brings us to the crux of the drama that Malagasy slaves experienced. While the British Parliament discussed whether slaves could be counted as any other cargo, like horses or bolts of Indian cotton, the captives—the subject of the debates—were confronted with the very human problem of survival and identity in a very different context, a problem of little concern to many gentlemen in Parliament.

The area that is now New York State, as well as some parts of New Jersey and Delaware, was named New Netherland by the Dutch and began as a settlement under the Dutch West India Company. It remained in the hands of the Dutch until a series of conflicts with the British, which had began in 1664 and ended in 1674, when the area from Albany, New York, to Delaware fell to the British Crown. Settlers in New Netherland came with the hope of making money; they did not come because of religious persecution, and many were not Dutch. The Dutch West India Company promoted settlement in order to gain value for their investment, and the first slaves who came to the settlement were brought by the Dutch.

The local Dutch trader Frederick Philipse of New Amsterdam was not among the most wealthy merchants, but he was successful in importing slaves to New Netherland and stayed when the British took over. Through his agent, Adam Baldridge, he facilitated the export of hundreds of Malagasy to New York during the seventeenth century, some of whom were further shipped to Connecticut, Massachusetts, and other points of New England upon their arrival in the New World.[30] He was also a major contact in Madagascar for other visiting Europeans.[31] Baldridge's trading post in Madagascar has been likened to the slave factories and forts that had already been established on Africa's western coast.[32] But instead of being financed and maintained by joint-stock companies and their shareholders, as in West Africa, the post at Saint Mary's was primarily created through the actions of pirates and ordinary seamen, as scholars have described quite vividly.[33] Complementing the existing trade networks was the financial backing Baldridge received from some of New York's wealthiest merchants, and he and Philipse maintained contacts with pirates, including some who had emigrated from the Caribbean to Madagascar.[34]

The latter period of Madagascar slave trading to the Americas is of particular interest to the story begun in this chapter. The slave cargo exports of 1719–21 that brought so many enslaved Malagasy to the trading posts on Virginia's York and Rappahannock Rivers were part of the increased slave exports that originated along Madagascar's eastern coast, just as the earlier slave exports to New Netherland had come from the same region.[35]

It was not until after the American Revolution that regular trade to the western Indian Ocean by North Americans resumed. By that time the Malagasy trade in slaves was not a significant part of U.S. Indian Ocean activities, largely due to efforts of abolitionists in Britain and the United States. The transatlantic slave trade was made illegal in 1808. By the second decade of the nineteenth century, the spice trade and whaling superseded the slave trade for American merchants in the Indian Ocean.

Captives

The Malagasy captives who arrived in Virginia in 1719 could not have known that their fate was very much tied to the political vagaries of the British Parliament and the East India Company's future. Due to persistent lobbying on the part of Anglo-Americans and private shippers in England, the protectionist policy allowing the British East India Company exclusive trade rights in the region had been repealed.[36] Evolving relations between North American colonies, European settlements in Madagascar, and the emerging Betsimisaraka federation, in northeastern Madagascar, reveal, at this stage, the complex workings of early modern colonizing projects that progressed in multiple directions, and these relations demonstrate the transregional nature of the slave trade.[37] The story of the slaves and early immigrants from Madagascar should be seen in this evolving global context.

The trajectories of the Madagascar slave trade to America were transregional and transnational, and actors entered and played the game both from the metropole (England, France) and from new territories that eventually were established as possessions of either crown. The historical record allows us to at least cobble together a *liste de présence* that reveals the dynamics that led to shipments between Madagascar and Virginia, and from this we can discern the local interplay of forces that, while leading to the Betsimisaraka federation, also led to the deportation of hundreds of people from the northeast of Madagascar.

For the purpose of their subsequent debarkation, and after traveling in canoes that plied the riverways of areas further inland, young women, men and children in slave coffles were likely forced to march to the northeastern coastal area facing Saint Mary's Island and to the port town of Fort Dauphin, further south along the coast. It is probable that they knew what they were in for. As we have seen, by 1716 this area was known for its brisk commerce with foreigners, including slave trading. Since slave exports had seen a peak in the late seventeenth century, some fifteen years earlier, the presence of Anglo-American foreigners circulating along the coast may have suggested to the captives that their destination would not be slavery within Madagaskaria, or the Red Island, as it was known to its European visitors. However, while captives probably suspected shipment abroad, they could not have imagined their coming voyage of thousands of miles to the New World.

Due to navigational constraints, such as ocean currents, seasonal monsoons, and the difficulty of sailing the Mozambique Channel most of the year, the greater part of the trade destined for the Americas traveled from Madagascar's eastern coast southward, stopping for provisions and trade at the Cape of Good Hope, in what is today South Africa, before crossing the Atlantic.

In 1721 Capt. Joseph Stretton entered Kingston, Jamaica, with 243 Negroes from "Africa" in the *Tunbridge Galley* of Bristol. Historian Virginia Platt suggests that often, when the generic term Africa was listed and the captain of record had Madagascar experience, it is probable that the ship was illegally carrying captives from Madagascar. Many captains simply reported Africa as the source of slaves in order to avoid discovery during the period between 1698 and 1712, when the Madagascar trade was illegal.[38] In 1721 the trade eventually closed again, which may be why Stretton listed "Africa" as his port of call.

Stretton's next post was as captain of the *Prince Eugene*, a vessel in which the British merchant John Duckinfield was an investor. The *Prince Eugene*, having been on an unlicensed voyage to Madagascar, arrived in Virginia from Madagascar after making a stop in Jamaica.

Later, a vessel named the *Duckinfield* (partially owned by John Duckinfield) entered Kingston with 280 slaves from "Africa," also probably in 1721.[39] That ship also continued on to Virginia. As it happens, Duckinfield was also among the owners of the *Rebecca Snow,* one of the other ships arriving in Virginia from Madagascar during this period.[40] These are four examples of ships partially owned by John Duckinfield that brought Malagasy slaves to Jamaica, three of which continued their voyages to the Virginia Commonwealth.

Family Oral Traditions

Scholar Alessandro Portelli suggests that the diversity of oral history lies in the fact that "wrong" statements are still psychologically "true," and that this truth may be equally as important as factually reliable accounts. Further, orality and writing, he points out, have not existed separately for several centuries. If many written sources are based on orality, Portelli argues, modern orality itself is saturated with writing.[41]

In the research for this volume, I discovered that for slave descendants today in America there is an interesting circularity between the received spoken word and the written word of professional historians. This has to do, I found, with family members who have a desire to know more about the stories they have heard and, as important, with their need to make a contribution to the ongoing narrative of family ancestors. A query that I received in 2001 on my e-list on "Madagascar ancestors" (managed through *rootsweb .com* from 2001 to 2003) is relevant to the story of early Anglo-American networks to Madagascar.[42] This query was from someone who thought he might be descended from a British slave trader and a slave from Madagascar. He had found his surname, Duckinfield, in archival records as he searched to identify the young Englishman who, according to family stories, took a slave concubine in Jamaica and brought her to the Anglo-American colony of Virginia, thus begetting an Afro-Virginian family. The present-day Mr. Duckinfield's archival search led him to discover the existence of John Duckinfield, one of the major slave ship owners for brigs going to and from

Madagascar in the eighteenth century. He learned that John Duckinfield was connected with several ships that traded between Madagascar, Jamaica, and Virginia in the eighteenth century.[43]

According to the family oral tradition, John Duckinfield's son became quite enamored of his concubine and consequentially became estranged from his father. The father was upset by his son's unreasonable demand to keep the concubine, and the son moved to Virginia with his concubine to settle there. This is the end of his family narrative as far as I was able to note it.

The contemporary African American Mr. Duckinfield did his own research to see if he could find any evidence of British Duckinfields trading in the Americas. He learned of the investor John Duckinfield of Duckinfield and Company of Bristol.[44] He did not at the time associate his family with Madagascar, but he did want to know his ancestry. In an e-mail, he expressed to me that, although his family did not mention Madagascar specifically, he thought that given the family story of his British forebear, there was a likelihood that the maternal ancestor in question may have been a Malagasy slave. He therefore joined our discussion group in the hopes of learning more. Thus, today's family narratives are transmitted by people who spend significant time looking through written histories. Unfortunately, as with other cases, the oral history does not in this case allow for a conclusive alignment of one story (familial) to the other (historical record). Portelli speaks of the inherent incompleteness of oral sources and of data that, once extracted from an interview, is always the result of a selection produced by the mutual relationship of interviewer and interviewee.[45] Certainly in this case the contemporary Mr. Duckinfield did seem to want more information. I was sorry that, in spite of my study, I had none to offer him.

The Duckinfield example reminds us that the "captives" and the "slaves" to whom archival documents refer were, after all, people. Like others who have been forced to migrate and endure horrendous ordeals, enslaved people left a mark on their descendants through their very anonymity. That is, the lack of information about forebears leaves its own mark, giving an unknown ancestor a different importance than that attributed to ancestors whose identities are known. That absence perturbs the consciousness like a missing limb. Though their personal stories do not appear in the historical record, the descendants of slaves continue to ponder the traumatic experience of slavery and to keep their own records, and their own counsel, about what they think happened.

2

Shipmates

THIS CHAPTER BEGINS an inquiry into histories of Virginia slaves and family stories by and about slave descendants, stories that echo a sense of separation and displacement. Through historical records we gain some idea of what happened to Malagasy slaves who were brought all the way from the Indian Ocean to the Americas, and through family oral narratives we get a glimpse of how families perceive a Malagasy descent that shapes their identities. These are families of African descent who also claim Malagasy descent, as well as Anglo-American and in some cases Native American ancestors. The term *shipmates* is a fitting description of the social attachments that occurred during the middle passage,[1] meaning here not only the crossing of the Atlantic but the larger idea of the period between when people were forced from their villages in Madagascar and when they were led off of boats plying the York and Rappahannock Rivers onto plantation docks.

The transatlantic slave trade created multiple sites of tragedy, of transformation, and loss, as it also created riches. Hardship and bereavement occurred on the level of national territories on the African continent and in Madagascar, as well as among individuals and families.[2] That is to say, kingdoms suffered and were reduced, and noble classes or commoners were variously bereft as the anarchy that the slave trade engendered increased over time. Some slaves came from centralized polities, and some kingdoms thrived precisely because of their role in the trade; other slaves were from loosely centralized, clan-based communities that fled their homelands or created elaborate ritualized customs to mark the impact of slavery on their societies.[3]

Disjuncture, Transformation, and Loss

There were several important sites of importation of Malagasy slaves in the Americas (see chapter 1). These included La Plata in Argentina, Barbados, Jamaica, Haiti, Brazil, Massachusetts, and Virginia. In eighteenth-century Virginia, an unusual number of captives, more than one thousand, arrived from Madagascar within a short period of time (three years) to a geographically and socially limited space in the Tidewater region. It is worth noting that of the 1,466 who arrived in Virginia during this short period, a little over a thousand were landed at the York River.[4] Such a large infusion of one language group during a short period would have made a noticeable impact on Tidewater slave communities. Over the subsequent century, Malagasy, continental Africans, and their descendants adjusted to a life of forced labor in Virginia, where their survival depended on their personal and community resourcefulness.

The Virginia planter families were proud of their heritage and power, and from the mid-eighteenth century on their descendants engaged in what I call hyperhistoricity, creating a society where family history, pedigree, and wealth were the currency that bound them together as the planter class. Partly in pride as Anglo-Americans, partly still identifying with elite families and individuals in England, the Virginians took the question of family social standing very seriously.[5] These preoccupations no doubt reverberated with their slaves, who were the children (and victims) of kingdoms, emirates, and chieftaincies. The planters' displays of power and pomp constituted a symbolic language that their slaves would have recognized. Like their captives, the elite Virginians of the eighteenth century also engaged in reinvention of their identities as Anglo-Americans on one hand and inheritors of a "homeland" culture, in this case British practices, on the other. Dutch, German, Huguenot, and Irish settlers were in the minority at this time, and few were part of the elite planter class in Virginia.

Historical records do not by themselves transmit the sense of loss and trauma that slaves experienced, but they do inform us of where slaves were, and when. Unfortunately, though the written record tells us where the "blacks" were, or where the "slaves" were, they do not tell us who those people were. They rarely refer to the captives as individuals and give little information about the lives of the slaves. Oral and written narratives produced by slave descendants may provide a means of adding texture and depth to the story told by statistics, but we cannot say for sure that these families are direct descendants of those Malagasy captives who arrived between 1719 and 1721. Their narratives do, however, fill a particular gap— What do American descendants of slaves think today? How do they feel?—and thus provide a new perspective on a shared story of America's involvement in the Indian Ocean slave trade.

In the first part of this chapter a historical discussion will present information from archival and secondary sources about the trade of slaves from Madagascar and their arrival in Virginia. In the second part, an example of a contemporary family narrative will be presented with a discussion about the possible meanings of a narrative apparently reaching back to the eighteenth century.

The Historical Record

The voyages that led to the deportation of captives toward Barbados and Virginia were exploratory; American investors hoped to acquire slaves and, under cover of this activity, trade with pirates for silver and India goods to which they previously had no direct access. They also hoped to find new sources of cheap slave labor. In the seventeenth century, slaves from Madagascar were selling for only ten shillings worth of goods each, while slaves from West Africa during the same period could sell for as much as three or four British pounds apiece. By the early eighteenth century, slaves from Madagascar were still cheaper than their West African counterparts, but the voyages to the western Indian Ocean were more expensive.[6]

The instability of Robert Walpole's South Sea venture (which eventually impoverished many British elite) led some Anglo-American colonists, such as Robert "King" Carter of Virginia, one of the wealthy great planters, to search for ways to offset the losses they anticipated from that fiasco.[7] Though they knew they were taking a risk, they did not foresee that their access to the Indian Ocean trade would once again be closed by the British Parliament by the end of 1723. It was general knowledge that such a long trajectory was bound to be deleterious to slave cargo, but the trip offered the bonus of direct access to East India goods. The slaves became the "legal" commodity of that commerce, and their trade was justified by their relatively cheap price compared to West African markets.[8]

Except for two short periods—between the 1670s and 1698 and from 1716 to the end of 1721—no goods (Negroes having also been classed as commodities) were supposed to come directly to the American colonies from east of the Cape of Good Hope during the period of colonial prohibition to the Indian Ocean trade.[9] In spring 1721 Capt. Joseph Stretton, whom we encountered in the previous chapter, was suspected by members of Parliament of having traded with pirates while in Madagascar on a slaving voyage. These actions had a serious impact on their view of Anglo-American colonist activity in the Indian Ocean. This is evident in a letter sent from London to Governor Alexander Spotswood of Virginia, relating to "Joseph Stretton of the Prince Eugene" and "his being concerned with Pirates." The letter suggested that Stretton would be called to England to go before British authorities.[10] Though trade with pirates was suspected of Captain Stretton, by that time the sanctioned trade had already transported thousands of Malagasy slaves and India goods, and most of the pirates had been chased away from their settlements in eastern Madagascar. After 1718 it was not pirates but private ships belonging to Anglo-Americans and their British commercial partners that traded in captives.

The Malagasy Middle Passage

The Malagasy slave experience was at the nexus of the western Indian Ocean slave trade and the trade of the Atlantic Ocean. Their tragedy was at the intersection of those two worlds and is an example of the globalization that began with the birth of capitalism and its transnational networks. Their movement, along with that of captives from Mozambique, describes the beginning of the end of the pirate heyday and the emergence of the nation-state, with its huge maritime companies, and the private slave traders, who competed with or were contracted by national bureaucracies.

North American planters contracted with British merchant houses in London and Bristol, such as that of Micajah Perry, in order to invest in the Madagascar slave trade and other enterprises.[11] From 1719 to 1721 roughly 1,450 slaves were brought from Madagascar to Virginia, and the average time for a voyage was well beyond the three months allowed for the West Africa trade; vessels bound for Madagascar were allotted about fifteen or sixteen months for the whole trip.[12] By virtue of surviving the traumatic experience of the Middle Passage together, captives were bonded by the terror and dislocation they experienced. The slave ship "was a strange and potent combination of war machine, mobile prison, and factory. . . . The slave ship also contained a war within, as the crew (now prison guards) battled slaves (prisoners), the one training its guns on the others, who plotted escape and insurrection."[13] The length of the trip once leaving the coast must have made it especially grueling, although the fact that captives could speak with one another was an unusual luxury in the context of the overall conditions of the Atlantic slave trade.

Historian Stephanie Smallwood eloquently states that "individual paths of misfortune merged into the commodifying Atlantic apparatus—the material, economic, and social mechanisms by which the market molded subjects into beings that more closely resembled objects—beings that existed solely for the use of those who claimed them as possessions."[14] Slave weight and the space they occupied had to balance silver, Indian cotton, and other pirate booty to assure a smooth and profitable voyage for ships traveling from the western Indian Ocean into Atlantic waters. Another scholar, Marcus Rediker, sees the slave ship as a factory that had as its mission the production of slaves; their transformation was from culturally grounded human beings to isolated, psychologically traumatized beings who would be manipulated by raw power. In his view, "sailors also 'produced' slaves within the ship as factory, doubling their economic value as they moved them from African based markets to those of the West, helping to create the labor power that animated a growing world economy in the eighteenth century and after. In producing workers for the plantation, the ship-factory also produced 'race.'"[15]

The production of race had its corresponding resistance from the object of its intentions. From the moment of their entry on the slave ship, we must imagine that the people who were captive began to plot their spiritual and psychic, if not their physical, response. As well, language undoubtedly played a critical role in sustaining a sense of personality for the captives.[16] We can visualize this encounter, situated as it is at the crucible of modern capitalism, as a conflict between the emerging modern epistemology of race and disappearing Old World epistemologies of culture.

One probable stopping place for ships leaving Madagascar was Saint Helena, an island in the South Atlantic Ocean. Descriptions of the conditions of slaves there give us an idea of the horror of the captive's experience and the dehumanizing effects the slave trade had on the slavers themselves. Among the archival documents that survive the busy shipping era of that island, there is a journal written by the nephew of Robert Brooke, the island's governor. In reading the journal, one is struck by the seeming stark loneliness and inhumanity of this place, which treated sailors only a little better than it did the slaves who were so unfortunate to end up there. Passages from the journal demonstrate that agricultural products from Madagascar were imported there along with slaves fairly regularly.

That many of the slaves on Saint Helena were from Madagascar is evidenced by written documents that highlight the importance of navigation routes of the time, and Saint Helena was undoubtedly a transnational space where the two ocean trade networks, the Indian and the Atlantic commercial routes, converged. For example, in 1715 the directors of the New East India Company (a later iteration of the East India Company that was formed in 1698) required that along with the privilege of trade licenses for the Indian Ocean and the Cape of Good Hope, licensees were required to deliver nine slaves at the company's settlement on the island for every £500 worth of goods: "those delivered were to be between the ages of 16 and 30, two-thirds male and one-third female, all natives of Madagascar, sound and healthy, and 'every way merchantable.'" This is corroborated by other scholars, who report that in 1676 all English ships trading to Madagascar that stopped at Saint Helena were required to leave one Negro, male or female, as the governor chose.[17] If all licensed ships were required to stop there, then that would have included those carrying Malagasy cargo to Virginia between 1715 and 1721.

In March 1716 licenses were taken out by Thomas White for three ships and a sloop, by Heysham and Company for one ship, and by Sir Randolph Knipe and Sir John Fryer for their vessel, the *Hamilton Galley*, for the Madagascar trade. The *Hamilton Galley* arrived in Barbados from Madagascar on July 23, 1717, carrying two hundred slaves, and continued on to Virginia.[18] It is possible that the "dangerous distempers" described in the text on Saint Helena were the cause of the "distemper of the eyes" that plagued a cargo from Madagascar that Virginia planter Robert "King" Carter complained about a year later (see below).[19] In 1758 two ships, the *Mercury* and the *Fly*, arrived at Saint Helena after having bought slaves in Madagascar. In all, twenty-six men were landed at Saint Helena from these two ships—sixteen men and ten boys.[20] In the Saint Helena archives another ship is mentioned that we earlier noted continued on to Virginia on at least one voyage, the *Prince Eugene*.

The ships that departed from eastern Madagascar were probably loaded with slaves from there, rather than slaves from Mozambique transshipped eastward across the north from Majunga (which occurred later). By this time the Betsimisaraka were already trading in slaves from the eastern regions (see chapter 1), and in fact some slaves were being transshipped in the opposite direction, westward by land, to the Bay of Boina. Ocean-bound Madagascar slaves were probably from the same or contiguous regions, and the ships almost, if not exclusively, filled with captives from Madagascar. These slaving vessels were not filled with people from starkly different ethnicities and nations, as was the case for most slave ships who packed in slave cargo from several ports along the West African coast.[21]

It is probable that at least some of the Malagasy destined for the ports of Virginia also were offloaded at Saint Helena for a short break. I have not been able to verify that all slaves on the five ships that arrived between 1719 and 1721 were actually disembarked there. However, it is likely that they were, because this was a chance to clean the lower decks, wash them down, and improve the health, however marginally, of the captive cargo. Further, the trajectory was a long one, and a stop at Saint Helena's was a way to keep valuable slave cargo alive. From the slaves' point of view, it is likely that some friends and relations were lost to each ship's captive community at this juncture. We do know that the *Prince Eugene* and the *Mercury* disembarked some slaves at Saint Helena. We can extrapolate from this that long before arriving in the Americas, the captives experienced many dislocations, losses, and tragedies that included but were not limited to death on the high seas. Indeed, death and loss lurked everywhere along the trajectory they followed.[22]

Arriving in Virginia: The Other Middle Passage

The shipmates' fragile communities were fractured again upon their arrival on the shores of Virginia and its inland rivers. Many authors have written about the trauma of this fourth great fracture for enslaved captives. The first trauma was the site of capture or initial sale—the moment when the slave was separated from family, familiar landmarks, friends, and an imagined future in his or her community. In fact, recent research has also shown that it was not uncommon for shipmates to find relatives and neighbors who were caught up in the same raid, although these would usually be a small group within the larger cargo.[23] The second great trauma was the slave factory— the holding pens where slaves from various origins within a region and even beyond were pushed together to become one strange, polyglot, frightened, and powerless community. For the captives of eastern Madagascar, small offshore islands were sometimes used to lodge women and men separately.[24] The next stage of the ordeal was the forced descent into the slave ship itself. This was the experience of the below decks, where suffering was great, people were disoriented, and sickness and death were as intimate company as the living bodies and the odoriferous wood to which people were chained. This situation, perhaps more than any other, gives proof of the resiliency of human beings. For in this floating prison, as Rediker rightly calls it, new relationships were built on the basis of shared suffering, shared witness, and shared survival.[25] The consequent disruption of these new and fragile relationships caused by ensuing sales at arrival points was another cause of trauma for shipmates arriving in the New World. Despondency, despair, and even "torpid insensibility" were common descriptions of the condition of the enslaved when they first came aboard a slave ship or arrived at their first American port.

We can thus imagine the Malagasy ancestors wrenched again from a newly familiar community, only to enter into other smaller boats, or to remain aboard the big ships, as people were dropped off at river ports, such as the docks along the James, Pamunkey, York, and Rappahannock Rivers that belonged to the great Virginia planters.

Thus came another round of painful separations, and it is easy to imagine the dislocation and shock that must have continued to settle into the psyche of these unfortunate travelers. Planters and ship captains alike saw this "melancholy" that afflicted slave cargoes as a management issue that had to be considered along with other slaving risks if one was going to make a go of the venture. Many slaves were thought simply to "pine away" or to go mad. If there was an advantage for those slaves who disembarked at Saint Helena, it must have been that they would find themselves in creole communities much marked by a Malagasy presence, which would not be the case for their fellows who continued on to Virginia.[26]

The *Prince Eugene* of Bristol made contact at Fort Dauphin in 1718 (Joseph Stretton, captain), and around May 1720, after leaving its cargo in the Americas, the *Prince Eugene* went out again, as did the *Rebecca Snow,* the *Gascoigne Galley,* and the *Coker Snow.*[27] The vessels on all five trips "made their way to St. Mary's, slaving as they went, and all were in contact with the pirates at some time."[28] The *Prince Eugene, Rebecca Snow,* and *Gascoigne Galley* went directly from Madagascar to Virginia. The *Prince Eugene* had already sold one cargo of slaves in Virginia by that time, in 1719. Another ship, the *Henrietta*, went to Pernambuco, in Brazil, tried to pass off its cargo as from Guinea (which failed—they were recognized as Malagasy), and proceeded to Virginia, from there to offload the remaining slave cargo from Madagascar. Platt describes the Madagascar vessels arriving in Virginia over a period of six weeks, all entering at the York River. The *Gascoigne Galley* brought 133 Negroes on May 15, 1721, the *Prince Eugene*, 103 Negroes on June 21, the *Rebecca Snow* arrived with 59 Negroes on June 26, and the *Henrietta* with 130 Negroes on June 27.[29] This makes a total of 425 people from Madagascar arriving at docks on the York River within a six-to-seven-week period.[30] It is significant, in cultural and social terms, that all these cargoes came from the same region of Madagascar, spoke the same language, and were disembarked along the same river in Virginia. Planters generally built small docks on the river some miles down from their neighbors' docks, to facilitate the loading of tobacco and the unloading of any goods they had ordered from Britain or elsewhere in the colonies.

Though 425 captive people is a large number in terms of cultural affinity, at a time when slave cargoes typically reflected two or more cultural and language groups per ship, the numbers carried were surprisingly small in terms of a vessel's average slave cargo. The captains, Virginia Platt tells us, "were in a hurry to sell for fear of embarrassing inquiries. They had come to a bad market and could not afford to extend credit, so that their sales forced down the prices generally."[31] The fact that they could not afford to extend credit no doubt affected who ended up with most of the slave cargo, as we shall later see. Moreover, their fear was based not on the fact of delivering slaves but perhaps on fears revolving around their activities with pirates. In one of the vessels, probably the *Gascoigne Galley*, the Negroes became practically unsalable because of a "distemper in their eyes," from which a great many became blind and "some of the Eye Balls came out."[32] This was perhaps a disease contracted at Saint Helena, as the slavers would not have initially accepted visibly ill captives to carry on such a long journey.

Much information about the sale of the Virginia-bound slaves can be found in John Baylor's account books for the period, who handled the Malagasy sales for Robert Carter, John Randolph, and William Waters. He was a well-known member of the elite planter community at Williamsburg. By 1719, no one at the time was as rich in this community as Robert Carter, who owned so many plantations he was called King Carter. Baylor often assisted Carter in disembarking and trading slaves who arrived in nearby Virginia ports. Although Baylor's account books and the letters of Robert Carter suggest that at least some of the Malagasy captives lingered in their Virginia coffles and pens for up to two months, many others were quickly shipped onward to the family docks that dotted the major riverways of Chesapeake Virginia.[33] This we must understand as the last iteration of shipmate—those who would make the final and, if not the most terrifying, certainly the most dreadful leg of the trip. At this time the captives would have seen continental Africans and African American creoles working around the docks and probably on the ships. They would wonder if they were going to the same places or different ports. And as many terrible circumstances do, these trips would have also presented opportunity. The slower river navigation from one place to the next—five, ten, or fifteen miles apart—gave captives the chance to notice that plantation docks were lined up along the riverways one after the other.

One might liken the slaves' painful itinerary to an unwinding ball of string. Their voyage wound along the eastern coast of Madagascar, in boats Platt describes as "slaving as they went," a phrase I find very graphic and direct, immediately calling to mind a sort of grim disorder in the order of things. They stopped at smaller ports, inspected potential cargo, and loaded people onto their smaller boats to take them to the larger slave ships. We know the names of those ships but not the names of those small boats, inconsequential in the historical record. The slave ships, as we have seen, are not anonymous, although the people and their descendants remained anonymous for many lifetimes. Once arrived at Saint Mary's Island, likely carried there in canoes or dhows, it was not uncommon for the women to be kept on a smaller island devoted to females and children, while the men underwent the same fate in different barracks. Then there was the long, torturous voyage around the Cape of Good Hope, up the southwestern coast of Africa, and on to a "rest stop" at the infamous island of Saint Helena. Then the ball of string uncoils, depositing bodies as they were accumulated, in lots, as the boats wound their way from port to port and river dock to river dock.

Sales and Settlement

Ira Berlin cites the Chesapeake's shift from being a "society with slaves" to a "slave society" at around 1698, when planters began to replace indentured (mostly white) labor with slave labor. During the 1680s, some two thousand Africans were carried into Virginia, and that number more than doubled in the 1690s. Nearly eight thousand slaves arrived in the colony between 1700 and 1710, and the Chesapeake briefly replaced Jamaica as the most profitable slave market in British America. The predominate African language in Virginia at that time was probably Ibo.[34] Joining those recently imported from Calabar,[35] the Malagasy slaves began arriving in 1712, just two years later. Initially, men outnumbered women in the general slave population, and the number of slaves grew slowly, if at all, by natural means. Local conditions, unbalanced sex ratios, occasional severe plantation discipline, an unhealthy environment, and possible conflicts between newly arrived African and more privileged creole slaves did not favor sustained family formation until the 1740s, while, on the other hand, local circumstances may have permitted the continued or reconstituted use of African languages and other customs, as well as the transmission to later generations of narratives of diverse African histories.[36]

Robert "King" Carter, John Baylor, (Sir) John Randolph, and William Waters had also invested in the slave cargo transport costs.[37] Of the three, Carter and Waters both held title to properties in Maryland as well as in Virginia, mostly in the Tidewater regions. Many slaves were sold among or retained by these major planters, whose own families were interconnected through webs of kinship, debt, favors, land ownership, and inheritance plans.[38]

Unlike the slaves who had been sent to ports of the Indian Ocean, those entering eighteenth-century Virginia did not benefit from contact with later waves of captives from Madagascar. Nor were they able to create residential communities, as far as we know, although some no doubt did not live far from each other. They were a minority among the other Africans, in contrast to the almost majority numbers of their compatriots on Mauritius and Réunion.[39]

The Malagasy captives lived the same isolation that all Africans experienced upon their arrival in Virginia. They were surrounded by "black people," but they were not surrounded by their own, in this case Malagasy speakers. They were outnumbered by people from West and West Central Africa, who had no idea of Madagascar. They arrived to find hundreds of Africans from various places on the African mainland (and their descendants), and soon after their arrival more followed, as imports peaked in the last half of the eighteenth century. It has been estimated, through the use of a Chesapeake database and the Trans-Atlantic Slave Trade Database, that from 1704 to 1718, a year before the Malagasy began to arrive (in the official record, as some may have arrived in 1712), 83 percent of the slaves for whom the port of disembarkation is known entered the York naval district, and another 11 percent entered the Rappahannock.[40] Of these, about a third were from the Bight of Biafra, or the Calabar coast, as it was also known. Further, the York naval district alone was the primary destination of about two-thirds of the nearly fifty thousand Africans transported to Virginia by 1745.[41] It has been estimated that slaves from Madagascar constituted 20 percent of the slave population in the York district at mid-century.[42]

Thus, the Malagasy joined a population that was made up of creoles (descended from the slaves brought in the early seventeenth century), Ibos, Senegambians, and West Central Africans, probably from the Angola-Congo coast. This polyglot workforce was divided into small units in order to assure close supervision and in response to the demands of Virginia's major crop, tobacco.

In terms of patterns of slave importation to Virginia, in some areas ethnic concentrations did occur as a function of slave selection biases. New evidence implies strongly patterned, rather than random, distributions of Africans in many receiving areas, particularly Tidewater Virginia. The evidence for the Lower and Upper James River districts tends to support older arguments for random mixing, while evidence for most of the older Tidewater (the York and Rappahannock districts) tends to support arguments for much more homogeneity among slaves than was previously supposed.[43] In general, the regional trade in slaves within Virginia more often concentrated rather than dispersed ethnic groups.[44]

Historical evidence, such as patrician and slaveholder John Baylor's account books (an excerpt of which is presented below), suggests that most of the Madagascar captives were sold in pairs or clusters of two and three slaves, except for the large lots that were bought by the investors, which may have comprised as much as 40 percent of the overall combined surviving cargo.[45] I have been unable to discern to what extent any of these slaves were resold. The large investors owned contiguous plantation lands, and as is depicted in the maps (figures 2 & 3) the investors' residential and spending habits reflected grandee patterns of kinship, marriage, financial debts, and credits. Because of these relations it is probable that the slaves they bought were kept within their elite networks.[46]

The sale and distribution of the slaves was no small task, as within three years more than a thousand had to be quickly disposed of. It was preferable to move them quickly for reasons of health and fatigue of the captives, and for legal reasons, as Platt has pointed out, such as charges of trading with pirates in Madagascar. Records indicate that some of the slaves did not survive, that some of the sick were sold, and that others were kept for a month or so before sale.[47]

An abbreviated excerpt from John Baylor's ledger list is reproduced here:

Baylor Ledger 1. 1719–1721

Elizabeth Sheppard 1719 1 Madagascar Negro Woman for 3,000 lbs tobacco

Robert Coleman 1719 one Madagascar Woman £23 (pays in tobacco)

Austin Bates 1 Madagascar Woman £23 (pays in tobacco)

Thomas Coleman 2 Madagascar Girls £40, (pays in tobacco)

Moses Quarles 1 Madagascar Woman £24, pay in tobacco

John Williamson, 1718 1 Madagascar Woman £24

From the *Prince Eugene*'s Cargo, May 23, 1719 to Jonathan Watson 2 girls, 1 boy £66

Thomas Randolph Sundry Negroes of *Prince Eugene* Cargo

Thomas Bayly 1 girl £25

June 2 Luke Smith 1 girl, 1 boy £42

June 12 William Bass 1 girl £25

June 23 Abraham Sallee 1 woman £27

June 24 Caleb Ware 1 girl £25

June 27 Jonathan Wale 1 woman £27

June 29 Richard Brooks 1 girl £25

Daniel Croom 1 boy £25

Two Madagascar girls were sold at York for £40

5 girls and 4 boys Madagascar sold at New Kent Court £135

An old Malettgasr woman and one sick boy sold to Doctor China for £25

Besides the complaints that Carter made to his associates about the preponderance of women in the Malagasy shipments, the list also gives evidence of more women than men, and more girls than boys.

Contrary to the gender ratio found among the Malagasy captives, records suggest that the slaves from Calabar were more equally balanced between male and female. In any case, Walsh shows that "salt water negroes" tended to cluster together socially. She points out that "there was a greater chance that many of the Africans coming to a large Virginia plantation after about 1698, when slave imports began a dramatic rise, lived with or near others who spoke the same or similar African languages."[48] We might ask whether the arrival of females from Madagascar had a decisive effect on the population's stabilization, which according to some accounts (see Kulikoff, chapter 3) started around 1730. This is an interesting question, because if the arrival of so many women did have such an impact, it was not by the design of the slave merchants, who were in fact dismayed by the preponderance of women and children in the cargo. Thus, the arrival of the Malagasy slaves also meant a large infusion of women into the Chesapeake plantation slave population, which at that time was not stable. The slaves who survived the Middle Passage and arrived between 1719 and 1721, and then survived the period of settlement and integration, would have been in their thirties, forties, and fifties at mid-century and would have created households.

Family Oral Traditions

Rather than a transition of narrative to myth, the pathways of the narratives run in the contrary direction, from homeland myths to historical narratives, from stories of "living dead" (see chapter 4) to reminiscences of deceased forebears. The more informal practices of remembrance that developed in North America are modest in comparison to many ceremonies that were practiced in various African-derived communities of South America. Consider, for example, what Richard Price was able to transmit to readers about the communities of Saramaka maroons that he visited in the Dutch colony of Suriname. His book *First-Time* is about the ways that Saramaka, descended from African slave maroons, transform the general past (everything that happened) into the significant past, their history.[49] There were some twenty thousand Saramaka living in villages in the forests of Dutch Guiana in the 1970s, and most had been there for more than two hundred years.[50] The Malagasy slaves who arrived in Virginia numbered approximately fourteen hundred people, and of those we can assume that as many as one-third died in the first year due to illness and exhaustion.

In contrast to the Saramaka, the self-described descendants of Malagasy slaves long ago fled the plantations where their ancestors were captive and have lived among other blacks of non-Malagasy descent, becoming integral members of the evolving African American community. Most live in urban centers, unlike the Saramaka, who remain largely rural. They have recited their histories at extended family gatherings in almost clandestine agreement that such histories are important. No significant Afro-Malagasy or creole Malagasy culture developed, nor have there been Afro-Malagasy communities in the recorded history of Virginia or elsewhere in the United States. Yet in family gatherings, the practice of memory takes on unique importance as older relatives recite the fragments of what they learned to younger kinfolk.

While to date no archeological evidence or historical documentation shows any singular Malagasy cultural behaviors in Virginia, there is some evidence of Africa-related community practices in the American colonies during slavery, particularly in New England. For example, kings and queens were selected by the African American community for the annual *junkanoo* festivals in New England. By 1755 the coronation had emerged as the central feature of Negro Election in Newport, Rhode Island, and subsequent observances were reported during the 1760s in Hartford and Norwich, Connecticut.[51] As early as 1799 blacks in Providence had created several institutions, including the African Union School in 1819, and the African Union Meeting House, a church organized in 1820.[52] The notion of Africa provided an ontological solution to the coming together of peoples descended from diverse African origins. In claiming Africa, one might say, there was "no blame," and no culture was put above the other. So what of slaves of Malagasy ancestry? Perhaps they celebrated Africa as they also celebrated, in private, Madagascar. What is likely is that Madagascar came to serve the same purpose of memory that the idea of Africa did. Although the Malagasy slaves may have been from different ethnic groups, once in America their important defining feature was that they were from Madagascar.

In order to effectively grasp the significance of the narratives, it is important to embrace both discourse and event and to pay attention to the slaves' "imaginative representational strategies that were employed over time."[53] For almost all the families in this study, one practice central to their black identities, which informs what kind of African American they are, is the passing on of stories they inherited from their parents, through their grandparents and their parents, about their "Malagasy" ancestor. Unlike the Saramaka villages of the 1970s and 1980s and their earlier villages, established two hundred years ago or more, blacks in North America rarely had opportunities to form strong maroon communities that had any permanence (exceptions might be found in Florida and Louisiana, and even these were short lived, in comparison to similar refugee communities in Brazil, Cuba, Dominican Republic, or Dutch Guiana). African and Malagasy descendants in North America were thus faced with a different *kind* of synthesizing and integrational work.

Many stories from African Americans who claim Malagasy ancestry state that their ancestors were kidnapped. This is a story that pervades the African American community regarding how people became enslaved. It avoids other details that may have been dropped over time due to shame—for example, sale into slavery due to debt, criminal behavior, or capture during war. One story tells of two sisters, kidnapped in Madagascar, who arrived in Virginia and from there were sold southward to Texas. Here is my transcription of that story:

> Two sisters were kidnapped in Madagascar and brought to America. They landed in Virginia and were taken to Texas. In Texas, they belonged to a man called Dr. Fine. Dr. Fine kept one of the girls in his house and the other on the farm (or a neighboring property). Dr. Fine made sexual advances to the Malagasy girl in his house and kept bothering her. One day, the girl grabbed a pair of scissors and stabbed him. She then ran from the house, ran to the other place to get her sister, and together they escaped. They left Texas and ended up in Missouri.[54]

There are several narratives from Texas (some others are presented chapter 4), and most of them refer back to Virginia. It may be that a "lot" of Malagasy slaves were sold southward after the Revolutionary War, or this may refer to another cargo that the current state of research does not yet provide information for.

During interviews, people repeatedly made reference to physical characteristics and behaviors that they associated with Madagascar. There are clear ideas, shared by all families, of what a Malagasy looked like and about how grandparents customarily instill a sense of pride about Madagascar. Thus, there was agreement among people who did not know each other but who were sharing narratives with me about defining factors such as the physiognomy of people, styles of family education, and the role of grandparents in transmitting tales of ancestors from Madagascar. Their willingness to discuss Malagasy slave ancestors and slave capture contrasts with the many African Americans who don't seek to know about Africa and who, for reasons we will examine later, do not have stories of any particular ethnic ancestor from Africa.

Acute feelings of betrayal do not seem to exist in the Malagasy stories. There are many ways to explain this, and one may be the average age of the captives. The captives from the eighteenth-century cohort appear in the record (for example, John Baylor's account books, Robert Carter's journals) as adults "with some children" but not as mostly children.[55] In contrast, most of the later shipments of "saltwater slaves" from West and Central Africa at the end of the eighteenth century were, indeed, mostly children, as supply markets fluctuated with the abolitionist attacks on the trade, and loss of local labor created a need for more captive labor to be retained in Africa. Another reason that people proudly remember Malagasy ancestors, which we will explore later, is quite possibly the way that Malagasy were perceived and perhaps treated differently by their white owners and other whites.

The slaves' bonds of newly constructed kinship—*situationally* created kinship—were typical of surviving shipmates from slave vessels.[56] The presence of several captives from the same or contiguous territories favored a sense of community, creating sentiments of "national" solidarity and identities based on common experience and origin. Even without these bonds, the common experience of enslavement was sufficient to encourage a new social contract based on that shared experience. The arrival of numerous slaves from Madagascar was remembered by the black community, for there are not only family stories of Malagasy slave descendants but later references in the African American community, such as a pomade promising hair "like a Malagasy" and stories of neighbors or other blacks who remember a family as "Malagasy." T. O. Madden, for example, wrote a history of the Madden family of Culpeper, Virginia, and makes reference to neighbors, the Bundy family, who were said to be from Madagascar.[57]

In summary, we now know that the arrivals of captives from Calabar and other points in the Bight of Benin resulted in clusters of households that were predominantly from these areas, that York County had greater concentrations of folk from particular slave-exporting regions than was typical in other colonial-American slave destinations, and that in fact these concentrations were unique to Virginia as well.[58] In Virginia, where the "charter generations" of the seventeenth century (as named by Ira Berlin) were often of Senegambian or Luso-African origins (or both), the eighteenth century saw large arrivals of captives from Calabar (southeastern present-day Nigeria) as well as Malagasy. As we have seen, the "middle passage" for slaves from Madagascar was long, and because it was so long, particularly arduous.

Captivity and Personhood

When Sidney Mintz and Richard Price wrote their seminal book on the beginnings of Afro-American culture, much of the historical data that we have today had not been collected. Mintz and Price wrote against the notion of cultural clusters and argued that meaningful cultural spaces could not have survived the harsh slave regimens of plantation life. At that time it was assumed that slaves were collected helter-skelter and that numbers of people sharing the same language on any given plantation were probably insignificant. Today we know that such cultural clusters did exist at certain times in particular places, that the periods during which such clusters existed may have been short-lived, and that at times they were replaced with other groups of new arrivals.

We can follow this pattern in the settlement of the captives from Madagascar. Slave communities of eighteenth-century Virginia were simultaneously heterogeneous and homogenous settlements. They were populated by Africans but by Africans from different geographic, social, and ethnic origins. The whites of the time saw them in this double identity as specifically geographically tagged and also as an amorphous gaggle of black people. The most usual discriminating classification was that of "saltwater Negro" (emigrating generation) and "country born" for subsequent generations of blacks. As part of the work of adaption that characterized these communities, people who spoke the same or related languages must have tried to live near each other, to speak to each other, or follow the welfare of each other.[59] There are certainly well-documented cases of this among creole country-born families.[60]

We can imagine a terrible personal conflict between horror at being witnessed in humiliation and shame and yet needing a witness for one's own shame. The traditional "Negro" song "Nobody Knows de Trouble I've Seen," born out of the slavery experience (although published in more recent times), evinces this need of witness to unfathomable troubles. I would argue that there must have been an ongoing tension within the community, particularly for those from the same or related ethnic groups. One wanted comfort, and at the same time, one suffered the knowledge of fellow slaves' witnessing one's humiliations. I suggest that this is the counterpoint dynamic that occurred simultaneously with the "exchange of country marks," which Gomez describes so perceptively and so beautifully.[61] It is a fact that violence created the need for diverse peoples to speak with one another, to converse, to share information. The human impulse toward survival was also the impulse that led to creolization. And if older slave stories and contemporary African American family stories have any basis at all, the other human impulses toward revolt, escape, competition, betrayal, and opportunism provided the acid that ate away at precolonial notions of ethnicity and identity that Africans brought with them.

The condition of slavery required that people weigh impossible choices: food for their children versus expression of anger; formation of ties with strangers instead of those with whom they shared a common language; the discovery that some strangers were more sympathetic than their own countrywoman; new hierarchies based on new and shifting circumstantial criteria. In the face of these very real internal pressures within slave communities, the complexity of the North American slave experience in the mid-Atlantic colonies of the eighteenth century becomes clear. If a sense of any precolonial identity prevailed under such conditions through the eighteenth to the nineteenth century, it must be explained.

In Madagascar the term *very* (lost) is used to describe the slave as a person who is lost, or more specifically, whose personhood is lost. Another term, *andevo*, is used to describe the nonbeing of an enslaved person, who becomes a nonentity within Malagasy society and in relation to the captive's lost kinship network.[62] Orlando Patterson's argument parallels this description. However, as I have argued elsewhere, it is precisely in the human fight to overcome "being reduced to dust" that the Malagasy slave, in a new context, recreated herself to become a person, once again, to her descendants.[63] Thus it is a personhood reclaimed for the benefit of the descendants, which in turn assures the survival of the original slave as an ancestor—and as a human being.[64]

The fact that societies of eastern Madagascar are mostly exogamous might have contributed to the practice of naming Madagascar as a specific lineage origin among others, and it may explain why slave descendants from Virginia could be comfortable with claiming "Malagasy" descent along with parallel claims of ancestry from continental Africans. In fact, the possibility that multiple lineages from different ethnic origins could be both socially acceptable and even *valuable* in early American slave communities needs to be explored more fully. For example, Mintz and Price noticed that in some African American communities, such as Para District in Guyana, families were organized or at least referred to as members of large ambilineal, or nonunilineal (not specifically matrilineal or patrilineal) descent groups "composed of all the descendants (traced bilaterally) of a particular person who had come from Africa." The authors go on to note, "After several generations, then, any individual would have belonged to a number of such kin groups."[65] Such affiliations could no doubt offer particular advantages for survival, multiplying the social options any individual might have in the face of adversity and emergency.

Perhaps the open quality of eastern Malagasy societies positively affected their ability to construct important affiliations, as it did in the case of Betsimisaraka collaboration with the Sakalava of the northwest and relations with European strangers.[66] It is plausible that the present-day slave descendants who claim Malagasy heritage descend from nonunilineal descent groups, claiming Madagascar, on the one hand, and other descent on the other. It might also be that Mintz and Price have discovered a trait that is shared more broadly than has been originally imagined, and that the ambilineal, consanguineous groups of Para had their counterparts here in North America, specifically among blacks in the Chesapeake.

In listening to oral narratives inherited and still performed in some form within contemporary families or reading such narratives now kept as family written record, it becomes evident that a new way of being in the world was created by the immigrant generation and their descendants. First and foremost, the narratives point to the importance of distinguishing one's identity from that of *other slaves* in particular, and then from other "Negroes" in general. Differences between blacks and Native Americans or whites would be secondary to assuring a social identity within the slave community.[67] Thus, claiming a "Madagascar" descent was a relational process and also a response to other identities and ethnicities present in the slave community.

This first imperative was the situating of the individual self as part of a kin group, fictive or real, and subsequently part of a community. This would have been a process wherein intra-African and African American (creole) cultural factors were at play. The second was the relationship of the black slave to the white master. The first process, in the view of some scholars, was by far the more complicated of the two, as differences and affinities among those born in Africa and those of African descent born in America were negotiated synchronously.[68] It is critical, then, to sort out what sorts of relationships may have existed among newly arrived slaves, and between them and the slaves they found already living on plantations. What the slave really believed, how the world was perceived, and how interpersonal relations were really conducted were all issues of life that were part of this transitional period.[69]

This cultural and psychological work of building a new identity in the context of Malagasy shipmates recalls the phenomenon of nation or community that has been much more often described for African diasporas of South America and the Caribbean. The nation may have corresponded to the "meta-ethnic system imposed by slavery,"[70] and this perspective is similar to my understanding of how and why the different people from eastern Madagascar became identified, and identified themselves, as slaves from Madagascar. Paul Lovejoy discusses the problem of ethnonyms and to what degree their application in the New World actually reflected ethnic and cultural groups on the African continent, and uses the term *panethnic,* which I understand to have a similar meaning as *metaethnic.* [71] My findings, in the case of the Madagascar slaves, supports these views, in that people once belonging to various ethnic groups from eastern and east-central Madagascar came to be known and to identify themselves as Malagasy, dropping earlier and more specific terms from home.

The Madagascar cohort also exhibits some characteristics of Berlin's "charter generations." Like them, slaves from Madagascar came from a region characterized by an enclave of European and local hybridity. At Saint Mary's and at Fort Dauphin, European men took local wives and mistresses, and the children born of these unions helped populate and sustain the enclave (see chapter 1). The Zanamalata were in some respects not unlike their Afro-Portuguese counterparts on the western coast. As in the case of lusophone Africa, the business of the Creole communities of these Madagascar ports was trade, brokering the movement of goods to Atlantic and Indian Ocean markets. The societies of the eastern coast became communities that produced and traded slaves and also where slaves became part of the local labor economy.

In chronological terms the Malagasy who went to New York arrived in the heyday of the charter generations, in the middle of the seventeenth century. Those who arrived later in Virginia came after the charter generations, but also emerged from a society characterized by intense trading and interaction with Europeans.[72] This bears out Lovejoy's arguments that the Atlantic creoles about whom Berlin writes were not one group in time but many groups over time.[73] There are important cultural implications in this. The possibly greater sophistication of Malagasy slaves may have given them an added tool for survival. This may be why, as early as 1796, a Malagasy woman in Saint Mary's County, in tidewater Maryland, protested her enslavement in court: "there had been some mistake, as she was from Madagascar" (see "A Particular Ancestral Place").[74] As Berlin reports it, the charter generations were particularly adept at intercultural communication as both negotiators and interpreters. If at least some of the people of eastern Madagascar had similar attributes, this suggests that they may have created a niche for themselves in the slave community, even though it is difficult to find written evidence of this. The appearance of a later generation of slaves who exhibit the "charter" characteristics has importance for our understanding of creolization and the dynamics of American slave communities, as well as evaluations of African agency and colonist repression of, or even dependence on, some Africans. It might be fruitful to use this lens to look at other immigrants from other such coastal communities, such as the Senegambian Wolof or the peoples of the Kongo, who also had long-standing interaction with Europeans in diverse ways—as merchants, as coreligionists, or as hosts. The key to such analysis is attention to the chronology of exports from slaving ports and arrivals at receiving ports in the Anglo-American colonies.

Was Madagascar, as it was used in Virginia, a metaethnic, or panethnic, term? I think so. But, even if we are able to answer this question, we are still left with the problem of the choice of this appellation, this chosen affinity, over others. Why, among the other ethnicities (or panethnic terms) that we know predominated in the eastern colonies of North America, did descent from Madagascar remain a theme in some African American family genealogies and historical accounts, instead of a discourse claiming, for instance, Ibo or Congo? Are there similar narratives about these other origins? Why Madagascar?

Several narratives contain language that underlines the specificity of Madagascar origins to the formation of a family identity. Juxtaposing archival evidence with recent works on Latin America[75] and contemporary family narratives helps us understand why people today remember Madagascar as an important family ethnicity, differentiating this origin from an "African" one. The choice of Madagascar reminds us of the internal negotiations that occurred in the (North) American slave community. Apparently, for external and internal reasons in these families, ethnic difference of a new sort was a sustained theme. We will return to the problem of aggregated ethnic identities later in this chapter.

The theme of being different is consistent throughout most of the family narratives. In their view, their families are different, because they have origins in both Madagascar and Africa. In these oral and family documented texts, the "Madagascar people" looked different, brought up their children in a "Malagasy way," and aspired to interact with whites on their own terms. Narratives show people referenced Malagasy ancestry in describing their difference within the black community. Thus, one example is a phrase that has shown up in at least three accounts, noting refusal to accept certain behavior because "I'm a Malagasy nigger." This was said during an early twentieth-century Mississippi trial when the plaintiff was defending herself before the judge (she had stabbed a man): "I'm no nigger. My grandma told me not to let nobody call me no nigger. I'm a Molly Glasser [Malagasy] and an ink spitter," the latter possibly being a reference to the chewing of betel nuts.[76] Such claims of distinction seem to have occurred most often in the context of drawing a line in order to define what behaviors on the part of whites or other blacks were acceptable and which weren't, and even in some cases inferring a specific kind of retaliation.[77]

These words of an elderly woman in the early twentieth century echo the protest, noted earlier, of the slave woman in 1796 in Saint Mary's County. This conviction of being different, and expecting to be treated differently, provokes questions about our common understanding of the black experience during slavery in North America.

The Constitution of a New Cultural Self

That the Malagasy slaves were shipmates in ships where the majority could communicate in the Malagasy language (which would have been mutually intelligible in spite of regional variations), and that they arrived and were sold in a fairly restricted geographic area, makes contemporary claims to Malagasy descent among Virginia families of today compelling.[78] Their stories offer insight into how African American family historical narratives contributed to the constitution of self in the formation of African American identity. These stories cobbled from memory and perhaps imagination are about making sense of disorder, the disorder of re-creating new lives in a new place that all slaves experienced. Materials from Virginia archives which present the sale and circulation of these early Malagasy slaves and their descendants help make sense of the disorder suggested by the appearance of the narratives themselves and the continued self-identification of some African Americans with Madagascar, as well as to reorder our thinking about how African Americans related to their history.

In spite of its communal purpose, the narrative and its inherent acts of remembrance probably survived because of personal habits in everyday, individual practice. The beliefs supporting these practices fall mostly into the category of unconscious adherence and reflect what I call a Malagasy sociocultural grammar that underlay everyday life. Mintz and Price speak of a core, deep "grammar" that functions as a sort of informal, organizing principle of personal and family culture. I understand the individual and group practice informed by such cultural grammar, the slaves' unconscious everyday life, as a site of Bourdieu's notion of habitus (see the introduction to the present volume). If people thought every day about their deceased grandmother watching them, then that idea would exert some moral tension in their lives every day. Moreover, thinking daily about one's deceased relative would not necessarily mean a conscious adherence to a formal system of belief. Such practices can be seen as belonging to an unconscious ontology of being, where spirits and ancestors inhabit space with living, flesh-and-blood people.[79]

In terms of ritual, the very notion and use of sacred relics, known throughout Madagascar, would have been reduced to symbolic gestures in the New World—the structure and rituals of society that supported remembrance in Madagascar were lost. Could one person be curator, practitioner of various rites, and also an ancestor intermediary through possession? It is more likely that simpler acts familiar to the slaves, such as pouring a libation for an ancestor, would last longer, while other rituals were discarded. Much would have been contextual and circumstantial, for a slave's life was rarely, if ever, his or her own to plan. Further, how does one revere both a Malagasy and an Ibo ancestor? How would one be judicious and not cause insult by choosing one ancestor over the other? Communication with ancestors was modified into more accessible and pliant forms of practice.

The example, earlier in the chapter, of the junkanoo festivals in New England shows how slaves constructed New World celebrations to respond to African needs for acknowledging ancestors and for pomp, ceremony, and pageantry. The sorts of activities described in New England were not permissible in the Chesapeake regions of Maryland and Virginia, where in some areas blacks outnumbered whites for almost a century. Yet the existence of the New England celebrations signals to us that Africans and their descendants of the eighteenth and even early nineteenth century were working at producing new identities that included fragments of particular African ethnic and cultural practices as well as borrowings from Anglo-Americans and the Dutch. Mintz and Price's discussion of unconscious "grammatical" principles that underlie and shape behavior are relevant here. What would have encouraged African creoles to acknowledge Madagascar as a credible entity comparable in some ways to an "African" place or identity? And what grammatical principles were in play that would have facilitated these negotiations of meaning?

Belief in living ancestor spirits is likely an outgrowth of the Afro-Malagasy experience and one of the core beliefs shared among slaves in general. The principles that underlie such a belief include a phenomenological outlook on the world that was at least partly Malagasy, which could coexist with and perhaps even reinforce beliefs of the other largely represented African groups in the Chesapeake during the first half of the eighteenth century, such as the Igbo and related peoples from Calabar and the Niger River delta. Later arrivals of captives from West Central Africa, such as the Kongo and Ngola kingdoms, are unlikely to have disturbed such beliefs since in these areas people believed in communion with departed family members also.[80]

Perhaps in the first country-born generation, people were looking back as much as they were looking forward, dreaming of Madagascar as much as they were hoping for survival in America. The starting point for many of the slave descendant narratives is (and I paraphrase here, having heard many versions of the following), "My grandmother said that we have an ancestor from Madagascar. She [the ancestor] was kidnapped in Madagascar and brought to Virginia. We don't know much more about her."

As we will see in the next chapter, the family narratives from this period are sparse, lack contextual description, and do not identify names or places in Madagascar. Most do not specify the original points of sale in Virginia or the identity of the original Anglo-American buyers. In fact, claims to Madagascar links from the period of slavery are little more than that: protestations of diversity in a context of homogeneous "blackness." Given the circumstances described above, perhaps their most remarkable characteristic is that these claims exist at all.

3

History and Narrative

Saltwater Slaves in Virginia

THE PREVIOUS CHAPTER introduced the slaves of Madagascar as a cohort of shipmates who, within just three years, arrived on the shores of Virginia's major rivers and their ports. From the archival record, we learned that ships carrying the slaves arrived at the York and Rappahannock Rivers between 1719 and 1721. We also established that these slave cargoes were unique, especially for North America, because the shipmates spoke the same language. They were able to communicate with one another and had similar, if not the same, cultural referents. Once in America, they landed in and were distributed to places not that far away from each other.

In this chapter the questions of settlement on the plantations where the slaves were sent, the new geography that they encountered, and how that geography affected their sense of identity will be discussed. How and where they were distributed among families in Virginia were variables that would greatly affect their cultural identities in the future. Thus, the relationship of the geography of planters' holdings and the developing identity of slaves from the Bestimisaraka territories is explored. In this new geography, the household or immediate family, rather than the village, probably became the site of reproduction of the Malagasy self. Reference to the island, Madagascar, replaced specific ethnic references from there.

We can historically locate the influx of slaves from Madagascar to the mid-Atlantic colonies, but it is difficult to go beyond conjecture in identifying the factors that led to the creation of narratives in which a slave could become an ancestor—a state denied any slave in Madagascar itself.[1] In eighteenth- and nineteenth-century Madagascar, to be a slave was to be *very*, or lost. By its very definition, the category of slave in Madagascar was synonymous with being without kin, without lineage, without the possibility of becoming an ancestor. A slave in Madagascar, as in continental Africa, was often a social appendage attached to the host lineage of the master, having lost his or her own lineage in the process of becoming an unfree member of the community. Slaves were most important simply as units of labor that served an individual, a group of lineages or a royal estate. Shipment to America was a twist in history that led such slaves to form a new kind of community that in time would become vocal about lost histories.[2]

While masters like "King" Carter prided themselves on winning the contest of names, insisting on new "slave names," the slaves themselves negotiated the more existential questions of identity, patrimony, and matriarchy among themselves. Slavery, though imposed and maintained by violence, was a social status that was continually negotiated.[3]

The Historical Record

In Virginia the racial balance was such that most whites were in both intensive and extensive contact with blacks. In the mid-eighteenth century William Byrd II thought Virginia would become known by the name New Guinea, and he and others came to fear the social results of the increasing number of slaves who were brought in during this period.[4] At the same time, slaves had a political sense of their position, and even in the absence of formally accepted institutions, the slave community and its constituent elements—families and households—were actively engaged in daily struggles for power, influence, and some measure of independence. This can be seen in the daily journals of various members of the Carter family. Patriarch Robert "King" Carter and his sons Landon and Robert wrote in their journals about some of the conflicts they had with their slaves, an inevitable feature of managing captive labor.[5]

Since the slave had an inherent material value (and occasionally a human and social one) for slaveholders, there was a disciplinary line that most planters did not want to cross, as that would eventually entail the loss of their investment. This valuation of slaves led to critical and sometimes perverse psychological games between master and slave. According to one source, Landon Carter was determined to root out "the Lazyness of our [black] People" in a systematic fashion through consistent and continued punishments. When "severe" whippings "day by day" did not increase his threshers' productivity, Carter, rather than considering they might have had a different approach to their task, was sure that outside agitators encouraged their dilatory pose.[6] Robert Carter III, named for his grandfather, had more visibly ambiguous feelings, and relations, with his slaves. Only recently the subject of serious research, Carter was a slaveholder who consulted his slaves on the performance of their overseers, who allowed his slaves to practice medicine, and who believed that ultimately slavery was unprofitable.[7] In short, slave-master relations varied according to owner prerogative, social pressure from peers, numbers of slaves, and how long the slaves had been on any given plantation.

This ongoing contest forced owners and slaves, even as they "confronted one another as deadly enemies, to concede a degree of legitimacy to their opponent. No matter how reluctantly given—or more likely, extracted—such concessions were difficult for either party to openly acknowledge. Masters presumed their own absolute sovereignty, and slaves never relinquished the right to control their own destiny."[8] Moreover, although the power of the slave owner manifested in clear and strict (if not impermeable) parameters beyond which slaves could not normally act, within those parameters slave life evolved on the household and community level, often according to personal need and choice. Thus, the creolization process took place as people negotiated social roles and cultural practice, in spite of owner hopes for total control. Before 1800 this process was continuous as new arrivals, "saltwater slaves," were introduced into a community. The world that the Malagasy slaves entered in Tidewater Virginia was such a place, and their children were born into that world. By the time their surviving children were adolescents, a new wave of saltwater slaves had arrived from West and Central Africa.

Lorena Walsh's study of Carter's Grove is particularly relevant to the history of the eighteenth-century captives from Madagascar and their descendants, as it suggests specific ethnic concentrations among slaves at that plantation.[9] According to her findings, the families of the Virginia plantation Carter's Grove (owned by Robert "King" Carter) showed a marked majority of Ibo, or Bight of Biafra, origins. She was able to deduce this from shipping, purchase, and plantation management records. This research suggests that the Malagasy of the 1719–21 cohort found themselves in a milieu that was predominately Ibo (and related ethnicities), with more people from the coast of Biafra arriving after they did. As they aged and had children, others arrived from places as culturally and geographically distant as the Senegambian coast and the Luanda/Angola/Congo ports of central West Africa. However, the most likely mates for the immigrant generation (statistically) would have been saltwater slaves from the Bight of Biafra, or creole children for whom at least one parent or grandparent had origins at the Bight of Biafra.[10]

However, Walsh also cautions that friction between saltwater slaves and creoles may have favored marriages among the former, as they would have shared experiences of disorientation and new settlement. At the time the Malagasy arrived, creole African origins would have been mostly Senegambian, according to statistical studies done by Walsh and others.[11] The concentration of men on large plantations suggests that most African adults were bought by the gentry (rather than small farmers)—a pattern documented by the composition of two planter properties in the Tidewater, one being Robert "King" Carter's. This tends to support my argument regarding the grouping of the surviving Malagasy shipmates and their young children, but questions of mortality and length of stay in any given place remain unanswered.[12] Considering the labor demands in the management of large numbers of adult slaves, it is understandable that smaller farmers favored fewer adult slaves and the purchase of more small children, adolescents, and young women, whom they could more easily train and supervise. Likewise, security risks were smaller with fewer adult male slaves to manage.

As we have noted, it may be significant that the period in which the Malagasy arrived just precedes the generation of Chesapeake slaves that began to stabilize demographically, while the gender structure of the Malagasy imports may have had an impact on the reproductive capacity of the slave community. If the Malagasy slaves did not contribute to the slowly growing stabilization of the eighteenth century, their children may have, as slave deaths were much less frequent in the late seventeenth century and the first decade of the eighteenth. According to Alan Kulikoff, the Chesapeake slave population began to stabilize around 1740, preceded by periodic highs in mortality rates throughout the century (1711, 1727, 1737, 1743). Philip D. Morgan, on the other hand, states that "by the 1730s—a decade when Virginia imported more slaves than ever before or again in its history—the slave population increased by natural means, at a remarkable rate of about 3 percent per year . . . the proportion of children increased significantly, too; there were now almost two children for every adult female."[13] However, if the slave population increased by a natural rate of 3 percent per year, it suggests that many of the new Africans imported did not survive resettlement.

Kulikoff estimates that one in four new captives died during the first year in the Chesapeake (among all new slaves). In 1727 Robert "King" Carter lost at least seventy slaves, almost a quarter of all his slaves born abroad and more than half his new "Negroes."[14] Most who became sick had developed respiratory illnesses in the winter and fall months. Kulikoff estimates very high mortality rates for new slaves in the 1720s.[15] While popular wisdom perceives the division of slaves as a consequence of owner desire to break up cultural groups, I would argue against that interpretation. If in fact slaves were viewed almost as livestock, and they certainly represented a monetary investment, it is more likely that slaves were divided into small groups soon after arrival in response to labor needs and to avoid the decimation of any large group of slaves by disease. This is a common livestock management strategy, and although it is abhorrent to reason in these terms, understanding the culture of Anglo-American slave societies during this period requires us to think about such possibilities. The large numbers of the slaves who arrived in the first half of the eighteenth century no doubt strained the management capacity of even the large plantations, which would have resulted in higher numbers of slaves settled, at least temporarily, in bigger groups.

Kulikoff asserts that between 1710 and 1740, 25 percent of slaves resided in units of over twenty (but usually under thirty), and that only 9 percent of Carter's slaves lived in units of over thirty in 1733. These statistics are critical in attempts to evaluate the living conditions of the captives who arrived from Madagascar and their first-generation descendants. Overall, it appears that a good number of slaves lived in units of twenty-one persons or more; of the areas which interest us here, thirty units of slave groups in this category were kept in York County from 1711 to 1720, and sixteen such units from 1721 to 1730. This is significant since the majority of Malagasy (one thousand) who arrived in Virginia between 1719 and 1721 arrived at the York River port.[16] It is not clear whether the deaths of Carter's slave property were dispersed among his many plantations or concentrated on a few.

Twenty-five to thirty people can plausibly create community. I would suggest here that these estimates could be usefully analyzed relative to the years that large numbers of slaves arrived; on the surface it appears that these large groups correspond to "seasoning" periods of newly arrived saltwater slaves who subsequently were broken into smaller groups once acculturated to plantation life. Although there are some indications to the contrary, suggesting that slaves upon arrival were broken into small groups, this infers a level of manpower (i.e., overseers) that may not be realistic. "King" Carter had a significant number of slaves living in large groups during this period; in 1733 he had forty-five units of twenty-one slaves each or more and forty units of eleven to twenty slaves. Unlike many of his peers, Carter listed slaves by families, apparently thinking of slaves in terms of households.[17] Nearly two-thirds, or 64 percent, of Carter's recent immigrant slaves during this period lived on plantations with numerous native (creole) adults and children, as well.[18] Given what we know about earlier slave imports, we can assume that in 1733 a good number of these "native slaves" were second-generation creoles of mixed Malagasy, Ibo, and Ngola descent (not discounting occasional Anglo-American, Senegambian, and Native American descent as well).

Kulikoff finds that husband-wife households were probably new creole households; seasoned immigrants often lived in conjugal units without children, while saltwater Negroes were placed in sex-segregated barracks.[19] From an ethnographic point of view, this data does not address the extended family practices of Africans and Malagasy that undoubtedly were in play, unless it applies only to the first year after arrival. If small children of new unions were kept apart, they were probably under the care of creole women who oversaw their daily activities. However, this does not signify that those children who lived on the same plantations did not see their mothers. Such an arrangement, keeping small children away from their mothers, would seem to be counterintuitive in terms of maintaining child survival rates.

The household, then, became the site of reconstruction and re-invention. Because men and women constituting couples, and their neighbors, were most often from different ethnicities, the community and the household were probably sites of contested identities, com-petition, negotiation, and regret between displaced people who were trying desperately to survive and reimagine their humanity. Somehow the new arrivals must have reckoned that the absence of their for-mer ordered lives also meant an opportunity to reinvent themselves. In order to survive, decisions had to be taken and adaptions made to new environments. One of those decisions seems to have been to inscribe oneself in the minds of descendants as an ancestor, and to instruct children on the importance of "holding history" and carrying the weight of the past for future generations.[20] In so doing, Malagasy reassured themselves of their humanity, including the right to have descendants and to create lineages.

Many slaves were "entailed," or annexed to the land, by the mid-1700s.[21] In 1728, Carter wrote a codicil for his will when slaves were reclassified as part of land properties.[22] This meant that slaves could not be sold but were to be transferred with the land to the person who inherited the land. It is thus understandable that the descendants of slaves came to refer to their places of American "origin," if that term can be used here, in terms of geography and titled landowners. It has been argued elsewhere that slaves often retained their original master's surname after being sold and that this tradition is grounded in the veneration, or perhaps recognition, of one's place of origin. This tradition may have been important to southern freedmen as a way to signify membership in a larger family network.[23]

Major plantations often had "greater concentrations of slaves and a larger proportion of immigrants in their slave population than areas dominated by small farms." Slaves on larger plantations with large numbers of blacks probably had more opportunities to "worship their gods, begin stable families, and develop their own communities."[24]

More than nine out of ten slaves brought into the Chesapeake in the eighteenth century either arrived directly from Africa or were transshipped from the West Indies after only a brief period of recuperation from their transatlantic ordeal.[25] By way of comparison, while in the seventeenth century blacks constituted a very small percentage of the Chesapeake population (Kulikoff says about 3 percent, or seventeen hundred people), the number of blacks in the Chesapeake colonies doubled in every decade from 1650 to 1690, while the white population grew more slowly. But from 1700 to 1740, roughly forty-three thousand blacks entered Virginia, about thirty-nine thousand of whom were Africans.[26] It is not mentioned whether the Africans referred to in this source included Malagasy; the remaining slaves (creoles) were probably transshipped from the Caribbean. Significantly for our discussion, over half or even three-quarters of the immigrant slaves went to a few lower Tidewater counties, while the rest were sent to the upper Tidewater region.[27] Until midcentury, more than 80 percent of imported Africans were disembarked on the shores of the York and Rappahannock Rivers, and Walsh reports that the region of embarkation for York slave imports is known for 60 percent of the Africans arriving by 1745. There planter wealth and political power was most concentrated and transatlantic mercantile connections most developed.[28] More particularly, from 1718 to 1726 an estimated 60 percent of slaves arriving in York were from Biafra (Calabar) and in the subsequent ten years again, immigrating Africans from Biafra or Angola made up 85 percent of incoming captives. Also during this period, about 20 percent of all slaves entering York, Virginia, were from Madagascar.[29]

The elite planters—and Robert "King" Carter was the elite of the elite—held plantations throughout eastern and middle Virginia, and sometimes in Maryland. These planters were the descendants of the earlier settlers of the Virginia Tidewater and, although generally "self-made" men, were the beneficiaries of tracts of land bequeathed them by their fathers and grandfathers (many of whom were landed gentry in England). Thus, Carter's sons—Landon, George, John, Charles, and Robert II—as well as their sisters (Carter had five daughters who survived to adulthood) received guardianship of all surviving slaves and their descendants, including Malagasy, whom Carter owned when he died. Others went to his children as marriage gifts.

A New Geography and New Identities

Though they were not all sold right away, the Malagasy were sold in the immediate vicinity of their arrival along the waterways of Chesapeake Virginia.[30] Maps 3.1 and 3.2 show planters' names and the location of their plantations. On map 3.1, ten plantations are associated with the Carter family. On map 3.2, five Burwell plantations are noted, and we find two Carter family–affiliated plantations on the southern bank of the James River (Burwell and, further west, Brandon, which belonged to the Randolph family). Further northwest are two Carter plantations and another Randolph plantation. Both of these families intermarried with the Carter family, and thus some slaves inherited by Carter's daughters traveled to other family properties when the daughters married, or were shifted between family-related plantations for special work duties. In the area shown there are two Carter plantations (including the famous Rosewell plantation) and four Burwell ones. Overlooking the York River, Rosewell was built by Mann Page (1691–1730). He was married to Judith Carter, the daughter of Robert "King" Carter, in 1718. As shown on map 3.2, the Rippon Hall plantation, belonging to the Carter family, is just north of Williamsburg and across the river from Rosewell, on the southern bank of the York, as was the plantation

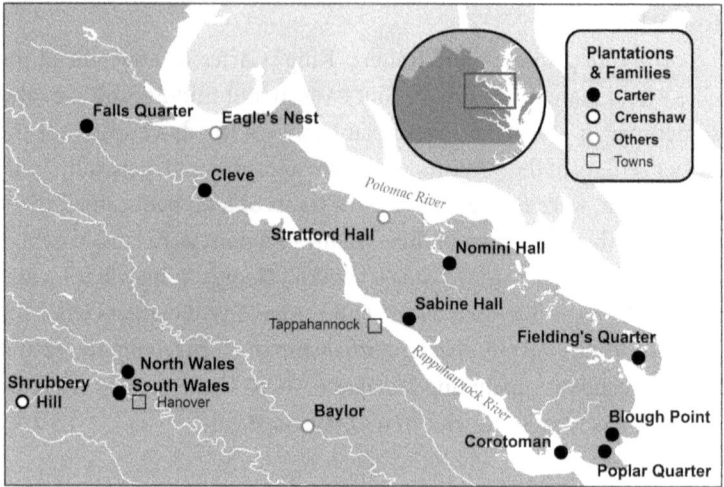

Map 3.1. Plantations near the Rappahannock River

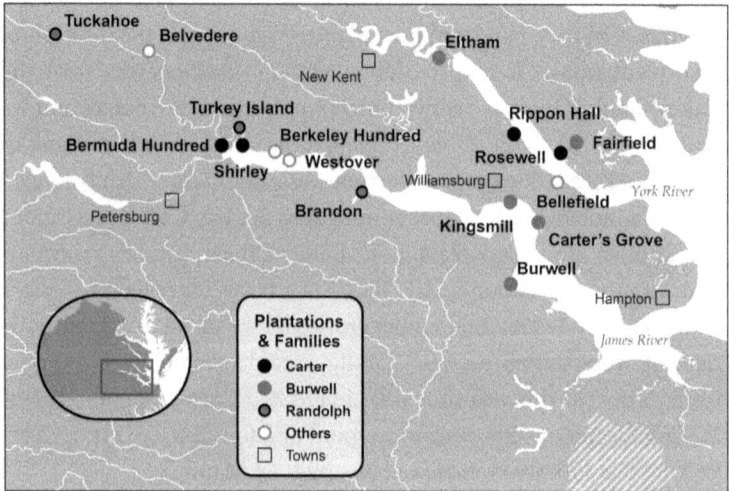

Map 3.2. Plantations on the York and James Rivers

of Cole Digges (in charge of customs when the Malagasy arrived), although that plantation is not depicted here. The three peninsulas of the Virginia tidewater can easily be identified. The map suggests how much river traffic must have shaped the life of the region.

The Carter, Berkeley, and Burwell families were closely related and linked by numerous marriages. The Fitzhugh and Page families also belonged to this network, along with the Harrison, Lewis, and Dandridge families, though their names are not depicted on the maps shown here. Of all the names on Baylor's 1718–19 slave list, only Ware appears, and they had a plantation on the southwestern bank of the Rappahannock. The plantations along the York, Rappahannock, and James Rivers lay almost back to back on opposite sides of the river, and river wharves ran side by side in intervals. The far reaches of one plantation territory bordered on another, both on their sides and across a river. This, too, may have played a role in the ability of slaves of different plantations to communicate with each other. Along the borders between the great plantations lay the possibility of encountering other captives while remaining on the master's land. Since planter properties abutted one another, it was also possible for slaves to send messages via slave boatmen on errands.

With the exception of the York district, to which large planters throughout the colony went occasionally to buy new workers, the numbers of slaves imported annually into the Rappahannock, South Branch Potomac, and Lower and Upper James Rivers were small enough to be absorbed mostly by purchasers living along these rivers and in their immediate hinterlands.[31] Moreover, since sales usually commenced within a week after a ship arrived, it was primarily local buyers who had sufficient advance notice to travel to the sale or arrange for an agent to attend it. The majority of slaves sent to the smaller naval districts likely remained within the hinterlands of the rivers where they had disembarked.[32] About one thousand slaves from Madagascar were imported to the York district alone between 1719 and 1730—mostly before 1722, as we have shown elsewhere. During the same period, 466 slaves from Madagascar were disembarked at Rappahannock ports.

No slaves from Madagascar are recorded as arriving to the South Potomac or the Upper or Lower James. Of those imported directly from Africa to these areas, origins of only 45 percent are known, and most of these came from Senegambia.[33]

Of the merchant planters who bought some of the slaves and put others in the Malagasy cohort on the local Virginia markets, chief among them were Robert "King" Carter, (Sir) John Randolph, and John Baylor, who had invested in their capture and transport. Many captives were bought by these major planters, whose own families were interconnected through webs of kinship, debt, favors, land ownership, and inheritance plans. Historian Rhys Isaac reports that "dependence on credit reduced the impersonal now-and-done-with quality inherent in cash transaction, sustaining in its place a network of continuing, face-to-face personal relationships."[34] The big planters typically owned several plantations along both rivers, as well as further north on the Chesapeake in many cases. John Baylor, one of the major, if not the major, dealers of the slaves, had a plantation not far from the courthouse, on the north side of the York River. Carter plantations are evident along both rivers as well.

We know that slaves were sometimes sent as messengers between plantations and kin, so it is possible that Malagasy kept up with each other's news via these opportunities. There is other evidence that the slaves who were owned by the Carters and transferred through inheritance and marriage to the Burwells may well have communicated with each other and that some were moved to areas on the James River. In the late 1730s two advertisements (presented below) were posted in the *Virginia Gazette* for runaway slaves (at the James River) that mention slaves from Madagascar. Sam, about thirty years of age; Gruff, who was twenty-six; and Tom, who was about thirty-five. The ad for Gruff and Tom remarks that these slaves arrived as children. Tom and Gruff apparently ran away together in 1745; Sam ran away in 1738. Interestingly, the Burwells are not mentioned as the owners of these slaves, which suggests that they were perhaps sold or rented out by the Burwells to neighboring plantations. Since we know the slaves came in between 1721 and 1738, it is interesting that twenty years later they were not so acclimated that they would not take a chance at escaping to freedom.

The physical proximity of the slaveowners' farms may have allowed children who were scattered among various planters to see their shipmates from time to time and to maintain some sense of shared culture as they grew up. Other former shipmates may have lived near one another in town (Williamsburg). One way to gauge the access that the captives had to one another is to compare Baylor's list with a map of eighteenth-century Williamsburg. The buyers on Baylor's list (in the preceding chapter) are not the great planters but seem to be town dwellers. A good third of the great planters also kept town homes in Williamsburg or Hanover, or both.

In reading the wills and correspondence of that period, we can imagine that from the point of view of the slaves, they were distributed helter-skelter, between different spaces on a given plantation and in different places on different plantations. They likely devised their own systems of guardianship. For example, if a slave's daughter was sent to a Randolph family property from the Carters, she might have hoped that a relative would look out for her at the Randolph plantation. The enlargement and expansion of African sensibilities of kinship to include Malagasy, Wolof, Bambara, or Ibo in an evolving "black" world was surely one of the greatest survival tools slaves had in that situation.[35] This created kinship did not preclude, I think, retaining individual cultural identities and embellishing them to create New World personae. Nevertheless, disappearing cultural knowledge was probably mourned by individuals and among people of different origins. Just as aging immigrant generations are known the world over to regret the things they can't remember or wish they could see again, so this must have been for the immigrant Malagasy and first country-born descendants. The primacy of kinship relations, fictive or by birth, helped them create vibrant, if subaltern, narratives of family and lineage. Thus the family relations among the whites unwittingly aided the kin and affine, in-law and friendship relationships among the slaves.

The letters of Robert "King" Carter and his financial partners in England (Micajah Perry and William Dawkins) give evidence that the immigrant generation of slaves from Madagascar, that is to say Malagasy-born captives, were mostly women and children.[36] Gender ratios alone suggest, therefore, that those Malagasy slaves who survived likely found themselves in communities where most of the men were either newly arrived from, or descendants of forebears from, Calabar and Senegambia. Carter, for instance, expresses his preference for "gambers," people from Senegambia, in his journals, and he was the owner of several extended families of southeastern Nigeria ("Ibo") heritage, in spite of his stated preferences.[37] Carter, of course, could not control which Africans would come on the market over time. For example, although he preferred "gambers," people imported from Senegambia to York ports in the first half of the eighteenth century accounted for only 20 percent of all transshipped slaves, matching the number of Malagasy imports.[38]

We have earlier noted that Virginia is especially known for the tight social relations that existed among its white elite in the eighteenth century. They married each other and fought with each other over debts and credits, land borders, and tobacco exports. This situation of dense social networks imprinted on the land through inheritance and marriage created a patchwork of plantations and households that were related financially and through kinship, linking white plantation owners, their children, and extended families from the Chesapeake coast to middle Virginia. A review of the investors in the Great Dismal Swamp, for example, reveals how closely capital and kinship were intertwined in this world.[39]

A visitor in the early 1740s found Virginians preoccupied with "Schemes of Gain."[40] An inventory of Virginia planter families who invested in the Dismal Swamp and who were related by marriage to the Carter family, or involved in business with them, is illustrative of the acquisitive character of Virginia's elite planters of the time. This example also gives an idea of the numerous family networks that might be destinations for slaves during their lifetimes. This density of familial relationships created opportunities for slaves to see each other or at least hear of each other through the information sent via carriage drivers, messengers, hired or loaned labor, or boatmen. The surviving Malagasy slaves and their descendants could be rotated and circulated among related households in a network that inadvertently provided a net of communication and interaction to its captive workers.

At least three contemporaries of Robert Carter's sons, whose families eventually became kinfolk, were involved in the Great Dismal Swamp project. These were Robert Tucker, David Meade, and Thomas Nelson. In the next generation one Meade male heir would marry a Page, herself the daughter of Judith Page, daughter of Robert "King" Carter. They would settle in Hanover, nestled at the end of the Pamunkey River, a western branch of the York River. Tucker married Joanna Corbin, whose plantation home sat just across the river from Ball property and a few miles west from Carter property on the northern bank of the Rappahannock. The aforementioned Thomas Nelson married an Armistead, and his brother William Nelson married a niece of John and Charles Carter (thus another Robert "King" Carter granddaughter). William Byrd himself married Elizabeth Carter, one of "King" Carter's daughters.[41] Robert Burwell was from the Isle of Wight County just west of Nansemond County and the Dismal Swamp. Tucker and Burwell were brothers-in-law; Burwell's wife, Sarah, was the daughter of the elder Thomas Nelson and Frances Tucker (Nelson), Robert Tucker's mother. Robert Burwell's father, Nathaniel Burwell, had also married one of "King" Carter's daughters. Burwell spent much time in York Town, where he owned houses, and he had a home estate that totaled close to thirty-five hundred acres overlooking the James River on its south bank. Burwell's daughter married another grandchild of "King" Carter's, the son of Mann Page who built the mansion at Rosewell plantation. Their uncle was John Carter.[42] Perhaps the diffusion of Malagasy slaves and their descendants also occurred in similar circumstances of desire, acquisition, and novelty.

William Waters, whose father was one of the main investors of the 1719–21 shipments of slaves from Madagascar, was also an investor in the Dismal Swamp Company. Retaining property in Northampton (the Virginia section of the Eastern Shore) and Halifax and Nansemond Counties, Waters spent most of his time after 1754 in Williamsburg.[43] That Waters participated in the investment in Malagasy slaves, visited the dock with Carter, and actually purchased some of them, is recorded in Baylor's notes of 1719 and 1721. Many great planters split their time between their plantations and the city of Williamsburg, where they made up the majority in the House of Burgesses, which suggests that at least some surviving Malagasy slaves might have visited Williamsburg with their masters.

Slaves often preferred to marry away from the home plantation. Certainly, having a spouse away from one's own plantation reduced the potential for coercion by masters and conflict with other slaves. Throughout the slave period, the custom of "night traveling" and visiting in slave quarters was noted.[44] There is a possibility that ethnic and cultural affiliations, as well as shared "shipmate" experiences, were part of the motivation for these visits. Slaves, therefore, saw each other on holidays and in the evenings, as well as at work. Sometimes they were reunited with family when they were deeded over to another branch of their owner's family.

Robert "King" Carter's will shows how first- and following-generation slaves were no longer thought of in terms of their ethnic or cultural origins. Perhaps for the planter, who lived relatively removed from daily slave life, these qualities were no longer important and therefore no longer existed in any critical way for the slave. King Carter was proud of his methods of organizing his slaves and integrating new arrivals into his slave communities. In a note to his overseer in 1727, he explained his approach to naming slaves and making them understand that they were his to name: "I name'd them here & by their names we can always know what sizes they are of & am sure we repeated them so often to them that everyone knew their names & would readily anser to them." After a few weeks at the home plantation, Carter forwarded his saltwater slaves (usually in small groups) to a satellite plantation or "quarter," where his overseer repeated the naming process, taking "care that the negros both men & women [Carter] sent . . . always go by ye names we gave them."[45]

As plantation sizes increased, more slaves lived in quarters away from the master's house and his direct supervision. These groupings were large enough to allow some degree of social invention that included saltwater cultural influences, such as Ibo and Malagasy, on creole slaves and on the saltwater slaves' own children. York County (destination of most of the Malagasy slaves), for example, had on average the largest number of units of eleven or more slaves in the region, and consistently from 1741 to 1785. Overall, blacks accounted for roughly 57 percent of the population in both 1755 and 1790 in York, James City, and New Kent, and 59 percent in 1790 in Richmond and Essex.[46] These statistics are especially interesting when compared to the cities, towns, and counties that contemporary self-identified Malagasy descendants name as their home regions. Walsh points out that if a number of well-to-do young planters living in particular neighborhoods (such as York) came of age at roughly the same time, which was a likely outcome of sequential white settlement in the Chesapeake, then their individual estate-building strategies could unwittingly result in larger concentrations of slaves from any given African region.[47] This is no doubt what happened when the majority of the slaves from Madagascar ended up with the Burwell, Berkeley, Carter, Randolph, and Fitzhugh families.

There are a few specific mentions of slaves of Malagasy origin in Carter's papers. On page 15 of his 1736 will, for example, he stated,

> Will is that my said Daughter Lucy have a genteel maintenance out of my estate until she arrive at such age or marriage, and that she live with her sister Page, or her sister Harrison as as they shall agree to be best and properest for her, I also give unto my said daughter Lucy, *the Madagascar Girl Belinda and her child* [emphasis mine].

There is also the case of "Madagascar Jack," also a slave belonging to Carter.[48] In correspondence to Robert Jones, one of Robert Carter's managers in Fairfax County, Carter mentions that he does not want Madagascar Jack to go to the "new design" at Corotoman plantation (1727, letter to Mr. Robert Jones). Whether Jack was himself from Madagascar, or had one Malagasy parent, it is evident that the term Malagasy was familiar enough to become part of a slave's name. In this case, the owner and the general community seem to have known this slave by a name indicating a place of origin.[49] There is some evidence in runaway slave ads that "saltwater negroes" tended to try to escape together, which was evident in ads throughout the South and applies to diverse ethnic groups. The Malagasy were no exception. For example, among first-generation runaway cases, people were often identified as "having the countenance of a Malagasy" or "hair like a Malagasy." Runaway slave advertisements, thus, show that Europeans perceived the slaves of Malagasy as a particular phenotype, and this theme emerges in the later family narratives as well. In the following ads from mid-eighteenth-century Virginia, ethnic referents were still being used for African and Malagasy slaves:

> RAN away from Coggan's Point on James River, opposite to Col. Byrd's, 3 Negro Men, viz, Bafil, a lofty, well-made, black Negro, Virginia born, about 25 years of Age. Glocester, a tall, slim, black Negro, about 50 Years of Age. *Sam, a Tawny, well made, Madagascar Negro,* about 30 years of age: They went away in a Canoe on Sunday the 25th of June last; they were seen to go down the River. (*Virginia Gazette,* July 21, 1738, emphasis mine) and
>
> RAN away from the Subscriber, living on James River, In Prince George County, on the 28th and 29th of April last, Three Negro Slaves; *one of them a short likely Madagascar,* named Gruff, about 26 years of Age; being imported young speaks very good English; was cloath'd in a dark grey Kersey Waistcoat and Breeches, with Mettal Buttons; he is a Carpenter by Trade: Another named Tom, *likewise a Madagascar;* cloathed in the same Manner; he is about 35 years of Age, a tall, lusty Fellow, and speaks pretty good English, by Trade a Sawyer: The other a Lad, about 17 years of Age, named Spark, and I believe Virginia-born, of a low Stature, pretty Black; . . . he has been used as a Waiting-man. (*Virginia Gazette,* Williamsburg, May 30 to June 5, 1745, emphasis mine)

From 1736 to 1745 there were numerous runaway notices for Malagasy slaves. In addition to those above, there was the November 1736 notice from Benjamin Needle of Prince William County whose slave had skin that was "yellowish" and whose hair was "like a Madagascar's" and the notice from Robert Chesley of Saint Mary's Courts, Maryland, who was searching for a white servant and Robin, a "Madagascar native."[50] Note that this Tidewater district, Saint

Mary's, is also the location of the woman Mary who, in 1796, wrote to the courts protesting that there had been a mistake, since as a Malagasy she should not have been enslaved. It suggests the possibility that Mary may have known others besides her mother who were "Madagascar born."

By the time of the American Revolution, most slaves lived in families, and most households included two parents linked to extended households. On the other hand, according to Mechal Sobel, most late eighteenth-century and early nineteenth-century plantation records list only mothers and children, although a minority of church records, account books, and especially Bibles record black families' fathers as well as mothers. Landon Carter was unique in referring to slave children as their father's in his journals and records.[51] In any event, analysis of plantation records, like those of Thomas Jefferson and George Washington, show that even when planters recognized slave marriages, slave couples were often not housed together. Thus, the central household often did not include a resident father. Similarly, slaves who worked in the "big house" most often were members of fractured families where some worked in the house, some on the farm or as artisans, and some on other plantations.[52] Nevertheless, about two-fifths of the slave women on large plantations and a fifth on small farms lived with husbands as well as children by the 1750s. The same proportion of men as women lived in nuclear households, according to Kulikoff's findings, and because children of separated spouses usually lived with their mothers, large numbers of men, even on big plantations, lived only with other men.[53] The Malagasy men, a minority in their shipmate group and a minority among the other men, thus probably lived more culturally isolated lives than Malagasy women and children of their group. It is important that we not transfer contemporary Western ideals to recent arrivals from Madagascar and West Africa when thinking of the eighteenth-century saltwater Negro family or household. Throughout most of the African continent and in Madagascar, leisure time and work was often gender segregated, and couples did not expect to live side by side and do most things together. This is not to diminish the difficulty and emotional hardship that such separations in Virginia caused but rather to caution that we remember the dynamic cultural context of Virginia's eighteenth-century captive workers.

If Malagasy slaves found themselves with few of their former shipmates on the same plantation, what conditions existed for them to pass on their ideas of Madagascar to the next generation? One factor may have been that several children were among those shipped. Those children may have provided a bridge between the first generations and those that followed, outliving the older captives and still alive when the children of the older captives matured. Tom and Gruff, we remember from the example above, arrived as children, according to the notice about their disappearance. Many examples can be found in planters' journals that give evidence of the practice of putting children with older women of the same background in order to enhance their survival chances. The use of such practices can be gleaned from looking through the account books and diaries of the major planters themselves. In most instances, small children stayed with older female slaves, friends, or relatives most of the day, learning how to do field work, helping around the grounds, or running errands. Morgan reports that over the course of the eighteenth century, women came to outnumber men as field workers, as slave men became the primary beneficiaries of the growth in skilled opportunities occurring in that era. At the same time, children generally were sent to the fields from age nine to fifteen, and were often used for the lighter tasks of weeding tobacco.[54] Fortunate youngsters eventually learned a trade, from blacksmithing to sewing. Opportunities for young children to hear stories from the old folks were probably frequent on plantations and in free households. One way to imagine the slave household is to include those elderly slaves and friends, sometimes but not always relations, who interacted intimately with the family even if they lived apart.

In the case of inheritance practices among the planters, Lorena Walsh explains that, aside from the Virginia elite, few Chesapeake planters practiced the tradition of passing slave property on to the eldest son, who could distribute them among his siblings or keep them and reimburse his siblings. She further explains, "Most parents commonly divided their personal property relatively equally among all their children, whatever the consequences for the slaves. . . . The Burwells' inheritance strategies unintentionally afforded their bondspeople more generational continuity and for a time more settled places of residence than was the lot of most slaves."[55] The (mostly Ibo descended) slaves of Carter's Grove, along with the land properties, eventually went to the Burwell family.

The children of the great planters, such as Robert, Landon, and Charles Carter, were community leaders and members of the old guard associated with the Church of England. By the 1770s public discourse expanded regarding older forms and institutions of worship, such as the Church of England, versus newer practices in the form of the Baptist and Methodist sects. Robert Carter III converted and became a Baptist, much to the chagrin of his community. The discourse of the time was especially directed against hierarchy, or symbolically legitimated inequality, in the highest levels of society.[56] Certainly, the move toward "grassroots" religious practice paralleled colonists' desire to be free of the "tyranny of the English." These debates heightened the fervor toward colonial independence and consequently heightened the contradiction of colonial planters representing themselves as exploited and miserable victims of the British while holding thousands of black slaves. Many of the planters, including Robert Carter III, son of Robert "King" Carter, upon seeing the increasing size of the slave community and the growing numbers of slaves of mixed heritage, responded by freeing large portions of their slaves. By the time the first country-born generation would have reached adulthood, ethnic references by planters began to disappear and, by the end of the century, slave owners increasingly turned to skin color as a descriptor as fewer saltwater slaves arrived.

By 1774 a band of Virginia slaves met to elect a leader "who would conduct them to the English troops should they arrive," and black rebelliousness in the Chesapeake increased in anticipation of the coming Revolutionary War. In the years leading up to the war, Thomas Paine denounced slavery, and Quakers began to manumit their slaves where the law allowed. By 1776 nearly fifteen thousand blacks opted for the royalist ranks, while five thousand served in the Continental army.[57] The national prohibition against black troops was not applied throughout, and though Congress never formally repealed a ban on black soldiers, army officers began to allow state recruiters to enlist freedmen.[58] The movement of black men resulting from the war is, perhaps, one explanation for the stories about Malagasy (Virginia) ancestors in New England around the end of the war, since we know that most imports from Madagascar, in the prior fifty years, were limited to Virginia.

Some white planters felt that those slaves who had remained loyal to them, or who had gone with their masters to war, deserved special consideration. Others were motivated by the spirit of independence and the call for justice that circulated in so many pamphlets of the era. In 1782 a law was passed in Virginia providing for the option of manumission of slaves in the new commonwealth.[59] Historical records indicate that a disproportionate number of slaves freed during this period and afterward were, in fact, people of mixed heritage with some Anglo-American ancestry. Robert F. Engs reports, for example, that in Hampton, Virginia, by the mid-nineteenth century, the town's free-black population "were not entirely 'free' and not entirely 'black' either. Most of them were mulattos, and many of them shared family names with the whites responsible for their complexion."[60] While Virginia passed the Manumission Act in 1782, by 1785 Virginia had fallen into a postwar depression, the price of cereals fluctuated and fell, and the value of slaves and tobacco declined sharply.[61]

As the nation took up arms for the Revolutionary War, African Americans joined both camps, with a majority casting their lot with the British. Most blacks expected the conflict to result in national manumission, but this was not the case. Instead, former white revolutionaries tabled schemes for gradual emancipation in Virginia and elsewhere in the South, crafting legislation allowing southern masters to recapture fugitives in search of freedom in the North.[62]

Some male slaves traveled as valets with their masters during the years of the Revolutionary War. Such was the case of Sterling Claibourne, the father of Claibourne Gladman. Gladman was born free, but his father was born a slave. Local historian Ted Delaney explains that Virginia freedman Gladman "was born in eastern Virginia in 1788, the son of Sterling Claibourne. Gladman's father Sterling was the slave and 'best friend'" of Revolutionary War general Butler Claibourne, who gave Sterling his freedom "one year after the Revolution as reward for bravery and loyalty during the War."[63] There is no record that suggests that Sterling was General Claibourne's brother, but this is a distinct possibility for that place and time. There is also the case of Cesar Tarrant of Hampton, a black veteran of the Revolutionary War who was given freedom and a land grant from the Commonwealth of Virginia in gratitude for his services.[64] During the Revolutionary War, however, there was only a minority of slaves who accompanied their owners to war. Many slaves took advantage of the chaos of that time to either join the Royalists or to run away to freedom.

Family Oral Traditions

All I know is that my family insists that we descended from a woman who was a Malagasy, and she was in Virginia.[65]

How much of the story of the eighteenth-century, immigrant slave generation is reflected in narratives claiming Malagasy descent? Very little. What family narratives tell of this period is in collapsed form, dense, and brief. The slaves' bonds of newly constructed kinship, *situationally* created kinship were typical of surviving shipmates from slave vessels, but over time the stories that described these bonds were lost. Certainly, the presence of several captives from the same or contiguous territories favored a sense of community, allowing sentiments of ethnic solidarity and identities based on common experience and origin. But even without these bonds, the common experience of enslavement was sufficient to encourage new social relations based on that shared experience.

There is, however, one narrative that explicitly refers to seeking a Malagasy marriage partner. Significantly, this is from the descendant of a man who was a sailor:

My great-great-great grandfather was a Malagasy and was in Connecticut in 1760. He fought in the American Revolution and later worked as a merchant seaman, possibly a whaler. He lived in New Haven and is said to have asked permission to stop and get a wife in Madagascar while out on a voyage. He got his wife in Madagascar and returned with her to Connecticut, where he remained until about 1815. He is remembered as telling stories about harpoons, which he associated particularly with Africa. The family remembers him as having dark skin and "hair to the floor."[66]

The man who recounted this story also noted that his mother's family was descended from maroons who lived "on the Virginia peninsula" in 1837.[67] The possibilities of ethnic and cultural enclaves among maroons, as Lorena Walsh has demonstrated in the case of Ibo and Calabar slaves on Carter plantations, are real, though understudied.[68] The fact that the above-described sailor wanted and was able to return to Madagascar to seek a wife raises other questions. It suggests that the sailor belonged to a network, in America or on the sea, that reinforced his feeling of "Malagasy-ness," for want of a better word, and that he also felt comfortable going to Madagascar to secure a wife. This raises questions about language, his ability to speak Malagasy, and what languages were predominant among black seamen at the time. Pier Larson, in *Ocean of Letters*, argues that the impact of the Malagasy language among maritime workers in the Indian Ocean has been grossly underestimated.[69] Perhaps there are reasons to believe that these maritime networks extended as far as the U.S. eastern coast by the beginning of the nineteenth century. Moreover, if the sailor spoke Malagasy, it is possible he practiced this language in America, allowing him to remain conversant so that he could communicate on trips abroad. This narrative is one of the most compelling, because it suggests possibilities of an enclave of Malagasy speakers in the Anglo-American colonies in the last half of the eighteenth century.

It is likely that the Malagasy cohorts sought each other out whenever possible and even found themselves together when occasional

plantation rituals required additional labor or favored large community efforts for celebrations such as Christmas. It would have been
their children, a new generation of transoceanic, multiethnic African unions who, hearing tales from Malagasy "uncles" and "aunts,"
began to emphasize, and perhaps privilege, their Malagasy ancestry.
It is unlikely that many of these children, or their parents, had much
power in deciding whom they would marry. It is doubtful, for instance, that parents could arrange for their children to marry others
of Malagasy descent. It is more reasonable to suggest that geographic
proximity of individual Malagasy slaves on various plantations and
the social proximity of masters favored close kin networks among
both slaves and among masters and thus included a certain number of descendants of Malagasy slaves who inevitably married each
other or had children together.

The slave descendants would later be dispersed to other planter
families, both through the westward movement of planters' sons toward the Piedmont regions of Virginia and through widening marriage networks among the planters. Many planters had begun to move
westward into the Piedmont after the revolution, in great part because
lands that had been used for tobacco were becoming exhausted, terms
of trade with England for tobacco had changed, and people were di-
versifying their farming strategies to include cereal crops, such as
wheat and corn.

At some point, the arrivals of 1719–21 would have begun to seek
news of their shipmates in the neighboring plantations and counties. Occasions to see each other may have been rare, though. They
were obliged to build a life where they were, as best they could. They
could not build a "Malagasy community" based on any residential
terms, although they may have had, in the first generation at least, a
language community.

The arrival of numerous slaves from Madagascar is remembered
by the black community and not only by those who believe they are
descendants but also by others who tell stories of neighbors and other
families remembered as Malagasy. T. O. Madden, born in 1860,[70] wrote
a history of his family from Culpeper, Virginia, in which he makes
reference to neighbors of his great-great-grandmother, the Bundy

family, who said they were from Madagascar (see chapter 2). Madden describes them as "tall, dark-skinned, and Indian or Asian-looking, with slanted eyes and straight hair. They claimed to have come from the island of Madagascar, off Africa (they still looked the same and still claimed to be from Madagascar a century later, when as a child I knew the Bundy family)."[71]

The most common phrase in the narratives is that "my ancestor was kidnapped and brought to Virginia." Following this statement, some allusion is made to the work this person performed on the plantation, and, interestingly, often this is a woman who worked in the "big house" as a servant. Numerous references to the placement of Malagasy in intimate relation to the planter's family raise questions about sexual exploitation, on the one hand, and the allure of the exotic, on the other. Consider, for instance, the story of the McCaw family from North Carolina, who claimed to have been owned by the Duke family. I interviewed the family matriarch by phone in the 1980s, when she was in her late seventies.[72] Mrs. McCaw said she learned from her parents that the Malagasy were used as "decorative slaves." They were coachmen and valets. She laughed as she remembered her grandmother telling her what she had learned from her mother: "They don't beat *we*." In other words, she remembered her grandmother remembering *her* mother's words revealing that the Malagasy slaves had a special position in the slave hierarchy.[73] This allusion to special placement suggests a world of reasons that claims to a Malagasy identity were attractive. This is supported by the runaway ads, where we learn that both Tom and Gruff were skilled workers, suggesting that they were placed as apprentices.

As Michel-Rolph Trouillot asks, "can historical narratives convey plots that are unthinkable in the world within which these narratives take place? How does one write a history of the impossible?" When Robert "King" Carter named his slaves, he did it with the intent of changing their ideas of themselves, and it was done as an exercise of power. It seems it rarely, if ever, occurred to him, or his sons, that slaves were simultaneously creating new identities from past experiences and the newness of their American lives.[74] Moreover, it is reasonable to postulate that it was the first generation of "country-born" slaves, living as they did between two imagined worlds—that of their parents' past lives and that of their dreams of freedom—who paid close attention to memories passed on to them in the form of stories, anecdotes, and moralistic parables. They would have been looking for tools to help them assess their position in the world and their value as human beings.

Trouillot argues that "the contention that enslaved Africans and their descendants could not envision freedom—let alone formulate strategies for gaining and securing such freedom—was based not so much on empirical evidence as on an ontology, an implicit organization of the world and its inhabitants . . . this worldview was widely shared by whites in Europe and the Americas and by many non-white plantation owners as well."[75] While first-generation "country-born" slaves watched their parents pine away, or emotionally close down, even while they fought to survive, the little that children could glean of what life was like for their parents before enslavement in America must have been very valuable indeed, for it suggested other ways of being. For the planter, on the other hand, the future belonged to the powerful, and this imagined future was based on the continued omnipotence of whites. In that world, a Malagasy slave would neither remain Malagasy nor remember Madagascar, because it was not admissible in the master's imagined future.

Early manumission probably helped some families maintain historical narratives, as freedom from bondage allowed more personal time. Robert Carter III eventually manumitted all his slaves, many of whom had, moreover, been trained in various skills at Corotoman plantation.[76] Through individual manumissions beginning in 1792 and later through a gift of deed, Carter himself or through his will had manumitted over two hundred souls by 1804. We can postulate that those slaves helped populate the growing urban centers where freed blacks congregated, such as Williamsburg, Hampton Roads, Petersburg, and Frederick, and Baltimore in Maryland. Petersburg, Virginia, stands out in particular as a place where many fled after being manumitted in the wake of the American Revolution, when manumission became popular for a short period, about thirty years. We have noted that bordering properties and kinship ties made it possible for country-born slaves of Malagasy descent to marry each other. For that matter, we can postulate that there were many marriages of people who were of mixed Calabar and Malagasy descent by the end of the eighteenth century.[77] It is also likely that manumitted people sought others of similar background with whom they could share rare moments of relaxation or celebration. Family histories became important as a means of defining identity and of bolstering morale. It may be that freed slaves of partly Malagasy descent purposefully married each other, although no written evidence exists of this.

The slave's and freed person's households were critical sites for engaging memory, where social space was created for building new historicized identities. First-generation, country-born slave culture favored the development of a transgenerational tradition of being Malagasy *and* black in the Americas.[78] Early descendants may have learned that they need not choose between Malagasy and other ancestors but rather that they could privilege one ancestor's memory over others'.[79]

As we know, most Malagasy slaves brought to North American mid-Atlantic ports during the eighteenth century were women and children.[80] Perhaps these children further developed a sense of Malagasy identity from the women who traveled with them. It is most probable that adult female captives, known to the children since their days of quarantine before departure from Madagascar, assumed roles of mothers, aunts, and big sisters, to whom the younger people looked for guidance, spiritual sustenance, and confirmation of their very much challenged humanity. The surviving child captives, whose lives overlapped into the next generation may have served as an important link to the creole children of the women as well, who ended up scattered throughout related Virginia households. It is arguable that early descendants of slaves from Madagascar insisted on this origin as a means to capture and produce future generations who would remember them, creating a symbolic space that would place them as ancestors and echo their understanding of what constituted a person.[81] We should imagine that there were sometimes conflicts between fathers and mothers of different ethnic origins, for example, Malagasy and

Ngola, or Malagasy and Ibo, who each saw in their children a chance to instill some ideals and concepts from their homelands. If, in Madagascar, families of the eastern regions were ambilineal, that is to say attributed inheritance from maternal and paternal lines, this was not the case of societies of the Biafran hinterlands. Thus from a gendered perspective, women may have had to actively instill an appreciation of Madagascar heritage in counterpoint to more patriarchal visions of child rearing and family belonging that characterized West African sensibilities that were carried to Virginia. Conversely, if Malagasy women were taken as concubines, the reference to Madagascar was what they could give their children in the face of the insecurity of their relations with white males in power.

The role of women in the transmission of culture has been much written about, and in this case should not be underestimated; nor should the possibility of their rape and concubinage.[82] Female ancestors appear in close proximity to white families in the majority of the slave narratives that I collected. They are spoken of as nannies and as maids, but rarely as workers in the fields. This, in addition to the fact that many of the families appear to have gained freedom before the Civil War, suggests that many of the Malagasy women were taken as concubines by their masters. It is probable that the reputation of Madagascar, the stories of pirates and "native wives," preceded the actual arrival of the women from that island. Some women may have actively tried to seduce their masters as a strategy of survival, while the majority may have been exploited sexually with no choice in the matter. Before closing on this subject, which deserves a study of its own, I would mention that close readings of court cases regarding race in eighteenth- and early nineteenth-century Virginia, as done by Joshua Rothman, show that straightness of hair was a very important racial marker of the time. Many whites were repulsed by African hair, which they found to be like "wool" and an indication of possible subhuman status. Many preferred mixed-race slaves for work in the house, as they considered them "improved" by white blood. Straight or wavy hair may have been a curse for many of the Malagasy women who found that white males considered them attractive.[83] We do not know if having a Malagasy girl was an act of conspicuous consumption, of possession of the exotic. However, the factors discussed above certainly point to the likelihood that many of the female slaves ended up as slave consorts to white planters.

It appears that some women arrived after the Revolutionary War and before 1820 as servants to British men. The fragments that contemporary African Americans share at family reunions and on genealogy websites sometimes refer to Virginia and England. The following is an example: "At the present time I am researching my family, who lived in Richmond, Va. I was told by my late great-aunt that we had a relative who came from Madagascar to England, and I believe came to Virginia."[84]

It is probably only in the last century that much of the detail of these narratives has been lost, as people became more educated and reasoned differently about what was most important in their lives. In today's generation of slave descendants, one is struck by the fact that the only remaining information is barely more than a list of place-names that can be correlated with lists of African American surnames from Virginia and claims to Malagasy ancestry emanating from such family groups. Still, the surnames associated with these claims present a striking record.

The following Internet query is from an African American who claims descent from the white Ragland family and from a Malagasy slave. It is interesting because it comes from Petersburg, a center for manumitted slaves in the late eighteenth century. The author, who used the title "Malagasy Ancestors Stolen," states on a genealogy website,

My name is Joi Dickerson and I am an African-American descended from the Ragland family. I have an ancestor John D. Ragland who was one of the many children of a slavemaster named Ragland in Petersburg, VA and his seamstress. . . .

My 92 year [old] lucid grandfather told me that a plantation owner left his plantation to my Madagascan maternal ancestor but she was denied the plantation due to the fact that she was black. She took her children and moved into the *Smokey* Mountains.[85]

This query demonstrates the writer's commitment to understanding the fate of her ancestor from Madagascar and the conditions in which she lived. This posting is then followed by a response from someone called Vollena, who shows an interest in establishing contact with possible relatives. This online dialogue gives an example of how people claiming Malagasy heritage use genealogy websites to validate their family histories and to find other people like themselves. Vollena also claims ancestors with the Ragland surname and refers back to Buckingham, Virginia, which is roughly one hundred fifty miles west of Richmond and one hundred miles northeast of Lynchburg.

There is documentation that suggests Malagasy slaves may have belonged to the Ragland family. For example, the customs official in Williamsburg at the time of the 1719–21 arrival was Cole Digges, who had a home in Petersburg. The Ragland mansion in Petersburg is not far from Digges's house, and Digges was the supervising official in the case of the *Prince Eugene*'s Captain Stretton. This suggests a link, though tenuous, among Ragland and Digges, Stretton, and the cargo of the *Mercury,* one of the ships mentioned in chapter 2 that brought slaves from Madagascar. The Raglands also held land in Hanover, Virginia.[86] Furthermore, there are other narratives of self-identified Malagasy descendants from African American Ragland families, suggesting that a Madagascar story was known among several Ragland slaves.[87]

In 2003 one African American woman mentioned to me[88] that one of her forebears, surnamed Lee, traveled from Virginia to Canada sometime around 1790, and family lore stated that he was from Madagascar.[89] In subsequent conversations, she mentioned additional family branches in Virginia, such as the Ragland family of Petersburg. It occurred to me that she was possibly descended from more than one Malagasy in Virginia, given the geographic distribution of her family in the commonwealth. When I mentioned this to her, she replied, "Your theory is quite intriguing, especially when I consider that the Raglands are from my mother's Virginia side, the Randolphs from my father's Virginia side, and the Lees from my father's Canadian side. Wouldn't it be amazing to find out that the Canadian Lees actually started out in Virginia connected to Robert E. Lee of Virginia [plantations], therefore, the Randolph line?"[90]

The above discussion of the Raglands shows how dense social networks remain in family memory, as both geographically embodied and historically rooted in the slavery era of Virginia. The rapidity with which family researchers establish connections based on surnames, origins in Virginia, and a story about Madagascar is striking. The African American family surnames of self-described descendants of Malagasy slaves, said to have been inherited from slavery times, are shared with the biggest Virginia planters of the colonial era: Randolph, Carter, Lee, Ragland, Ragsdale, Brown, Meriweather, Lewis, Dandridge (the maiden name of George Washington's wife), and Catlett. Interestingly, there are no Burwells. Perhaps slaves inherited from Carter by the Burwell family retained the Carter name. There are also African Americans claiming Malagasy ancestry with the surnames Belsches, Beckinridge, and Steptoe,[91] names of Virginia planters less widely known today but nonetheless connected by kin and social convention to the families listed above. Family stories claiming Malagasy origin today often refer to towns, counties, and plantations throughout eastern and middle Virginia, particularly Richmond, Culpeper, Essex, York, Hanover, and New Kent County.

The enacted "narratives" themselves are lengthy, open discussions in which the common but majestic stories of love, loss, marriage, death, and birth are recounted from the far past to the present. I have been fortunate to be present while some families recounted their Virginia histories. As Portelli points out regarding oral histories, it is the occasion of the visit, and the researcher's request, that in some fashion creates the narrative that is recorded, even if the researcher has been invited, and even if efforts are made to maintain distance. The performance becomes a layered oratory as intimate and other meanings are woven together for the benefit of a new listener. Fortunately, at times my presence was forgotten or minimized in importance as storytellers gained steam.

The narratives sometimes take the form of short lectures and are intertwined with dialogue and discussion as various family members add or dispute details. These talks can go on for hours and may continue through a meal. The Malagasy story is key to ensuing generations' stories, and the narratives gather more detail as they get closer to contemporary times. These performances are valuable not just for the history they infer but for the attitudes and behaviors they present. Pride and sadness, loss and tenacity are themes that repeat throughout, and more than one family has sheepishly admitted to "cousin marrying," which also answers some questions about how information circulated within lifetimes and was passed down over the generations.

It cannot be surprising that the trauma experienced by that first generation precluded the creation and passing down of detailed accounts of their suffering. The bare quality of these testimonies is itself a marker of the conditions under which the stories originated and were passed down. The silences speak loudly of the limited social space and time that was available for first-generation (American-born) descendants to learn about the country of their mothers and, very occasionally, their fathers (since women were the majority among the slaves arriving from Madagascar), and the importance of this information relative to their day-to-day survival. Within this silence, however, one also notices a yearning to know more about Madagascar.

To some extent, whether they merely *believe* that they are the descendants of slaves from Madagascar or they materially *are* the descendants is not the most important or interesting problem. These stories are about more than genealogy; they are the stories of insiders. The fact of being in a family network that holds a Madagascar story is important to people; they go to great lengths to find substantiating historical evidence for the logic of the narratives. Moreover, knowing the story about Madagascar places a person in a particular cultural framework, the framework that Bourdieu calls habitus, a dynamic aggregate of particular tastes and positionalities that in this case bestows signifying cultural capital. They are people, descendants of slaves, who have a story about where their black ancestors came from.

It is especially worth noting that within a community where few people knew world geography, and where generations of people led largely isolated lives in segregated black southern communities, the notion that someone *could reasonably* self-identify as a descendant of a Malagasy slave has not been strange or new. The concept—the idea—of claiming a Malagasy slave as an ancestor is important to those who assume this history, and furthermore it is believable to their neighbors. It is a concept that has had local valor for the claimants' families and for their public lives. This suggests that the idea is historically rooted in the African American community, reflecting realities of ethnic difference and compromise that prevailed many generations ago, as long ago as the Revolutionary period and beyond.

4

After the American Revolution
Undocumented Arrivals

MANY SLAVES WERE FREED following the Manumission Act of 1782 in Virginia. Given the high proportion of Malagasy-descended slaves at "King" Carter's own properties and those belonging to others in his social network, it is probable that a good number of those who were manumitted in the turbulent years between 1782 and 1806 (when Virginia passed new laws restricting manumissions) were people of Malagasy and Ibo descent. The tendency toward manumission, however, had started before the Revolutionary War. As early as 1769, Richard Bland, who was in the House of Burgesses, proposed that masters should be allowed to free their slaves whenever they chose, but he was called "an enemy of his country," and his bill, composed and seconded by Thomas Jefferson, was never even put to a vote.[1]

John Randolph, whose grandfather had been an investor with Carter in the Malagasy slave importations, "scrupulously provided for the Negroes set free by his brother, although he described them as 'a burden to themselves, and a pest to the neighborhood.'"[2] Freed slaves, some of them formerly attached to the Carter, Randolph, and Page properties, worked in towns and on farms, joining already established free-black communities.

Free blacks were usually seen as a menace by the white community, and they found it necessary to work continuously to gain a living. They had to keep a watchful eye, as freed persons were often the object of abuse or even kidnapping for resale as slaves. A review of court cases of the period in Virginia shows how many, and how often, freed blacks were obliged to go to court or to jail for failure to pay taxes—something that was often beyond their means. By 1813 laws were passed restricting free-black movement and requiring them to leave Virginia unless they were sponsored by an influential white person. Such sponsorships required a court-issued document proving legal status. Everywhere in the slaveholding states, free blacks were disdained. They were often suspected of harboring or assisting runaway slaves, and because they competed with slave and poor-white labor, it was often difficult for them to find work. Many free blacks moved to Ohio, only to return in the 1830s so that they could be closer to family and familiar territory. This historical period is reflected in some of the narratives, which describe migrations to and from Ohio. Others went north to Baltimore, New York City, and New England.[3]

For the enslaved, things became more difficult as planter families switched from tobacco to cereal crops or invested in iron mines where slaves were sent to work. Many slaves left loved ones and familiar environments as the children of the great planters migrated westward to take advantage of newly available fertile lands in the Piedmont. Moreover, due to a swell in slave imports right before the revolution that coincided with westward migration, the Piedmont region of Virginia for the first time had more first-generation slaves than the Tidewater. Up to 40 percent of slaves in the Upper South worked as hired labor during this period, including children, who turned their earnings over to their masters.[4]

Laws making transatlantic slave trading illegal, passed in 1808, also meant that few, if any, saltwater slaves now arrived in Virginia slave communities. This development had important and lasting cultural and psychological consequences for the slave community. African cultural infusions slowed considerably, and if, on one hand, slaves were glad not to witness the pitiable and violent passage of the first months of a newly arrived captive's life, they were also no longer hosts and teachers to newcomers and no longer would gain information that new slaves might bring. It was now up to parents and grandparents to tell children about what that period was like, what it meant to see arriving saltwater slaves walking confusedly down a wooden plank to their new "homes" on plantations.

With the eventual closing of the transatlantic slave trade[5] (and in spite of the illegal trade, which continued clandestinely), the domestic slave market was reinvigorated. Facing the declining returns on tobacco crops and the wavering prices of cereals, planters of the Upper South decided that keeping large communities of slaves was no longer economical. Thousands of slaves were traded west and south during this period to newly settled lands in Kentucky, Alabama, Tennessee, and Mississippi.[6] Many were taken as far south as New Orleans, which had a thriving slave market at the time, and from there hundreds were sold to newly established cotton plantations. These events, too, are reflected in some of the narratives of self-identified Malagasy descendants presented in this chapter.

In addition to a bustling domestic slave trade in the United States, illegal transatlantic slave trading brought in huge profits as landowners in the Lower South looked for more labor to sustain their new plantations. At this time domestic slaves, already acclimated to life in America, were often more expensive than clandestinely imported saltwater slaves or Afro-American slaves brought in from the Caribbean and South America.

The illegal trade was complex and geographically diverse. To avoid British antislavery brigs and American customs officials who had not been corrupted by the brisk and voluminous winnings available, slavers bought transshipped slaves who had been brought across the Atlantic to the markets of Cuba, Brazil, and Mexico and even made occasional daring trips back to the continent of Africa. Often saltwater slaves were brought in from the Caribbean and South America under the guise of being natives of the Americas. Others were contraband brought in clandestinely to the numerous river ports of Alabama, Florida, and Georgia.

The Historical Record

Having stabilized by the 1750s, the slave community was growing at a rate faster than the white population by the end of the American

Revolution, and white Virginians were beginning to worry about the size of the black population. In 1772 the House of Burgesses beseeched the king to "remove all restraining . . . on laws as might check so pernicious a commerce [which] we have too much reason to fear will endanger the very existence of your Majesty's American dominion." The petition was ignored by the English king. By 1782, Virginia had 270,762 slaves and 296,852 free persons. Many Virginians agreed with Thomas Jefferson that the chief task was to free the commonwealth from the bondage of its 50 percent Negro population.[7] This was not just a concern of freeing Negroes from bondage but of freeing elite white planters from the dangers of living with so many unwilling black captives in their midst. The new move toward manumission was the composite product of these fears, the Anabaptist movement, the pressure to free slaves emanating from Quakers and to a lesser extent Methodists, and the spirit of liberty and liberation that followed the American Revolution.

In 1785 a bill that would have repealed the 1782 Manumission Act nearly passed in the House of Burgesses and Thomas Jefferson's second emancipation proposal never received a hearing in the Virginia House of Delegates. Also in that year, the general committee of the Baptist Church passed a motion that declared "hereditary slavery to be contrary to the word of God," but it was met with unfavorable responses, especially when the committee tried to compose a gradual emancipation plan. Still, some Virginians did begin to contemplate measures that might ameliorate slavery or liberate some of their black labor force. For example, planter George Wythe liberated several of his slaves, providing them rents and interest in trust, a plan so generous that the grandnephew who had expected a greater inheritance put arsenic in Wythe's coffee.[8] Detractors complained of dangerous, dirty, free-Negro communities growing in their midst, but manumissions continued.

In 1791, Robert Carter III, who had slaves distributed on almost twenty plantations across a broad swath of Virginia, began individual manumissions. Over the next year he wrote a deed of gift that would eventually free all of them (much to the chagrin of his children and other family members).[9] In February 1792, through his deed of gift,

Carter undertook the largest private emancipation in American history. Recognizing family bonds among slaves, he staggered it over time, and couples were freed together.[10] Some freed people moved to cities in Virginia and Maryland, and others to Ohio. Others continued to work for Carter for wages, and a sailor, Gloucester Billy, continued to work on Carter's ship but as a freeman. By 1797 entire plantations owned by Robert Carter, such as Leo, were occupied by free blacks living on small farms.[11] On the other hand, some slaves who had been promised freedom in consideration of their service during the Revolutionary War were reenslaved. George Washington's "mulatto man, William, who calls himself William Lee," found that this promise for freedom did not become reality until the death of his master.[12]

Many free blacks went hungry while slaves were eating their meager, but daily, meals. Although life was very difficult for free blacks, slaves considered this a better future than remaining captive workers on plantations. In the following text we will look at descriptions of life for free blacks at the end of the eighteenth and in the first half of the nineteenth centuries, using descriptions from Petersburg, the Hampton-Richmond area, and Lynchburg.

Petersburg

Hundreds of former captives settled in or around Petersburg, just southwest of the James River and the town of Hopewell. Petersburg was an urban hub characterized by a large percentage of manumitted slaves and, particularly, numerous free African American women who were heads of household. Suzanne Lebsock suggests that the presence of the more liberal new Christian sects may have been part of the reason for the high number of manumitted slaves who lived there.[13]

Hopewell, near Francis Eppes's plantation, was initially known as Bermuda City, and later Charles City, becoming a part of Prince George County in 1703. Charles City is often mentioned in Robert "King" Carter's journals. Notably, the Shirley plantation was in Charles City County, much of it having come into possession of the Carter family through marriage in 1723.[14] These towns and settlements were not far from Petersburg. Freed slaves would have likely migrated to the larger and more cosmopolitan center of Petersburg. Hopewell, however, provides a good example of the evolving social networks that resulted in manumitted slave migration to urban centers.

The history of the Eppes family leads back to the early Tidewater families of the Jeffersons, Carters, and Randolphs. For example, the Eppes family owned three plantations along the Appomattox River. The Shirley plantation, on the James River, owned by Charles Carter, lay just to the north of their property.[15] Francis Eppes's descendant, John Wayles Eppes, married his first cousin Maria Jefferson in 1797, the younger surviving legitimate daughter of Thomas Jefferson, whose wife, Martha, was a Wayles. Eppes owned the mother of Sally Hemings, who we now know was the mistress of Thomas Jefferson. When Maria died, shortly after the birth of their daughter, her husband, John Wayles Eppes, took the niece of Sally Hemings, Betsy "Critta" Hemings, as his concubine, and she remained with him for over forty years. We know that there were numerous interracial relationships. Places and people were enmeshed in close property and kin networks, and the geographic distribution of the slaves who migrated to Petersburg in later years, we should recall, was determined by earlier inheritances, marriage gifts, and slave-hiring practices. This was true across the entire Tidewater region, often with multiple generations repeating the pattern of master/concubine, and slave families who had become linked to master families were circulated among relatives. Typically, when they were emancipated, they sought to live near one another.[16] They were sometimes known as "white slaves."

Although Jefferson did not manumit members of the enslaved Hemings family until later years, many of his cohorts did free their mulatto children and concubines. In view of this, we cannot exclude the possibility that many of these liaisons included Malagasy women or their descendants. The historical record indicates that a good portion, perhaps more than half, of people manumitted during slavery were mulatto and had familial ties with whites. The high proportion of free black women in Petersburg thus deserves special attention in this context. The possibility that many Malagasy women were used as concubines (see chapter 3) poses questions about the proportion of people of mixed Malagasy and Anglo-American descent who became part of the free-black population. In talking of the period from 1790 to 1810,

Susan Lebsock reports that "the most spectacular growth rate . . . was registered by free blacks, who more than tripled their numbers during the two decades. . . . This manumission trend ended in 1806, when new legislation put an end to slave emancipations in Virginia and installed severely repressive laws for free blacks.[17] By 1810, there were more than a thousand free blacks in Petersburg."[18]

Hampton

Hampton is located at the southeastern tip of Virginia's peninsula in what was formerly Elizabeth City County (1634–1952), and the town was the county seat until it eventually merged with the city of Hampton as we know it today. On its southward side near the city of Newport News, the James River empties into the harbor of Hampton Roads, and to the northeast, the York River terminates in Chesapeake Bay. Seventy-five miles northwest of Hampton, alongside the James River, is Richmond, and across the harbor from Hampton are the cities of Norfolk and Portsmouth. Hampton Village, surrounded by water on three sides, was an important port in pre-Revolutionary days and served as a gateway to the wealthy plantations along the James and York Rivers. Free blacks there could make a living through fishing and oystering, in addition to working as servants, boatmen, and at artisanal occupations such as carpenter or metal smith.[19] It is not surprising, then, that many of the narratives about Malagasy ancestors point back to this area of Virginia, as it was a veritable gateway to the plantations along the two rivers and had favorable employment opportunities for those who were emancipated. A narrative from Hampton will be discussed below.

Richmond

Richmond was a significant destination for runaways, who mingled with the free-black population, trying to evade capture or planning to move onward from there. Richmond's grand jury complained to city authorities of the "numerous evils" resulting from the tolerance of "vagrants, beggars, free negroes and runaway slaves."[20] By 1790 roughly thirty-seven hundred people lived in Richmond; half the population was black, and over 90 percent of the black population was enslaved.[21]

In 1800, due to the news of Gabriel Prosser's Rebellion,[22] the city of Richmond and the Virginia General Assembly took action against the free intermingling of whites and blacks, as well as the intermingling of free people and slaves, and police surveillance increased. Many slaves were shipped to the Lower South from Richmond after 1800.

Still, slave labor was critical to nearly every important sector of Richmond's economy, for in addition to tobacco-related work, enslaved men also worked in iron foundries, flour mills, coal mines, railroads, tanneries, and textile manufacturing. Some slaves worked as carpenters, blacksmiths, plasterers, shoemakers, and bookbinders, while others worked as boatmen, fishermen, porters, stevedores and drivers. With this broad use of slave labor, free black males (and poor white males) were regularly marginalized on the labor market. On the other hand, free women of color in Richmond, many of whom had moved to town from surrounding rural areas, particularly dominated the laundry business or worked as domestics.

By the fourth decade of the nineteenth century, Richmond was the regional center for the processing and manufacturing of tobacco, the milling of flour, and the smelting of iron, as well as being the largest slave market. A relatively new town in the area, located at the falls of the James River, it was an entrepot for all river traffic of goods to and from western Virginia. National and international trade passed through Richmond, and it attracted people from all neighboring counties.

Anne Carter Wickham, daughter of Charles Carter and granddaughter of Robert "King" Carter, was one of the inheritors of Carter's estate including slaves. She lived in Hanover, about one hundred miles north of Richmond,[23] where her family had become involved in the Ana Baptist movement. The Hickory Hill plantation, located in Ashland (Hanover), was an appendage to the Shirley plantation in Charles City County. Hanover also had many Quaker residents, including the sister of Johns Hopkins (after whom the current university in Baltimore and Washington, DC, is named). She was married to Nathaniel Crenshaw, who at one time housed more than one hundred free blacks on his estate.[24] Four narratives were collected from Hanover, two of which are connected to the Crenshaw household. Three other narratives claim that Malagasy ancestors passed through Richmond as slaves. Some are presented below in the following section. As well, many Baptist churches were established by families claiming Malagasy descent in Richmond, and Richmond and Hanover are mentioned in several of the family narratives.[25] We can thus cautiously propose that some of Carter's slaves inherited by Ana Page were of mixed Malagasy heritage, and this poses the question of whether there were clusters of such people, free and enslaved, joining the same churches during this period, perhaps with white Baptist support.

Lynchburg

Of free-black life in small towns in the Piedmont region, Lynchburg offers a representative example. Historians Ted Delaney and Phillip Wayne Rhodes recount that "free blacks, like slaves, were generally hated as a class, although often beloved and praised as individuals. White Lynchburgers publicly expressed contempt for 'local free blacks as early as the 1820s." Delaney and Rhodes quote from an anonymous letter to the editor of a Lynchburg newspaper in August 1829: "As citizens [free blacks] contribute nothing to the beauty, harmony or strength of the country—nothing to its wealth or prosperity, and nothing to its happiness. . . . They are worse than dead weight in every respect . . . indolent, improvident, luxurious and vicious." The two historians note that "the rhetoric denouncing free blacks was always . . . vitriolic."[26] These descriptions were generally typical of white opinions of free blacks as a group in Virginia, in spite of evidence given by Robert Engs and Joshua Rothman, who report that many freed individuals connected to white families had broad access to various opportunities and that such exceptions were numerous. In these complex communities, individuals could be accepted and even praised, while as a group free blacks were disdained and mistrusted.

Lynchburg is situated just southwest of Charlottesville and Monticello, the home of Thomas Jefferson. It typifies the small towns (such as Culpeper) that grew up among large plantations and small farms in emerging Piedmont economies following the Revolutionary

War. Like Hopewell, Lynchburg did not attract large numbers of free blacks, who preferred the bigger towns, where they were less isolated, found community, felt greater security in numbers, and had a greater chance of getting work. By the beginning of the nineteenth century, there was a growing trend of migration of white planters to the Piedmont, and slave families were often fractured, as some family members were chosen to accompany their white masters to new homes in the West and South.

Transshipped Domestic Slaves

> Dis time tomorrer night
> Where will I be?
> I'll be gone, gone, gone
> Down to Tennessee.
>
> —Traditional[27]

In the eighteenth century, the main farm crop in Virginia was tobacco. Because tobacco exhausts the soil, a century and a half of unceasing growth impoverished Tidewater Virginia's once fertile lands, and the oldest part of the commonwealth began the nineteenth century as an agricultural community with no money crop. While some planters abandoned these farmlands for new regions in the west of Virginia, the fertile and low-priced lands around the Gulf of Mexico basin soon proved too strong an attraction and pulled settlers from the Upper South.[28]

Between 1820 and 1860, more than four million slaves were sold from one owner to another in the United States. Nearly a fourth of those were carried across state lines. Susan Eva O'Donovan reports that this forced migration dwarfed the transatlantic traffic between Africa and British mainland North America and "decimated enslaved families and communities that had been generations in the making." She adds that "smaller boys and girls accounted for better than 30 percent of all those who were sold into the interstate trade." One reason was that governments in slaveholding states often "exempted those who bought and sold children across state lines from many of the administrative requirements attached to the importation of older slaves, making it easier . . . for slaveholders and traders in South Carolina [for example] to import slaves under the age of fifteen without having to present official certificates attesting to those slaves' good character and orderly behavior in their previous homes."[29] This had a significant impact, increasing the circulation of children as guarantees for loans or to pay debts, and it may have also facilitated the importation of saltwater slaves, including perhaps slaves from Madagascar (see "Family Oral Traditions," below).

Transshipped Saltwater Slaves: The Illegal Slave Trade

Although the transatlantic slave trade was abolished in 1808, attempts to enforce the law stretched through the next decade as the British High Commission worked from West Africa to Cuba to intercept slaving vessels. Though the transatlantic slave trade was coming to an end, slavery itself was not, and through transshipment of slaves many traders were able to pretend that a saltwater slave was born somewhere in the Americas and thus eligible to be resold anywhere in the western Atlantic region.

Hundreds of slave cargoes arrived in Brazil from southeastern Africa during the nineteenth century. The Trans-Atlantic Slave Trade Database covers approximately thirty-five thousand slaving voyages for the entire period of the trade, representing four-fifths of the number of slaves who were actually transported.[30] Of 436 voyages originating in Brazil or Spanish America reported in that database, more than one hundred went to southeastern Africa to purchase slaves. Of the recorded shipments from 1817 to 1836, approximately 160 voyages were from southeastern Africa to southeastern Brazil, or Bahia. However, the tables show that almost all these slaves were purchased in Mozambique. It is not known if these voyages included stops in Madagascar or if they also purchased slaves at the Cape of Good Hope.

The numbers of slaves clandestinely shipped from Brazil and Cuba to the North American mainland after 1808 are not known, and estimates remain contested. Approximately 235 ships sailed into Cuba from ports unknown, or at least unrecorded, during the first half of the nineteenth century. Of recorded voyages to Cuba as noted in the Trans-Atlantic Slave Trade Database, only three are from southeastern Africa (rather than explicitly from Mozambique) during these years. The large number of unidentified ports exporting to Cuba poses a problem that future research may solve; perhaps Madagascar ports were among them. However, even if we were able to establish that a shipment or shipments of Malagasy slaves arrived in Brazil or Cuba from 1808 to 1836, we would still need to identify if and how they could have been transshipped to the United States. Of those two challenges, it is easier to demonstrate how slaves were transshipped from the Caribbean or South America to the United States than to know if a particular group from a particular place of origin in Africa and its islands was among them.

In *The Final Victims,* James McMillin discusses the foreign (transatlantic) slave trade to North America from 1783 to 1810 and describes how, during the first decade of the nineteenth century, slaves were moved along the southern coasts of the United States.[31] McMillin points out various terms used in advertisements, such as *several, a few, a group, a gang,* and *a parcel,* as well as the phrases used for larger slave importations, such as *a small cargo, a shipment, a cargo,* or *a shipload,* the latter usually referring to one hundred enslaved people or more.[32] These words show well that slaves were depersonalized and objectified in the language of the trade, and understanding the differences among these terms affects how illegal activity in the trade might be assessed.

Not only is estimating the numbers of captives problematic, but getting a true number of ships that arrived in the Lower South during those years is also extremely difficult. For example, though customs officials were responsible for reporting all state imports and exports in South Carolina, only a few arrivals and clearances for South Carolina ports other than Charleston were listed. Before the transatlantic trade was outlawed, merchants evaded reporting to avoid taxes. McMillin reports, "Although more than a hundred vessels entered Beaufort and Georgetown annually in the 1780s, duties officials recorded only five arrivals for the four years the report covered."[33] From the time of the Revolutionary War to the year that the trade was banned, small cargoes of slaves "ranging from one to thirty slaves arrived regularly and constituted as much as 10 percent of the Charleston trade."[34]

The disarray and inconsistency of recorded data is true of the Lower South in general. Estimates based on the carrying capacity of American slaving vessels during the 1790s suggest, for example, that ships carried eleven thousand more African captives to North America than incomplete records of arrivals indicate, of which seven thousand probably landed in South Carolina while another four thousand arrived in Georgia.[35] It is suspected that the total number of foreign imports to the North American mainland may have been as high as 109,200 for the first decade of the nineteenth century, including French and Spanish imports into North American ports.[36] While these figures are still under debate, allowing for errors or overestimation still demonstrates that a large volume of captives was illegally brought in after 1810. The latest recorded cases are for the decade 1860–70.

Transshipment of saltwater slaves to the U.S. mainland was attractive because of the huge numbers arriving in Cuba and Brazil (where they were outside the British mandate against the trade for more than forty years after 1808), the insistent need for slave labor in the Lower South, and the rising cost of American-born slaves after the prohibition of the transatlantic trade. Slaves were brought into the Lower South through the abundant waterways of the Florida and Georgia coasts. In closing this short section with its brief survey of a very large subject, I must discuss the examples of Florida and Cuba as two likely candidates for the illegal trade. The existence of numerous family narratives about ancestors from Madagascar arriving in the early nineteenth century suggests that these southern routes of trade were probable trajectories that brought Malagasy captives to the United States after the prohibition of the transatlantic trade.

D. R. Murray wrote an early article on statistics of the slave trade to Cuba, years before the Trans-Atlantic Slave Trade Database project was established by David Eltis of Emory University and others.[37] Though Murray did not benefit from that project's findings, there is information in his article that is of use for our discussion. The two main bodies of archival material on which Murray draws are the customs house records of Havana, covering the years from 1790 to 1821, and the reports of the British commissioners stationed at Havana from 1819 to 1824. He examines the period from 1790 to 1867, since 1790 was the first year of the "open" slave trade under the cedula of 1789,[38] and 1867 was the last year in which a documented slave landing took place in Cuba. From 1790 to 1820 the African slave trade to Cuba was legal according to Spanish law.[39] In 1825 one British official in Cuba figured that an average of 250 slaves per ship for the period 1822–24 was low and that the arrivals in the Havana area alone would have been approximately 2,500 in 1822, 1,000 in 1823, and 4,250 in 1824.[40] The volume of this trade must then take into account the trade from there to Florida, and the implications of *that* trade for states bordering Florida territory, even given the huge demand that we know existed in Cuba at that time for slave labor.

There were American ships involved in this trade. The publication of an anti–slave trade tract by the Society of Friends in 1824 and a federal case involving slave-trading activities in 1860 show that slave importations continued to be an issue of public concern.[41] Frances J. Stafford explains, "So notorious was American participation in the slave trade after 1808, that President Madison in 1810 informed Congress of the necessity of devising further legislation for its suppression."[42] Stafford further states, "A long and sparsely settled coastline and a close proximity to Cuba made [Florida] an ideal location from which to operate."[43] Florida was known as the avenue through which "Negroes" were regularly smuggled across the border into the southern states, particularly via Fernandina and Amelia Island, which served as headquarters for slave smugglers. One trader was able to dispose of one thousand transshipped slaves in less than two months from his post on Amelia Island in 1817.[44]

Thus, there is some evidence that slaves from Cuba were transshipped to the United States via Florida and the coast of Georgia. There is also evidence of American merchants traveling to Brazil to purchase saltwater slaves, whom they later identified to U.S. customs officials as Brazilians. However, documents indicating the provenance of many of these slaves do not exist or have not yet been found.

Family Oral Traditions

The Domestic Transshipment of Slaves

We have noted that after the Revolutionary War and the close of the transatlantic slave trade, many slaves were sold south from Virginia, as domestic, locally born slaves became more valuable. It is probable that some among those sent further south in the domestic transshipment of slaves were the grandchildren and great-grandchildren of the Malagasy slaves who had come to Virginia between 1719 and 1721. The Stith family of Mississippi and Texas claims that their Malagasy ancestor was brought to Mississippi by the daughter of a Virginia planter, possibly accompanying her new husband. The family notes especially the trek southward, for they did not take any of the ships that by that time were making the circuit between Virginia and Mississippi. The family speaks of the master's daughter with little rancor, although they pass on very bad memories of the long walk south. This ancestor traveled with another slave family from the same Virginia plantation, and the two families have remained close, intermarrying over time. Most links with other black families in Virginia were lost.[45]

Undocumented Slave Arrivals

There are several references to Madagascar, both written and oral, that come from the Lower South. Texas and Mississippi, in particular, are the loci of several Madagascar stories. In a segment from an online genealogy discussion under the heading "Lost Relatives," one gentleman posted this in the hopes of making contact with other family members: "I am trying to locate any family ancestors of Oscar McKizzic [of Texas]. Do not have any information other than possible family in Madagascar. Born in 1800's."[46] He received an answer from a woman who claimed to recognize the surname

McKizzic, although the surname she had been looking for was Scott. She, too, was looking for relatives and claimed a Madagascar origin, and she evidently thought that her family and the family of Oscar McKizzic were from the same Texas town: "Hi, I'm also looking for lost relatives. I read your message and the name you used was familiar to my info. . . . The ancestor I'm looking for is name [sic] Scott. I believe they're from the same town. Any info on the town or how I can get info will be greatly appreciated. I spelled it Matagaska, going by the sound."[47]

Another writer, also from Texas and looking for evidence of family from Madagascar, responded: "What part of *Texas* was she supposedly sold in? I too; from what I'm told have Malgasy ancestors but the only thing I know is they ended up in *Sherman, Texas* with the last name *Burnette*. So I'm trying to find any information I can. Anything you have may be helpful."[48] This last hopeful statement demonstrates the importance to descendants of slaves of locating not just contemporary relatives but past relations to people and places. It is also interesting that the narrator refers to how people "ended up" in Texas with "the last name Burnette," giving a sense of the haphazard nature of the family's past experience.

Here, the writers are not sure if they are all descended from the same Malagasy ancestor or if there were several enslaved Malagasy in Texas. Their posts also do not make it clear if they are from families who were transshipped from the Upper South or whether their ancestor from Madagascar is remembered as a more recent arrival. This confusion suggests there is no memory of a group of Malagasy slaves or slave descendants arriving in Texas. However, as we shall discuss later, the absence of an intergenerational reference to a past event does not signify that an event, particularly a traumatic event, did not exist.

The author of the above narrative concerning the ancestor "Scott" says "Matagaska," and in various narratives the terms "Malagasy," "Molly Glasser," or "Madagasky" are also used. An example is the story from Mississippi recounted in chapter 2, regarding the woman who said, "'I'm no nigger. My grandma told me not to let nobody call me no nigger. I'm a Molly Glasser and an ink spitter."[49] As we know, words orally transmitted over time are often mispronounced and misremembered. In fact, it is the irregularity of how the words Madagascar and Malagasy are remembered that adds to the credibility of these oral transmissions. These distortions originating from diverse sources suggest that there was, indeed, a root word—a root concept of Madagascar—that people in the African American community were referring to. A phrase later in the same text refers to the use of betel nuts and thus the term *ink spitter*. This is provocative since betel nuts are an Indian Ocean product and suggests that commodities other than slaves were also traveling these transoceanic routes.

There is another instance of reference to Madagascar from a recorded former slave narrative. In a 1930s interview an eighty-four-year-old Texas man named John Barker stated, "I was born a slave. I'm a Malagasser nigger."[50] Published accounts such as this one mirror the other spoken narratives that have been presented here which I collected. Of course, my texts from family stories are also only representations; and as Portelli argues, even recorded voices on tapes cannot truly reproduce the performance of the oral narrative. Though third-person accounts are more removed from the emotion and rhythm of the original interview, the existence of such narratives is important to this study because of their content.

There are several other such narratives from individuals who claim that an enslaved ancestor from Madagascar arrived in the first half of the nineteenth century. Among these people are William H. Robinson, pastor (North Carolina); John Davis (Hampton, Virginia); Mohammed Ali (Kentucky); and Pascal Beverly Randolph (Virginia). Pastor Robinson was born in 1848 in Wilmington, North Carolina. In the opening section of his book, he recounts, "In reading Stanley and Livingston on Africa we notice that the negro race is divided into different tribes. Among them is the Madagascar tribe, who are noted for their mechanical skill. To this tribe my parents both belonged. . . . My parents, Peter and Rosy, belonged to a very wealthy ship and slave holder, who owned two farms and over five hundred slaves."[51] In the context of our discussion above regarding the timing of the abolition of slavery in Mauritius, the large percentage of skilled laborers who were slaves there, and the marked presence of Indian Ocean workers in the British maritime industry, it is interesting to note that Robinson's father was a maritime worker. He states, "My father was an engineer and towed vessels in and out of Wilmington harbor into the Atlantic ocean. He pursued this occupation for over fifteen years and received many tips by being courteous and always on the alert for ships heaving in sight."[52]

There is more than one narrative from Kentucky and Tennessee. One is by a contemporary of Robinson's, Isaac Johnson, who also wrote and published an autobiography, "Slavery Days in Old Kentucky: A True Story of a Father Who Sold His Wife and Four Children (By One of the Children)." In the opening paragraphs he states,

> I was born in the State of Kentucky in 1844. . . . The family at that time consisted of my father, Richard Yeager, my mother, Jane, an older brother, Louis, a younger brother, Ambrose, and later on another brother, Eddie. . . . As I look back to my boyhood days I can see that my mother was an intelligent woman, considering her station in life, and it is from her, and my paternal uncles in after years, I learned as to my ancestry.
>
> My grandfather was an Irishman, named Griffin Yeager, and his brothers were engaged in the villainous vocation of the Slave Trade. Their business was to steal negroes from Africa or wherever they could get them and sell them as slaves in the United States. My mother was stolen by these people from the island of Madagascar in the year 1840. She was brought to America and given to my grandfather who concluded she would make a good servant. He gave her the name of Jane and kept her till he died, which was soon after. By the terms of grandfather's will, Jane was bequeathed to his eldest son Richard, commonly known as Dick Yeager.[53]

Isaac's mother ended up becoming the common-law wife of Richard (Dick) Yeager, until the white community stepped in and expressed concern about this interracial couple. Since there are several narratives from this region, one wonders if Griffin Yeager and his brothers were responsible for bringing in "lots" or "cargoes" or "parcels" of Malagasy in the clandestine trade sometime between 1830 and 1845.

The next report on a family narrative, published in the *Washington Post* in 1980, also leads us to Kentucky. The reporter who conveyed the family story of the famous boxer Muhammad Ali (Cassius Clay) wrote that of the two paternal aunts that Ali spoke of, Coretta and Eva, only Eva Clay Waddell was living in 1980:

> Eva Clay Waddell still lives in Louisville, and she remembers with warmth and pride her family's history. "My father was Herman Clay," she said, "and my mother was Edith Greathouse Clay. They were Muhammad Ali's grandparents, and they were still living when he was growing up. . . . I never knew the names of my father's parents. They both died before I was born. All I ever heard about them was that my grandmother was a woman from Madagascar, and that she and my grandfather [Muhammad Ali's great-grandparents] were married in Louisville, and their children were born here."⁵⁴

It is striking that all three of these stories refer to the same generation for their Malagasy ancestors' arrival, but the appearance of a cluster of narratives from the Kentucky-Tennessee region raises questions. It may be that slaves brought in illegally from the Gulf were moved through Kentucky and then transshipped to Virginia and North Carolina; that slaves were brought in from Charleston, Richmond, or Hampton and then moved south and west; or, perhaps least likely, that there was more than one clandestine importation of slaves from Madagascar in the nineteenth century.

The texts of these narratives respond to a traumatic experience: the captivity and enslavement of a mother (and father, in one instance), who was forcibly taken in a ship from somewhere in Madagascar and transported to the United States. Deriving from geographically dispersed families with no apparent knowledge of each other, the slave descendant narratives in this section suggest the arrival of young adults or youths in mainland North America between 1800 and 1850. There is a loud silence in these narratives regarding the trajectories of their transatlantic routes to America. O'Donovan says that the domestic transshipped child slaves of the period "lacked the most basic understanding of local and regional geography, a phenomenon that created badly distorted maps even in the minds of those who attempted to attend to the direction and distance of their journeys."[55] On the other hand, we recall that many of the narratives refer to women and men who were kidnapped and, once arrived at their destination, worked closely with their masters and captors. This may have put them in a social position that allowed certain liberties of limited privacy, which may have permitted them, if they were placed on nearby plantations, to continue to talk about their land of origin and perhaps even to speak their own language. But this was probably not the case.

It appears that once arrived, most of the slaves who came through clandestine routes were placed individually, and most of them were women. The fact of not having anyone with whom to share a story of Madagascar or, indeed, of a transatlantic journey has probably contributed to the scarcity or absence of any detailed information about the trajectory followed in America or of life in Madagascar. They did not have the benefit of continuing shipmate relationships that the slaves of 1719–21 who arrived in Virginia from Madagascar had. Hence, children were no doubt the main audience for such stories and may have been the only company such nineteenth-century slaves had for speaking of Madagascar.

Robert Levy's notion of "hypocognition" is useful in understanding the selectivity of the slave's memory. According to Michael Harkin, Levy argues that "certain emotional experiences may not find expression since they lack an appropriate cognitive structuration in the culture that would allow them to become the subject of discourse. In such cases, 'the unarticulated, un-nameable, and chaotic qualities' make them disturbing and dangerous, and . . . potentially creative forces, in revitalization movements, for example."[56] If no descriptions of life aboard the slave ships or arrivals to mainland America remain as family narrative, this was either a choice or the result of trauma the migrating person experienced that made such descriptions impossible. Such absences in the narratives are not the result of simply forgetting what happened. We know from chapter 2 that although descriptions of the Middle Passage don't exist, relations established during the Middle Passage were important. In the case of the 1719–21 slave cohort in Virginia, the possibility of sharing and communicating the shipmate experience probably sustained many people through a very difficult time. In contrast, it does not seem that the shipmates of the mid-nineteenth century had the luxury of living near each other or even knowing whether they were placed near each other. They were likely sold off as quickly as possible, especially if they were sold in the clandestine trade, although it appears that at times they were bought and kept as couples. In the latter case, they may have been brought in as personal servants.

Among the narratives I collected and those that were published, I found no text that refers to circumstances of arrival. Arriving at their destinations in the United States twenty, thirty, or in some cases fifty years after the majority of slaves they came to know, only shipmates and family could have provided a certain kind of psychological haven for the nineteenth-century slave. In the absence of those shipmates, such slaves would have had to create the families they would tell their stories to.

Virginia

The acclaimed African American writer Arthur Davis was descended from a slave in Hampton, Virginia. William Roscoe Davis, his ancestor, was "nominally [a] slave of Mrs. Shields, mistress of the 'Little England' estate in Hampton. Davis was the son of a Madagascar slave woman smuggled into Virginia in the 1830s, twenty years after the American slave trade was outlawed. His father was a white sailor aboard that slave ship who raped his mother during the voyage." Davis's mother's case appears to be an example of an isolated experience in which shipmates were not part of the social environment once arrived in America. Davis, reports Robert Engs, "was born and raised in Norfolk where he learned to read and write from his master." He would later become a spokesman for Hampton's postbellum black community.[57]

Another such story is that of Pascal Beverly Randolph, the man responsible for establishing the Rosicrucian movement in the United

States, in the mid-nineteenth century. Randolph was born in New York, at 70 Canal Street, on September 5, 1825, and grew up in the Five Points section of Manhattan, a notorious slum. He is described in the literature as "mulatto." His story of an illegal Malagasy arrival is only five or ten years earlier than that of Roscoe Davis's story. Randolph reported that his mother was a "princess from Madagascar" who was kidnapped and brought to Virginia. He was a product of her union with a white Virginian who, Randolph claimed, was a nephew of John Randolph of Roanoke (of the same family as Sir John Randolph, friend of Robert "King" Carter, one hundred years earlier). Pascal claimed that his names Beverly and Randolph were not coincidental (reflecting his ties with the Virginia Randolphs) and that his mother's master had brought her to New York due to her illness.[58] When she was later abandoned, she took up fortune telling, or as Randolph said, she became a "seeress." This is an interesting detail, which may have some truth in view of the importance of possession in Malagasy life. Through this vocation she sought to save herself and her son. Her name was Flora Clark, and later in this chapter we will find evidence of other African American Clarks in Virginia who claim Malagasy ancestors arriving between 1825 and 1840. We might postulate that some, if not all, of these women arrived in the same illicit cargo. Some narratives mention the general area of Virginia but not the names of plantations or descendants.

The following is an e-mail message sent to me in 2004 about the Madagascar History Project (actually a reference to my website (freepages.genealogy.rootsweb.com~Malagasy4us): "I'm e-mailing you to find out if this project is still in effect? My great grandmother was a slave [in Virginia] and she was from Madagascar. Please let me know the status of your project. I saw an article in the local Richmond, Virginia, newspaper over a year ago that referenced this project and listed your e-mail address."

The following is a story of someone born around 1795, who thus must have arrived in his youth:

My Name is Monica Thompson and I am a descendant of George Henry Thomson born in Madagascar, Africa in 1795, taken as a slave from his native land to Virginia like most slaves. . . . We know through stories past [*sic*] down and documented that he was sold in Virginia and taken to a plantation in Kentucky. He ran away to Pennsylvania where he lived with Quakers. Then he ran to New York [in the] Niagara Falls area and began working as a coachman and blacksmith for a white family from Liverpool England. . . . His complexion was also black with slanted eyes and very long silky smooth hair.[59]

We find here a connection between Virginia and sales of Malagasy to Kentucky. The query concerns someone "born . . . in 1795" and, thus, not a part of the cargoes in the earlier eighteenth century. It offers an example of the kind of contextual detail some families hold on to, and it mentions dates.[60]

The above quotes also mention themes that appear in other later narratives: starting out in Virginia and moving north, perhaps to Canada; physical characteristics referring to a supposed Malagasy appearance; and royal descent. The physical characteristics mentioned conform to the physiognomy often described in other narratives, in which long hair, in particular, is used as a marker. Later in the same account the narrator mentions Indonesia, which is problematic; it reflects a racial description that suggests a familiarity with the slave trade of the Western Indian Ocean. It is not impossible that this comparison was made by the slave himself, especially if he came through the Cape of Good Hope, in southern Africa. The reference to Indonesia could also have been added to the story by the family much later. I have discussed the issue of royal affiliation elsewhere but will say here that I read this as attempts to declare origin from a place perceived of as civilized, of having a kingdom.[61]

Claims to distinct physical features can be interpreted several ways. First, we can read them as a persistent referent to being different from continental Africans. Second, the references to physical appearance bring up the question of racism—a significant issue. The use of hair as a marker to suggest Malagasy, as opposed to continental Africans, is part of this preoccupation. The basic prejudice or ethnocentrist view of desirable, or superior, physical features had important ramifications. In addition to being a criterion for recognizing compatriots, physical appearance also had to do with rejecting African heritage. In the racialist world of nineteenth-century America, Malagasy definitions of beauty and superiority were no doubt reinforced and remembered in comparison to the perceived "ugliness" of continental African physiognomies.

Another family narrative comes from the Morgan family of Tidewater Virginia and Maryland, who remember their "slave mother," Felicia. A young woman born in Madagascar, perhaps arriving with her Malagasy mother, Felicia was a household slave for the Courtney family in Maryland near the Virginia border in the early 1800s, having been brought there by her English master, who is remembered as belonging to the British military.[62] It suggests there may have been a slave ship with Malagasy on board that was intercepted by the British antislavery brigades, or alternatively, that Felicia and her mother arrived as personal servants.

Other stories mention England, too, as in the following narrative concerning the Clark, Gordon, and Winston family network of Hanover, Virginia. The Clark family bases its paternal line on the marriage of a young woman from Madagascar who was sent to Virginia at about thirteen years of age, probably around 1836. It appears that Lucy Clark arrived free with her sister, Mariah, or was freed upon arrival, perhaps through the white Winston family, who were Quakers. Once there, she was settled with and adopted by the black Winston family in Ashland. The Winstons were an extended family of manumitted blacks freed by the white Winston family.

The black Winstons were also apparently familiar with another well-off white Quaker family in the district, that of Nathaniel Crenshaw, whose wife (the sister of Johns Hopkins) was also related to the prominent Page and Henry families of Virginia. The Malagasy girl, then named Lucy Ann Winston, married a free black man, John Clark. In interviews with the great-granddaughter of William "Buck" Clark (John Clark's brother), it was stated that John Clark claimed to have "danced his way across the Atlantic from England" and that for several years he was unwilling to take up agricultural work, like the rest of the family, due to his aristocratic Malagasy background.[63] Clark and his brother, William, were free and sent to live with the Crenshaws at their home, Shrubbery Hill, by a white

Clark (Quaker) patriarch. The Nathaniel Crenshaw household was known for offering sanctuary to freed blacks and at one time had as many as one hundred free black people living at Shrubbery Hill.

John's brother, William, is said to have married Lucy Ann's sister, Mariah, who arrived with her from Madagascar. Mariah did not fare as well as Lucy and for some time lived either as a servant or slave in Hanover. There is some disagreement in the family, for only one branch of the family claims that John and William Clark were also of "Madagascar" descent. John Clark eventually worked as an evangelist and established several Baptist churches in and around Richmond, having been ordained by the Baptist Historical Society in the mid-nineteenth century, at the University of Richmond.[64]

A relative, Dabney Winston, remembered as the husband of Lucy Ann's sister Mariah, also established several churches to the northeast, in York County, during the same period, principally near Tappahannock, Virginia.

A likely explanation is that Clark (and possibly other male relatives) worked as part of a British ship's crew, as the claim is that he sailed from London to Virginia. If John was not of Malagasy origin, the claim that he was is nevertheless interesting, as it indicates a high value being placed on that identity. In this network, all the families' histories are entangled in the history of local Baptist congregations, the Quaker community at Cedar Creek, and the free blacks who were protected under the sponsorship of the Crenshaw family during the early to mid-nineteenth century.

It is provocative that the stories above from Virginia suggest a contraband of Malagasy slaves that were brought into Virginia and intercepted by British and American slave ship patrols. In such a case, it would appear that some were placed with Virginia whites who subsequently freed them, while others were bought as slaves and served white households such as the Courtney family, mentioned just above in the Morgan oral tradition.

The Lower South

One of the participants in the Malagasy Ancestry Project (remembered by some as the Madagascar History Project, as above), which included a conference at the Library of Congress in 2001, shared the following:

> Our family oral history for this story came mainly from my deceased Aunt Ethel Johnson Cherry, who told it on her sick bed in Los Angeles in the late 1990s, to various members of the family, including myself. She affirmed that a slave woman from Madagascar had a daughter in Vicksburg, Mississippi, sometime round the 1850s, from a union with a man named James Grimes. Aunt Ethel asserted that she was beautiful, and perhaps sold by her own family. James is reputed to have been, at least in part, Native American. Extensive search of family papers, and genealogical, probate, civil and local church and mortuary records have produced no details of any sort regarding either of them—not even the woman's name. Betty [her descendant] was, according to family lore, born near Vicksburg, Mississippi, on a plantation owned by a family named Butler.[65]

The narrator goes on to explain that by the 1870s, Betty appears with children, at least two of whom they suspect were children of one of the white Butler males. In the memory of the narrator's family, these unions were considered "amicable," their generation had grown up as "friends," and the Butler family acknowledged "these mulatto children" and attempted to have them educated. Afraid that they would be sent to boarding school and out of reach, Betty bundled them up and took a boat up the Mississippi River to Kansas. There Betty married and later divorced a man named George Johnson, but the children had taken his name.[66]

The dislocation of family and de-territorialization from a homeland provoke acute feelings that come through the simple language of these narratives. The following are examples of searches for family who were at the Stockdale plantation in Alabama. An unusual aspect of one narrative is the use of a name that the posting individual understands as inherited from Madagascar, Cochina Eley. The post was titled "Looking for Evidence/Cochina Eley of Madagascar":[67] "One of our older family members said we came from Madagascar . . . the 1870 census records show our family in Talladega County, Alabama. They were living on the Stockdale Plantation."[68] The dialogue continues, as people discuss different family stories: "I don't know anything about the Alexander side. One of the older family member said, 'we were Alexander before being changed to our slavemaster name Stockdale.' Maybe someday I will be able to connect the two families."[69]

As in the case of the Burnett family narrative, we note that surnames are seemingly something that happens to the family, a result of external forces. The Alexander comment seems to refer to a resale of the family, or parts of it, from one slave owner named Alexander to another named Stockdale. Such transactions—and name changes—were numerous and widespread by the 1830s.

The stylistic and substantive differences between the "late slave arrival" set of narratives and the ones from the earlier slave cohort are abundant and obvious. What these queries have in common is the absence of any documented existence of their arrival. When slaves arrived as listed commodities, we know of their arrival. When and if they arrived as illegal contraband cannot at this time be established; there was no record of such an entry into the United States.

The relatively high number of testimonies referring to an enslaved ancestor identified as Malagasy in the 1830s and 1840s caused me to re-evaluate my material and accept that not all of these narratives, from such diverse sources, could be attributed to erroneous chronology. It is unlikely that different people in different places (who did not know each other) would all make the same mistake in chronology, placing a Madagascar-born or second-generation Malagasy descendant in the 1830s. I therefore accepted the possibility that all these stories derived from a common experience of illegal transport to the United States sometime between 1808 and 1850.

My research leads to the tentative conclusion that some of the narratives I collected from African Americans emerged from late slave arrivals rather than early free immigrants such as merchants, as I had formerly thought (and have written about), or from descendants of the 1719–21 cohort.[70] Yet none of the family stories or narratives states clearly that their progenitor arrived during the period of the illegal slave trade, and reasons for that are discussed below.

The most remarkable differentiating quality of these narratives is their comparatively high level of detail and description of places, people, and events from the second generation onward in comparison to the thin quality of information and description in the narratives deriving from the first generation. Perhaps this is a reflection of the first generation's efforts to integrate into the existing black community and slave community, through kin networks, residence, and so forth, as well as the trauma their parents experienced. The later dense description and efforts at chronology of events contrast significantly with the absence of any information regarding their arrival or the trajectories they traveled before arriving to the shores of the United States.

In many ways, the slave stories in this chapter recall the lives documented by historian Sylviane Diouf in her memorable volume *Dreams of Africa in Alabama: The Slave Ship Clotilda and the Story of the Last Africans Brought to America*. Like those in Diouf's book, these narratives relate to a period after the official abolition of the slave trade, in 1808. There are more questions than answers for the Madagascar material, even though the families concerned generally have made considerable effort to document themselves since the first generation of descendants. Descendants of those who appear to have been illegally imported slaves have been able to track the family's subsequent history, in stark contrast to the lack of description of how or where their ancestors arrived, when they arrived, or where they were originally placed—in spite of their ancestors' comparatively recent arrival. This differs from the stories in Diouf's book, where families remembered place-names and other details of their lives before capture. How the Malagasy slaves of this period were brought in (if, in fact, they arrived during this later period) is not to be found, therefore, in family stories or in the archival record.

How might Malagasy slaves of the nineteenth century have been pulled into the Atlantic slave trade? Gwyn Campbell has written about the growth of the slave trade on the Madagascar plateau from the eighteenth to the nineteenth centuries, and Richard Allen has demonstrated that children were often sold into the external slavery network.[71] A few likely scenarios can be considered here. One is that a person arrived in the United States from Mauritius, where he or she had already been enslaved or was the child of enslaved Malagasy and had Christian training or contacts (or both).[72] Another is that the person in question was already a slave in Madagascar and, for some reason unknown to us, was sold to slave traders working external (Atlantic) trade networks. A third possibility is that this captive person, and perhaps the others who have been discussed here, was sold from Madagascar and then shipped to Cape Town, where he or she was again put on another ship departing toward the Americas. All these scenarios are equally possible for the other narratives in this set. A related possibility for some of the scenarios, particularly the slave ancestor Felicia from the Morgan family, is that a person arrived in the United States as a personal servant of a white person who, after coming into the country, decided to sell that slave.

There is a theme throughout the slave descendant narratives that is a counterpoint to shared bereavement and loss. Hovering below the surface of these narratives—sometimes evident in the silences and other times in the questions brought forward—is a sense of bewilderment. How can I not know more about my ancestor? Why do I know this about her, and not that? This bewilderment was especially evident during group discussions when invited informants and members of Washington's Malagasy community met to discuss the "inheritance of narratives" and the historical and social meanings of such oral histories for the American and Malagasy participants.[73] Not a few respondents bemoaned the fact that "they didn't know anything else" besides the apparently important fact that somebody was from Madagascar and that this was not to be forgotten—the two messages that have survived into the twenty-first century.

In closing this section, I should mention some other well-known African Americans who claimed ancestry from Madagascar: Judge William Henry Hastie (judge of the United States Court of Appeals for the Third Circuit, in office 1949–71), artist Elizabeth Catlett, dancer and choreographer Katherine Mary Dunham (whose father, Albert Millard Dunham, was said to be a descendant of slaves from West Africa and Madagascar), and Mary Church Terrell, an activist in the early days of the NAACP. Hastie was from North Carolina, and the Catlett and Terrell families were from Virginia. It is unsure whether their stories come from slaves or free immigrants, but they remain with us today.[74] Through a review of historical research on clandestine slave trade activities in the Lower South during the first half of the nineteenth century, and with awareness of the social turmoil in Madagascar during the same period, we may begin to find historical context for the appearance of African American family narratives claiming an ancestor from Madagascar who arrived after 1721 and before the Emancipation Proclamation.

5

Free, Undocumented Immigrants

THE ABOLITION OF SLAVERY for African slaves and their descendants was not limited to the new nation of the United States. The period from the American Revolution to the mid-nineteenth century saw the abolition of slavery for thousands of Africans and their descendants in Haiti, in some of the islands of the Indian Ocean, and in South Africa. Britain began to expand its naval capacity, using contract labor to substitute for slave labor, although the difference for most nonwhite workers was scarcely discernible. By the mid-nineteenth century, sailors from diverse territories now colonized by the British traveled on a global scale; the integration of the Indian Ocean and Atlantic Ocean networks was completed during the next century; by the end of the nineteenth century steamboats had expanded maritime capacities. Because of the increasingly broad movement of people along maritime routes, it is difficult to know the routes taken by Malagasy who arrived in the United States after 1810. Many people traveled both voluntarily and involuntarily to England, France, the Caribbean, and the United States during this period.

The Historical Record

During the same period that illegal slaves were being brought into the United States, it seems that Malagasy merchants and sailors were also arriving as free immigrants. Although no documentation has been found regarding their entry, there are a few possible reasons for this. The early nineteenth century was a period of profound change throughout Madagascar. The Merina state of the central highlands

129

expanded and began a series of wars, conquering region after region, almost subduing the Sakalava kingdoms of the north and west. These disruptions changed the balance of power on the island, and many people from Sakalava territories emigrated to nearby islands, such as the Comoros and Zanzibar. Others from the eastern and central highlands were sold into slavery on the islands of Mauritius and Réunion or migrated to Mauritius as free people. The central highlands became an area of slave export. An Anglo-Merina treaty was signed in 1817 with a representative of the British Crown, and although it was intended to herald the end of the slave trade, it continued clandestinely for more than a decade. The 1820s and 1830s were marked by conflict within the Merina region (Imerina) as King Radama I (r. 1810–28), and later Queen Ranavalona I (r. 1828–61), used arms supplied by the British to consolidate state power. Under Ranavalona I, the Crown impressed the labor of thousands of free people (*hova*), and new levies impoverished hundreds of families, many of whom ended up in slavery. Queen Ranavalona also initiated a repressive campaign against the rise of Christian conversions in the country. Many Christians fled the central highlands, some emigrating to Mauritius, while others found themselves enslaved within Madagascar itself.[1] Due to the social disruption from forced labor, repression of Christianity, expansion wars, and slavery, the population of Imerina (the central plateau) went from 750,000 to 130,000 between 1829 and 1842, according to historian Gwyn Campbell. Similarly, the overall population of Madagascar is estimated to have declined from around five million to two and one-half million between 1833 and 1839 under the rule of Queen Ranavalona I.[2]

In terms of what may have favored the emigration of free, or *freed*, Malagasy into the United States, the most likely would be the Madagascar-Mauritius slave trade, the movement of indentured servants from the western Indian Ocean region to the Caribbean, and the spice trade—which at times may or may not have been connected. There were many American traders traveling to Mauritius in the last half of the eighteenth century and the first half of the nineteenth century. An account from the office of the administrator general of the region states, "Of the last twenty years, the greatest number from any single nation are those from the United States [which was] 414 during the last 10 years, and 391 of these directly from the United States."[3] By the end of the eighteenth century, American traders were well established at Majunga, the commercial port of the Bay of Boina in northwestern Madagascar. Waters, West, Pingree and Waters was an important trading firm out of New England that had established a trading house at Majunga, in northwestern Madagascar, by 1824, and they also traded to Zanzibar. It is reasonable to suppose that in the course of such regularly established trade at Majunga (also known as Mahajanga) some Malagasy sailors may have been employed by these and other American firms. It is also possible that the large number of American ships plying the combined trade in livestock, hides, opal, and other products such as tortoise shell, and who made up a big percentage of ships stopping in Mauritian and South African ports, acquired sailors from Madagascar or those port towns under quasi-contractual conditions.

Historian Pier Larson reports that "Malagasy captive laborers were drawn principally from [Madagascar's] east coast and its densely populated highland interiors" and that "captives from Madagascar were typically funneled to a limited number of embarkation points along the island's eastward-facing Indian Ocean coast," while some western-coast ports played a minor role in slave exports during the last decades of the eighteenth century.[4] Larson describes how people from Madagascar made up a large portion of the slave population in Mauritius and how they arrived in successive waves; in 1765 most Malagasy slaves in Mauritius had arrived only within the last few decades, and that more than half the creoles were children of at least one Madagascar parent, reflecting the high estimated 42 percent of slaves and 36 percent of the island's entire population.[5]

Richard Allen reports that the number of merchants and traders residing in Port Louis (Mauritius) rose from 103 in 1776 to 365 in 1808, while the number of vessels calling at the port rose from 78 in 1769 to a record high of 347 in 1803. The number of slaves in Mauritius had soared from 2,533 in 1746 to 63,281 in 1810 due to planter need for labor for sugar cane production. The Slavery Abolition Act for British possessions was passed in 1833, and in February 1835 emancipation took place in Mauritius. Many of the slaves in Mauritius were first-generation Malagasy, and a good percentage of all slaves were skilled craftsmen.[6] Others worked in the maritime industry. Thus Mauritius in the mid-nineteenth century had a large newly emancipated labor force, many of whom were skilled in maritime trades. Mauritian slaves by the time of emancipation included many men skilled in crafts related to ship repair, sails, and carpentry. In light of the large number of American vessels in Mauritian ports during this period, it is not unreasonable to conjecture that some of those ships picked up freed Mauritians (Malagasy) to join their crews. Recently manumitted persons of Malagasy descent may have also joined American and British ships at Cape Town, South Africa.[7]

The case of the Prize Negroes of the Cape might also be instructive. Assumed to almost exclusively be descendants of liberated "Negroes" taken into service from intercepted slaving vessels at the Cape over the four decades following the 1808 British abolition mandate, they played an important role in the transition from slave to "free" labor following the end of British involvement in the transatlantic slave trade.[8] A naval squadron was based at the Cape of Good Hope to intercept such ships in the southern and southeastern waters, and to land their slaves on the Cape peninsula. Such captives were to be seized and forfeited and then apprenticed so that they might be trained in presumably marketable skills.[9] Over twenty-one hundred such slaves—all but thirty-four from Madagascar or Mozambique—were then indentured as apprentices by the collector of customs. They became the bulk of the population of Prize Negroes.[10] Furthermore, in 1808, when a Portuguese vessel ran aground northeast of the Cape, though most of the slave cargo also went into indenture, many escaped and were still being sought in 1814 and 1815.[11] Among Prize Negroes indentured in the decade after the abolition of the slave trade, 108 were apprenticed to the navy and 111 to the army. A further 151 were indentured for colonial government service, and the remaining 1,750 were apprenticed to private individuals. In total, well over half the Prize Negroes landed in the colony were apprenticed in Cape Town itself.[12] By the early 1830s some two thousand Prize Negroes had been absorbed into the colonial population, having served the maximum fourteen years indenture and become "free blacks."[13] In subsequent years, notably from 1841 to 1844, Portuguese ships slaving on the eastern coast of Africa were intercepted and the slaves brought to the Cape as new Prize Negroes, though during those years most of them were children. In 1846, 202 slaves were captured from a dhow off the western coast of Madagascar.[14] Their lives spent in conditions of virtual slavery, many of these unfree workers elected to run away, and according to historian Christopher Saunders, newspapers regularly carried reports of escaped Prize Negro laborers.[15] As Saunders points out, discerning the fate of the Prize Negroes after indenture is fraught with problems: "How many of the fifty to eighty persons who on average attended a service in the Malagasy language in the London Missionary Society's chapel in Cape Town in the 1830s had come to the colony as slaves before 1807, how many as Prize Negroes after that date?"[16]

From 1801 to 1890 roughly four thousand persons a year were exported from the western coast of Madagascar, especially Maintirano and Mahajanga. Likewise, roughly three thousand Malagasy traveled to Mauritius from 1836 to 1843 as contract laborers.[17] Pier Larson argues that by 1800 it is likely that more people spoke Malagasy than Kiswahili and all southern African languages combined, and that any history of the southwestern Indian Ocean "must account for the numerical significance of Malagasy speakers in the area and their extensive oceanic travels, including to Cape Town during certain years."[18] In summary, Larson's descriptions of the "vernacular life of the streets," where many Mauritian bondspeople were of mixed Malagasy descent and quite likely multilingual, present important possible scenarios for imagining life in the early nineteenth-century ports of Richmond, Charleston, and Lower South ports such as Galveston and Savannah.[19]

Family Oral Traditions

Family oral narratives count back in generations (rather than years) to their Malagasy ancestor, and in the cases discussed below, they do not go back any further than the late eighteenth and early nineteenth centuries. Against all publicly accepted truths (and recorded information in the United States), there are families who insist that one of their earliest American ancestors is a child born sometime between 1800 and 1850 to a Malagasy mother.

Here narratives are presented by people who claim descent from Malagasy sailors and merchants who arrived in America during the first half of the nineteenth century. By the time the surviving children of the original slave cohort were grandparents (1760–90, approximately), Malagasy sailors on American and British ships may have been arriving to the United States and settling in the segregated communities of free blacks, perhaps unknowingly among descendants of the 1719–21 cohort. Just as Prize Negroes and occasional contract sailors came to constitute another layer of creole Malagasy culture in the Cape of South Africa, settling where descendants of earlier slave imports from Madagascar had now become creoles, the United States probably also experienced another wave of Malagasy immigrants, overlapping with the illegal importations that were discussed in chapter 4.

Sailors and Merchants: Unregistered Immigrants

There is a noticeable difference between the narratives of those self-identified as slave descendants and those self-identified as descendants of free immigrants. By the early nineteenth century, Malagasy sailors on American and British ships were arriving to settle in the segregated communities of African Americans that earlier Malagasy survivors and their descendants had helped found. In addition to sailors, some seem to have been merchants, and yet others beneficiaries of Christian missionary projects. It is unclear how many of these travelers were enslaved before their arrival in America. Although they arrived as individuals or small family groups and did not arrive en masse, as did their earlier less fortunate compatriots, their story is critical to an understanding of the durability and attractiveness of the Madagascar ancestry story among all the families in the study.

In contrast to narratives about enslaved parents, there is a tone of confidence in the stories and narratives collected from descendants of free, voluntary immigrants who arrived roughly during the same period. They are marked by a complex pride based on a known former nationality, ensuing new citizenship, and privilege. The stories overlap geographically with those from the cohort of slaves arriving in the nineteenth century, which prompts interesting questions regarding possible roles of those Malagasy who arrived free during this period.

The settlement of nineteenth-century immigrants into areas that previously were sites of arrival and installation of the earlier slaves from Madagascar, and the former group's various genealogical histories as far as they are known, suggests that some form of dynamic interaction likely existed between these families, whether by accident or intentionally. Like their earlier counterparts, the emigrants taught their children to revere their memory.

Collected via e-mail exchanges over a three-year period, the story of Rakekata and her descendants is one that echoes later tales of emigration from Madagascar to the States. Rakekata, according to the descendant whom I interviewed, left Madagascar sometime in the nineteenth century under the sponsorship of a Captain Davis. It is not known whether there is any connection between this family and that of the earlier-discussed William Roscoe Davis, whose mother was sold as a slave at Hampton Roads around the same time. Once arrived in Virginia, Captain Davis arranged for Rakekata and her family and their goods (of which, apparently, there were many) to be sent on to Elyria, Ohio. Once in Elyria, the family set up house and joined (or perhaps helped create) a community centered around the church. The informant shared stories of growing up in a house full of heavy wooden furniture brought from Madagascar and admonitions from her mother not to confuse herself with the ordinary black folk whom she met at school or in her neighborhood. According to this descendant, Cammie, her mother believed avidly in the spirit world and ancestors. Once, when walking down the street, Cammie asked her mother what religious branch they actually belonged to, and her mother responded, "I belong to the Church of the Living Dead. All around us are the spirits of people who have died, only we just can't see them." Cammie informed me that her "great-grandfather [was] Lewis Davis and his wife [was] Martha Davis. Martha was said to have been a Madagascan Royal in exile from the same island. She kept her Madagascan name in secret."

Lewis Davis is listed in the 1880 census of Elyria, Ohio, as a drayman, black, born around 1832. His birthplace is listed as North Carolina. Martha is listed as forty-one years old in the same census, and her birthplace is listed as Ohio.[20] The family claims that Lewis Davis was a Malay. Thus, this story also points to a connection in South Africa, particularly Cape Town. As Christopher Saunders explains of Prize Negroes in Cape Town, over time many were absorbed into the ambiguous community that would in time become the Coloured, and among those, many were proud to be known as Malays.[21]

The Townshend family members are the descendants of Charlie Townshend, who is said to have moved to South Carolina at the suggestion of his white American friend, a shipper and "tradesman" named York Townshend. The story was passed down from Oscar Townshend, a grandson of Charlie, to his descendant who lived in the Washington, DC, area in the 1980s. The narrative states that in Madagascar, Charlie Townshend gathered some of his immediate family together ("he brought the whole tribe") and set off for America in one of York Townshend's ships. This suggests that he befriended Isaac Townshend in some port in Madagascar. After arriving in America, the family lived for some time in South Carolina (possibly near Union Springs), helping Isaac with his shipping business and living "under his protection." After an undetermined number of years the family left South Carolina with the help of their friend. The cause of their emigration to another state was the occurrence of racist attacks on the family, apparently the result of white jealousy and disapproval of their successful role in Isaac's business. The family moved to Alabama and were again aided in their settlement by Isaac Townshend. In Alabama, not far from Tuskeegee, they established a base from which some members of their family traveled to and from Cape Town, South Africa. The descendants do not remember or decline to say what the commerce to South Africa was. However, they remained in Alabama without encountering the same trouble they experienced in South Carolina. The narratives state that the granddaughter of Charlie Townshend still referred to herself as Malagasy. According to oral tradition, she grew up in the same neighborhood as George Washington Carver. Together they played games of collecting and identifying various plants that grew in the woods near their homes.

Many of the narratives are characterized by an interesting quality, in that people of second, third, and even fourth generations are continually referred to as Malagasy, in spite of the obvious marriages that they made here in the United States with people of diverse African, Native American, and Euro-American origins. This points to the complex meaning that the term Malagasy may signify for the carriers of these traditions. An informant from the Townshend family indicated that her grandmother (who was the granddaughter of Charlie Townshend) admonished her children to remember that "they were descended from a Malagasy" and that that descent meant "they had to carry themselves in a certain way, a respectful way."[22]

Another narrative is the tale of two brothers who ended up in Natchez, Mississippi, in the early 1800s. The story seems to fit the model of the arrival of sailors from Madagascar who settled near their ports of entry, or of a Lower South arrival of illegal slave cargo from Madagascar during the first half of the nineteenth century. The family is not sure if the brothers were slaves or freemen who worked for wages.

The descendant who shared this story made it clear that it involves the history of two brothers who arrived in America together, according to the family, with the support of two white men, one with the surname Calhoun and the other named John Puckett. They settled in Natchez, where they worked as horse groomers and were well-known "horse people." An interesting clue in this story is the name of one of the brothers, Ali ben Ali "Butcherknife," which remains a source of pride and mirth for his descendants. The epithet Butcherknife is salutary one that Ali earned for his proficiency in knife fighting, presumably before his arrival in the United States. Though known by his family as Ali ben Ali, he took the name Eddie Puckett, and his brother also assumed this surname. This narrative is frustratingly short, yet the details which it contains actually suggest quite a bit of information. First, the name Ali ben Ali has definite geographic connotations. When I first heard the name, his descendant pronounced it as Alipenali, and it was only due to my familiarity with Arabic names and Swahili coast history that I was able to surmise a mispronunciation.[23]

Ali ben Ali was a famous name on the Swahili coast, popular in Zanzibari, Comorian, and Lamu communities that claimed descent from Oman. It would have been a common name among "sidis" (Afro-Indians) and lascars working on British boats in the north-western Indian Ocean.[24] The fact that Ali ben Ali claimed Madagascar as his home of origin suggests that he was either part of one of the coastal communities of northwestern Madagascar, which was much involved in the Swahili trade, or from the northeast or north of the island, where there are families of Arab origin.

Robert Brown, perhaps the fifth or sixth generation from Ali ben Ali Butcherknife, still evinced pride in his knowledge of his ancestor and his family history. In other words, Brown clearly *owned* this story, which seems to have been an important part of his family identity.

The family narrative of the Gregory and Mahomet/Maham-mitt families of Baltimore and Frederick, Maryland, offers another example of an arrival from Madagascar with a Muslim name. The family believes that their ancestor, Ali Salaha Mahomet, arrived circa 1822. This year is significant in light of the Brown family's nar-rative about Ali ben Ali Butcherknife. Both men appear to have arrived within a few years of each other, if not together. This is also provocative in relation to the stories of the Townshend family, who seem to have arrived around the same time as well. It is worthwhile to pose the question of whether Ali Mahomet, Ali ben Ali, and the Townshends traveled back and forth to Madagascar in collabora-tion with, or in the service of, their white business partners. The social positioning that these immigrants seem to have enjoyed also recalls Pier Larson's argument that asymmetries of power could re-inforce cultural differences within black creole communities where Malagasy immigrants lived.[25] If the stories of the immigrant Mala-gasy are more coherent and detailed than those of the slave descen-dant narratives, it may be because the lives they lived allowed for relative access to power (probably in the form of contacts with influential whites) that few other blacks enjoyed at the time.

According to family tradition, Ali Salaha Mahomet, as he was perhaps named according to family informants, arrived in Baltimore before moving to Frederick, taking the name Jeremiah Mahomet. One side of the family claims that he left Madagascar at the suggestion of his father, who wanted him to further his education in France. In this version, Mahomet is a part of the nobility of his region. This branch of the family (the Gregory family) descends from Mahomet's daughter, Margaret. In the other version, kept by descendants of Mahomet's son, John, Mahomet fled to escape political turmoil. He is said to have left at night on "a French ship" but under the direction of "an Indian captain." Furthermore, the family member interviewed in 1988, Jeremiah Mahammitt, shared a piece of wisdom he had received from his forebears about Madagascar at the time the family left: "You had to have something or be a slave" (suggesting wealth provided protection from enslavement). His version describes conflict at sea on a ship wherein "one group of Indians and Africans fought another group of Indians and Africans."[26] The cause of the fight can only be conjectured. It might have been over rations of food, or over the management of the crew—this remains unknown. The ship is said to have made an eventual stop in France, or a French territory.

The tombstone of Jeremiah's great-grandfather, John Mahammitt, who was born in 1857, lies in the family cemetery in Frederick, Maryland. The two family stories converge at the arrival of Mahomet from his transit in "France," when he settled in Baltimore and became acquainted with Chief Justice Roger B. Taney and Frederick notable Edward Delaplaine. This story, too, seems to allude to some sort of commercial engagement of Mahomet with his two American contacts. Mahomet eventually married a free mulatto girl under bond in Taney's household and settled in Frederick. His marriage to the girl, according to the Gregory (Margaret's descendant) side, created some conflict with his father, who, having received a letter from his son, cautioned him not to marry outside his status and culture.

The 1850s census shows numerous Mahomet and Mahammitt households in Hagerstown, Frederick, and Baltimore. Members of the family are listed variously as mulatto or black, and there are several children in four different households.[27] The narrator, Jeremiah Mahammitt, shared (in 1988) that the children in the 1850 census were the first generation born in America, and mentions a brother of the immigrant, "Thit," and an aunt, "Soraya," suggesting that Ali Salaha Mahomet/Mahammitt did not arrive alone. The preponderance of female-headed Mahammitt households in the 1850 Maryland census of Washington and Frederick Counties suggests that the men were engaged in some sort of peripatetic work, perhaps working as sailors, except for one family member, Jerry Mahammitt, a seventeen-year-old listed as a farmhand; Josiah Mahammitt, a laborer at twenty-four; and the elder Jeremiah Mahammitt, fifty years old.[28]

In the 1860s Margaret became an entrepreneur, set up a laundry in Baltimore, and then moved to Rochester, then Saratoga, in New York State (where a Hannah Mahomet is also listed in 1850) and finally Williamsport, Pennsylvania, where she established a business, a health clinic that used "electricity for healing," a popular treatment of the time.[29] Another cousin, Thomas Mahammitt, moved to Nebraska around 1900. Just before World War I, a nephew of Margaret, Walter Mahammitt, was listed as an attendee at one of Washington, DC's numerous black cultural "salons" of the period, as recorded in the *Colored American*.[30] Descendants of the Mahomet/Mahammitt family remain attached to this narrative as an important signifier of unusual cultural heritage and as a marker of class in a context where this marker no longer bears social significance. In the Frederick commercial publication of *Polks* (1928–29, 1931–32), one son of the family appears as a laborer for an antiques business, and Joshua Mahammitt worked for Charles Kline in town on North Market Avenue.

The story has been passed down to each generation, as is the case with all the narratives presented here. Jeremiah Mahammitt of Frederick and Baltimore, Maryland, descendant of the male line, remembered Malagasy vocabulary well into the twentieth century, and these words have been identified to be of northwestern Madagascar, probably Antalaotra, origin. The words seem to fall into two categories:

words for family relationships and words related to flight or sailing.[31] This narrator (Jeremiah) also referred to ceremonies and rituals conducted at their home or in the woods near Frederick during the 1920s and 1930s. These activities were confirmed by an elderly neighbor of the family in Frederick, who explained to me that her parents would not let her join the festivities, as they were considered "very strange."[32]

One of Margaret's descendants, T. M. Gregory, was a scholar and social activist who wrote for the NAACP's *Crisis* magazine, was one of the initiators of the New Negro Theatre movement, and was responsible for setting up the drama department at Howard University. He was there at the time of Arthur Davis and probably knew Ann Petry (an African American writer from Connecticut who also claimed Malagasy ancestry), discussed in my recent essay on Madagascar stories in the edited volume *Crossing Memories* (2011).[33]

There is a possibility that at least some of the free-immigrant stories are linked to the histories of the slave descendants. It would not have been uncommon, for instance, for Rakekata (Martha Davis, above) to travel with a few slaves and to sell one or more upon arrival in the United States to finance her settlement. The same could be said for other stories in this set, and as we have discussed above, servants of free people were not classed under the restriction of the transatlantic slave trade acts. Stories passed down by families who claim a free-immigrant ancestor have a clear, if limited, reference to how they got to the United States. These stories always refer to a white patron or ally who takes a hand in the immigrant's settlement, and often, his or her choice of occupation. However, they lack written evidence of relationships such as work contracts, correspondence, or entry and travel documents. This is not surprising, as most of these narratives seem to be colored by a sense of furtiveness and secrecy. It may be that these people were connected to other illegal trading activities. Further, in the early nineteenth century, when slavery was still a significant and critical part of local and national economies, details about any particular black person were often not considered of significant value (in local government documentation) unless that person was involved in a court case or political activism such as the abolition movement. On the contrary, these families seem to have existed in a parallel world, where they suffered in poverty like other free blacks but at the same time enjoyed occasional privilege as a result of their close relationship with white allies, many of whom probably also owned slaves.

The narratives of this group also seem to suggest early communities or extended families in which more than one person came from Madagascar. Thus, Larson's idea of multilingual enclaves among slaves and free people from Madagascar in Mauritius is especially pertinent and provides a way for us to think about the arrival and settlement of these families. Referring to slaves and free people from Madagascar in Mauritius, Larson states that the recent emphasis "on interconnection and mixture has been an important correction" to past social science and humanities research that restricted its focus to creolization. He cautions us, however, to look at processes of ethnic distinction that are simultaneous to cultural and linguistic hybridity processes.[34] Larson challenges the "incorrect assumption in most studies of creolization that European creole languages were necessary for interlingual communication and rendered the native tongues of slaves irrelevant, expeditiously reducing them to inutile memories."[35] Although communities of Malagasy language in North America may have prevailed for only the first one or two generations in instances where there was a family group, the implications of Larson's view for those instances in the American context should be considered. For example, in my research on the Mahomet family, I recorded and verified in 1989 twenty-two vocabulary words that were from northwestern Madagascar from Jeremiah Mahammitt, who was sixty-five years old and living in Baltimore at the time. His retention of this vocabulary was probably because his branch of the family had consistently lived in proximity to each other in Frederick and Baltimore from the time of their ancestor's (or perhaps ancestors') arrival. The recorded vocabulary all evidenced the influence of coastal Swahili (see the appendix, "Jeremiah Mahammitt's Malagasy Words," where some examples are given).

Significantly, Larson insists that students of Madagascar and its diasporas must be conscious that "in previous centuries [Madagascar] served as one of the demographic and cultural pivots about which the histories and economies of the French and Dutch slave colonies of the Indian Ocean spun." Larson warns that scholars should not commence with "modern Malagasy-speaking or identifying groups outside the Big Island and trace them back to vernacular homelands."[36] This is an important point. It is through listening to the pronouncements of subaltern voices such as Jeremiah's that we should be motivated to turn to the archives and other historical sources, rather than dismissing such voices out of hand or, alternatively, creating imagined lives that exist outside historical fact. The endeavors of historical and ethnographic research both depend on cumulative process, though those processes differ significantly. Observing behaviors over time, and documentation research over years and across diverse spaces, require extended reflection and commitment to exploring the possibilities of human behavior in all its diversity.

6

The Problem of the Metanarrative

IN THIS VOLUME I have discussed documented evidence of the arrival of slaves from Madagascar to the United States between 1719 and 1721. I have also described some aspects of the life of black slaves and black freed persons from the mid-eighteenth to the mid-nineteenth centuries, allowing us to imagine what life may have been like for slaves and their descendants. Some slave descendants, we have learned, claim to be of Malagasy origin. Yet after 1721 there are no other official written records known at this writing that speak of arrivals from that island until after the Civil War. In addition to stories of people from Virginia who claim descent from the captives who arrived in the eighteenth century, there are numerous families who claim descent from a Malagasy ancestor who was either brought in as a slave or who arrived as a free immigrant in the first half of the nineteenth century. The diverse voices that speak of Madagascar origins share certain characteristics, although they come from different places and speak of different eras in a time span of almost 150 years. Through reading the narratives together, we get a sense of a larger text and a common message. Is there a metanarrative to be seen in the assemblage of these various and diverse family stories?

A metanarrative is not necessarily a conscious construction, but it is an observable one. In that sense, one might say that the various Madagascar narratives do, indeed, constitute a metanarrative. That metanarrative is largely one of geographic, cultural, and racial conceptions that endured in contradiction to popular perceptions in the postrevolutionary period and onward about what constituted a "Negro" or an "African."

The terms Madagasky, Madagasco, Malagasser, and Molly Glasser would have gone the way of all the African ethnicities whose names have been forgotten within African American families, if some implicit agreement over ethnic difference had not evolved among African and Malagasy forced and voluntary immigrants in America's black community. In that sense, the emergent African American community conceded and recognized its diversity and was the midwife of the Madagascar metanarrative. There were observable physiognomic and cultural differences that characterized Malagasy, and those differences played some part in the persistence of naming Madagascar. However, in the eyes of the saltwater slaves and their immediate descendants, were not all Africans different from each other?

Perhaps the end of this process was also the end of self-conception in cultural rather than racial terms among black people. At some point color became more important than geography and more important than language. Africanity became a burden to many. The pervading prejudice against Africa encouraged the attractiveness of a "Madagascar" identity for blacks. Initially and through generations, descendants were identified, one learns in the narratives, by "long hair, Asian eyes, bronze skin." The emphasis on these physical features shows us that these physical characteristics mattered. Perhaps people were proud to have features considered beautiful (long wavy or straight hair; bronze, not black, skin). This emphasis also may have allowed racially mixed slave descendants to avoid having to admit to "white blood," with all the connotations that such admission carried, even when (or especially when) they also had abusive white ancestors.

How does storytelling figure in the family that routinely attempts to regain its past? Of course, each society lives its past in material and nonmaterial ways. Beyond the genetic stories imprinted in each generation's birth, there are geographies that hold powerful mnemonic messages for each human settlement. There are also landscapes that reverberate with images, smells, and panoramas that express the past. Plantations, courthouses, market squares, rivers, trees, and meadows can all be figures in the memory's archives. But there is something beyond even the continual reordering of such archival configurations of a people's, or a person's, imagination.

By contrasting family narratives with historical evidence, my purpose has been to offer some reflection on how people constructed a vision of themselves and passed that vision on to successive generations of their descendants. Their confrontations, negotiations, and innovations speak through family narratives in their sense of dignity, dislocation, questioning, tenacity, confusion, and loss. Their stories give us one window through which to look at the complex social and cultural processes that characterized chattel slavery in America's mid-eighteenth and nineteenth centuries. Through looking at the Madagascar ancestor stories as a body of texts, we are able to conceive of particular histories in an otherwise almost inaccessible ethnic and cultural African American past. Within the negotiated cultural spaces of the emergent African American culture, families and individuals created narratives that evolved from memory, experience, local histories, and even dreams. Certainly, one condition of slavery was to dream of a different future, to imagine a different, less hostile environment, and to construct a communal as well as individual personality that was resistant but not rigid.

In chapters 2 and 3 cultural logics of West and Central African ethnicity and cultural belonging were discussed. The fluidity of ethnic identity in the African context was no doubt a factor in enabling the resistant flexibility that black people needed as the United States moved forward from the Revolutionary War and, later, toward the Civil War. Intimate relations blacks had with white Americans and Native Americans also required a worldview that allowed for an aggregate identity that could build on diverse cultural elements from Africa, Madagascar, and the panoply of other cultural practices and ethnic identities found and created in America. Being "a Malagasy" or having a "Malagasy ancestor," I have argued, was recognized within the community as one element of this cultural complex.

On the other hand, political pressures from outside the black community have called for a certain amount of consensus about being of African descent, although names used to describe this identity have varied over time, as Sterling Stuckey reminds us. The black (Negro, colored) community was for very long the only place to be for people of African descent. The community was not just a safe zone, however; it was also a place of joy, of artistic creation, of spiritual fulfillment, and a place with an imaginable future because it was made up of people who wanted black people to have a future; its denizens—as black people—were invested in that future. In chapter 3 we saw that the black experience in slavery and in freedom, occurring in hostile environments, led to certain cultural protocols. We could provisionally say that from the many "deep grammars" (to refer to earlier discussions on the work of Mintz and Price) of West and Central Africa and Mozambique, a new creole cultural grammar and worldview were created. This was a process of fusion and of compromise.

The Noble Savage

One key theme in this book has been what being a Malagasy or having a Malagasy ancestor has meant for those who self-identify in that way. Throughout the text I have suggested why families find it important to remember Malagasy heritage as culturally and racially apart from African heritage, instead of seeing it as a sort of subset of a slave identity or African identity. The answer is not in one event or in one process but rather in the cumulative history that Madagascar evolved in the black community and also in the white American gaze, which was an imagined history of exotica and folk simplicity.

Exotica and folk simplicity were images associated throughout the nineteenth century with the conquered peoples of the "south," the newly colonized societies of Africa, the Caribbean and elsewhere, giving rise to the idea of the noble savage. Michel-Rolph Trouillot has pointed out the ironic and dialectic nature of the construction of the noble savage in the mind of the West, and Madagascar has from the start of its encounter with Europe and America been a site of imagined noble savagery par excellence (remember, for example, the pirates at the beginning of this story). As Trouillot sees it, in defense of a Western colonial vision, the savage became evidence of a particular version of utopia.[1] This is not the place to engage Trouillot's discussion of the origins and nature of this category, but we can say here that the "exotic other" of the nineteenth century was the significant trope that accompanied European expansion, adventurism, conquest, and the project of colonization. As Trouillot suggests, historical events and the evolution of ideas about the "other" in anthropology call for a deconstruction of both the concept and the popular image of the savage. Drawing on these themes from Trouillot, my preceding discussion of oral traditions of some African Americans and their engagement with the past is also a project of deconstruction of their historically supposed savagery. Put another way, the preceding texts are inscribed in the project of recognizing the humanity of Africans and Malagasy who became slaves in the United States and of depicting their problems as human problems. In terms of the questions that are posed in the text, it should now be clear that the Malagasy narrative has been a tool in refurbishing self and humanity. In that context, one might assume that the image of Madagascar as an exotic, ordered place in the public discourse of the larger white society (in the sense of a tropical, disordered order) consciously or unconsciously provided a counternarrative against continental Africa, which, using Trouillot's framework, represented the barbaric savage in American imaginations. Perceptions of who were noble or barbaric savages were not static. For example, early in the period of slavery, some plantation owners and journalists referred to Equiano in terms that recall the noble-savage trope, and the same can be said for Africans thought of as Moors, such as Abdul Rahman, a slave in mid-nineteenth-century Mississippi; Omar ibn Said, a slave in North Carolina; or Job Ayuba ben Solomon, another slave who was able to gain support for his return from America to West Africa.[2] These historical figures are now familiar to scholars and laypersons because of documented historical evidence. To date there are no known narratives emerging from people who say they are their descendants. What happened to them? We will return to the apparent absence of narratives from families of African origins later in this section, but first we can evaluate what elements may have favored the sustained "Malagasy voice," as the absence of one and the presence of the other are intrinsically linked.

There have been factors both internal and external that sustained the value of a Malagasy self. We have discussed some of the internal factors at length—these range from geographic specificity (from Madagascar the island rather than Africa the continent) to growing obsessions with straight or curly hair as a preferable physical trait to African kinky hair. The importance of family and ancestors as a deep grammar shared by African and Malagasy cultures is also certainly a factor. This would be particularly strong in the Madagascar case, where ancestors are ever present to watch over, guide, and even frustrate their living descendants. Finally, it appears that many Malagasy arrived in the United States much later than most other slaves, and also much earlier than most other African or African-related immigrations. The arrivals occurred early enough that the idea of Madagascar had not disappeared entirely from slave descendants of the early nineteenth century, and late enough that people living today can remember learning about these arrivals, whether voluntary travelers or slaves, from their grandparents, who tell the tale of *their* grandparents. It remains to explore aspects of the external forces that favored nurturing a family history of Madagascar.

A look through America's newspapers in the last decade of the nineteenth century provides an important clue. At the end of the century, France had deported the queen of Madagascar, Ranavalona III, from Madagascar's capital of Antananarivo to the island of Réunion and then to Algeria, as the colonial government felt that her presence incited undesirable elements of nationalism among the Malagasy population. The U.S. press and, one imagines, the public, were fascinated and enthralled with the deportation of the queen; it was presented as a David and Goliath metaphor. The Malagasy were depicted as a unique people, perhaps recalling the people of Hawaii, in whom America was developing an increasingly imperialist interest. The queen of Madagascar was shown as a victim of French avarice and underhandedness. The Malagasy were described as civilized, in their way. Evidence of this is available in reports describing how the queen occasionally entertained while in her exile status in Algiers and her travel to Paris. Some journalists were enthralled with her graciousness, her "orientality," and her natural dignity, while others declined to see her in a good light, stating, "The Queen is but thirty-six years of age without any mental or physical attractions."[3] Articles appeared in the *Washington Bee,* an African American newspaper in Washington, DC, and elsewhere around the country (including Kentucky, South Carolina, Pennsylvania, and the territory of Hawaii) describing the queen with her servants, her finery, her vision of Madagascar, the problem of her exile, and, by 1894, the growing conflict between France and England over the island.[4]

Dependence on maritime travel was a major factor in the continued global importance of Madagascar (see chapter 4), and markets for india rubber, nutmeg, vanilla, and essential oils for perfumes stimulated public imagination of places east, whether Zanzibar, India, or Madagascar. The latter half of the nineteenth century also saw an increase in the volume of Christian missionary activity on the island. The reports from Washington, DC, show evidence of African American identification with Madagascar and "the dusky queen," as she was named in several newspapers. Moreover, in 1891, Mr. John Lewis Waller, an African American, was named diplomatic counsel to Madagascar for the United States.[5] Of significance to the black community and with certain diplomatic ramifications for the country, Waller's daughter married the nephew of Queen Ranavalona III while the family was living in Madagascar. Their son, Andy Razaf, was born in Washington, DC, in 1895 and became a well-known jazz musician and composer in the first decades of the twentieth century.[6] The coverage of these events in black and white newspapers no doubt kept Madagascar alive in the minds of African Americans beyond the mid-nineteenth century, when illegal slavery finally brought the last captives to the United States.

In spite of the ongoing reference to Madagascar in the black community as a place of origin or as a subject of news reports, family narratives about Madagascar escaped the notice of scholars of the African diaspora and of African American folk culture. Some salient reasons are the lack of precise information, until recently, regarding the transatlantic slave trade; the absence of scholar-community linkages that could motivate a recording of such stories: problems of credibility and, alternatively, habits of secretiveness that each family consciously or unconsciously practiced. To better understand the implications of these habits of secretiveness, the meaning of silences in the narratives, and the symbolic importance of Madagascar to black families, we will now turn to ethnography.

Ethnographic Sense

In 1996, Ruth Behar stated that anthropology is "the most fascinating, bizarre, disturbing, and necessary form of witnessing left to us at the end of the twentieth century." She joins other anthropologists in declaring, "An anthropologist's conversations and interactions in the field can never again be exactly reproduced. They are unique, irrecoverable, gone before they happen."[7] This, she says, is what Clifford Geertz meant by the "burden of authorship."

In spite of knowing that I cannot "bring the ethnographic moment back," I have presented these oral narratives that teach about human tenacity, the conditions of slavery, and aspects of America's history with Madagascar, because I believe that they should be discovered by and appreciated by a wider audience.[8] This makes me guilty of altering not only the form but the purpose of the stories (at least in this iteration), but it seems to me that the value to be gained by sharing is worth the risk. Few Americans outside of those whose history includes enslavement have much insight into how descent from slave ancestors is experienced. Fewer ever think about how and why that experience would have an impact today.

Inevitably, stories that we hear and scenes that we observe are housed in new forms when recorded and presented in a scholarly context. The ethnographer struggles with this contradiction, intending that some essence of the material experience is successfully transmitted. This is true of the collection and presentation of the narratives in this book.

The narratives that I listened to, the performance of family oral traditions in living rooms, libraries, meeting halls, churches, and gardens that I observed, were not presented with the benefit of written histories of Madagascar or Virginia. As I followed the stories people told, there were no maps they showed of plantations in Georgia, Kentucky, Tennessee, or Mississippi. There were no discussions of illegal slave trading, except references to being kidnapped and transported. Although some of the narratives were collected from well-educated people, they were not historians or anthropologists. The Malagasy stories were part of their personal and not professional identities.

In this book I have positioned the Malagasy ancestor stories in a new and collective way. Historically documented events have preceded presentations of family oral histories. The possibility that there may be some cross-pollination from one perspective to the other on this and related topics is part of the purpose of my effort. The result places the texts close to what historian Natalie Zemon Davis has called "fuzzy studies,"[9] but it also places my argument in the fruitful context of "the between," as discussed by anthropologist Paul Stoller. Stoller argues that in a world of multiple realities, there are several paths to the apprehension of social reality, and that multiple realities exist within distinct and permeable universes of meaning.[10] To understand how families and individuals (tacitly) agree to be, or habitually and unconsciously accept being a descendant of a Malagasy person, we must look deeper. Whether the ancestor who came to America was a slave or early immigrant, the fact of a Malagasy ancestor is a historical truth for descendant families, even if within and outside their communities it is not given much credence. This family conviction operates against generally accepted understandings of when slaves came to America, where slaves came from, and commonly held beliefs about early black immigrants. For many, their truths are not in the historical record and have been saved in spite of it. The stories from their grandparents are as true as, or more true than, what the documented evidence suggests. Since these narratives evolved in environments of very disparate economies of power, the telling in itself is an exercise in power—the power to define oneself, in the sense that J. L. Austin discusses "performative utterances" and speech as act.[11] The narrative is also a performance of choice. That their (Malagasy) ethnicity would exist in a distinct but permeable universe of meaning (how to count one's ethnic and cultural inheritance, for example) is not surprising in this context. To contemplate or accept these claims is to accept that "the between" is fruitful and productive, and that for those of us looking from the outside in, confronting unsettling views of the world situated between what is documented and what is claimed, can be a creative and enlightening opportunity.[12]

One point I have argued is that the logic of pushing for and emphasizing Malagasy ancestry was a project of ancestor creation, or more correctly, the creation of descendants. In my analysis, this discourse has sought to nullify the violence that created the slave by safeguarding the concept of the lineage, as slaves by definition do not enjoy the prerogative of lineage. Through the creation of lineage (descendants, family) the slave was able to wrest control of time and space from the master's worldview to her own. Children, thus, could be defined as people (human beings) by the fact of having ancestors and could belong to a universe that extended back in time before the act of capture and that extended forward in time. This was in direct response to the ancestor who named the need and function for a progenitor whose death could only be the fault of descendants who would not remember. Thus, one informant (a descendant of Raketaka, presented in chapter 4)[13] explains that her mother said she believed in "the religion of never-die," a creed where ancestors walk unseen among their descendants.

While particular sentiments remain about Madagascar among self-identified descendants, the same people express feelings common among most African Americans regarding the overall tragic and debilitating experience of the transatlantic slave trade and its aftermath. All descendant families are also part of the African American community and ethos, and although they do not know the origins of their other ancestors, they do not deny their existence, either. This interplay of loyalties and bereavement is part of the layeredness that is typical of African diaspora identities.[14] What is different in the Malagasy stories is the continued interaction of the narrators with the past. Unlike romantic attachments to a generalized idea of Africa, these interactions with the past occur through the conduit of a particular primogenitor and are personalized attachments.

Today it is difficult to imagine the world of the nineteenth century, when many African Americans spoke of their preslavery origins, and the descendants of these Americans are not easily visible within the black community in our era. The Malagasy were noble savages among other noble savages of the nineteenth century, and people who claimed Malagasy descent were not the only blacks to claim their non-European heritage during that time. But this does not completely explain why African Americans appear to have lost other African, slave origin stories, while stories of Madagascar appear to have persisted.

The negative portrayals of the peoples of the African continent that predominated in American public discourse of the past, and that continue today, have had a great deal to do with the erasure of particular African pasts. Likewise, problems of credibility face slave descendants, some of whom most certainly are the great-great-grandchildren of slaves who were brought into the United States illegally after 1810. The elderly in such families, in particular, face the risk of appearing absurd or foolish to younger relatives who do not believe or do not know that thousands of African slaves arrived only thirty years before the Civil War. Very often black and white people assume these stories are contrived; very rarely are the stories taken seriously and investigated. We cannot confirm that other family narratives exist about continental African origins, but in light of this work on Madagascar, Sylviane Diouf's work on families in Alabama, and what we know of the volume of the slave trade after 1810, it is possible that there are other narratives about other slave experiences that name or suggest particular places, linguistic groups, or cultures in Africa.

The families whose narratives are represented here evince a great love for their history and for the idea of family. They have also communicated, in narratives and in their questions, the angst, sadness, and pride they feel in knowing the particular identity of a black ancestor whose story refers to a specific place beyond the shores of America. For a descendant of slaves, such knowledge represents great wealth. It represents a sort of auxiliary resource for maintaining human dignity. Belief in such stories has served as a psychological cushion through generations of hardship and of living with the contempt of the majority population over many years. Moreover, since the late twentieth century, with the advent of online genealogy resources and increased (though modest) television programming on "African roots" and African American history, many families have become more public about information that at one time circulated mostly among relatives and friends. The changing social and media environment has rendered the stories of Madagascar more credible than before.

The Burden of Memory

Knowing the narratives has led me to reflect on the burden of memory. Memory, we recall here, can be a burden and affect generations of people with its messages of trauma, betrayal, and loss. Absences in the narratives are part of the material that is remembered, because silences, in their way, also record something.[15] The absence of answers to questions that are stimulated by the text of each story is a strong absence. It points to silences and to decisions made not to transmit certain information, or to situations where the information that could have been passed on was simply too painful, too fraught with contradictions and embarrassments, or, conversely, considered too insignificant to be included for the next generation. There are also silences that hint at forgetting—people and places omitted because they did not at one time or the other figure in the importance of things.

Who people are is closely linked to what they think about memory, what they remember, and what they can claim to remember, and the invocation of memory is part of an identity discourse.[16] Some anthropologists have addressed the problem of culture as a memorial practice.[17] Communities may work on narratives in order to make the past intelligible in the present. Paul Antze points out that memory and its tokens provide the substantive grounds for claims to corporateness and continuity. In the same volume, Lawrence Kirmayer explains that among survivors of the Holocaust, many are overwhelmed by memories and unwilling to recount their tale for fear of the pain it will evoke. Thus their problem, he points out, is not the limit of memory but of language—the inadequacy of ordinary words to express all they have witnessed.[18] This predicament also describes the absence of descriptions of arrivals and settling that characterize the Madagascar narratives, so that although sometimes there are mentions of kidnaps, there are no descriptions of arrival, of sale, or of transport to any plantation or river dock. Violent and painful experiences cause reactions of numbing, detachment, or suppression so that stories "work around the edges" of such events. Remembrances and memory are conditioned by what Kirmayer describes as "the culturally constructed *landscape of memory*," which he sees as "the metaphoric terrain that shapes the distance and effort required to remember affectively charged and socially defined events that initially may be vague, impressionistic, or simply absent from memory."[19]

Earlier I wrote of a metanarrative, the cumulative voice of many slave descendant voices. Kirmayer speaks of *metamemory*—implicit models of memory that influence what can be recalled and cited as veridical. Narratives of trauma, then, may be understood as cultural constructions of personal and historical memory.[20] The Madagascar stories diffuse among extended family members at holiday gatherings or other family events. What people feel they know is what they have heard or read before from relatives. Each time the narratives are performed, wrapped around and extending from key events that occurred during slavery times (and presenting a void in critical places), the family members listen and observe, and thus the story of how the narrative is related is also retained for future performance (including the silences). For example, we note the absence of any discussion or reference to problems of integrating into eighteenth- or nineteenth-century black communities, problems stemming from difference such as language, appearance, habits of dress, and so forth. The most painful sequences are left out of the vocal and written narratives, and that silence has its own message. These remembrance experiences operate in the cultural context of the slave descendant or early immigrant family, and both are enlisted to engage historicity. In these cases of history making, the object is to reconstruct a story that reaffirms social meaning and addresses the history of identity as the family has lived it.

If there is an important issue here in this question of memory—its vagaries, its foreboding or capricious silences, and its gifts—it is the question of how much the past is consciously allowed to inform, and to form, the present. It is the problem of what memory counts for that is of significance in this regard. In speaking of the significance of the values of memory, in the Madagascar narratives we note spoken references to remembered scenes, landscapes, and people. Remembrances are not purely recreational and they have therapeutic value. Stories offer a sort of pedagogy: how to treat elders, how to eat, whom to socialize with, when to laugh, when not to cry, when to tell family stories, and how.

The family narrative created dense meaning in times of chaos and erratic, incomprehensible change (see chapter 2). It also created stable meaning and order in an environment of capricious meanness and shifting frames of reference. However, I would argue that such stories also provided other very important value for the families that recited them. That value is the point at which the sacred and the profane interfaced in everyday life.

The Weight of the Past

It is not by accident that I have chosen here the phrase "weight of the past," borrowed from anthropologist Michael Lambek's volume of the same title.[21] The Madagascar family narratives are the site of a transition from a specifically sacred normative practice. They signal a past location of sacred experience and process, such as possession ceremonies, libations, cemetery rituals, and land tenure rules that provided formal ways to remember ancestors. By this, I mean that the commemorative activity of reciting and reading family narratives is, for the descendants of Malagasy early immigrants and slaves, a way of signifying the continued presence of the ancestor and of honoring a social contract with the dead. In recognizing this contract with the dead, the living are at ease in their interactions with each other, as their (embodied) meanings to each other are partially defined by their relationship to that ancestor (thus practicing a certain exclusivity). To break that contract would mean not only to change or diminish family coherence but also to alter the coherence of the individual's identity—how that individual has been defined by the larger society compared to how the person "reads" and names herself or himself.

The holy became the secular as an ancestor was invoked without formal ceremony, but the present became the spiritual fulcrum upon which the eternal and spiritual nature of the ancestor is projected toward the future. This transfer of the sacred from an object of reverence (the ancestor) to the subject of a story suggests how the conceptualization of the world and the cosmos changed over generations. It is likely that this occurred for many families of African origin as well as of Afro-Malagasy descent. As Lambek has argued, memory is "less a completely private yet potentially objective phenomenon stored *within* the mind and capable of remaining there than it is activated implicitly or explicitly *between* people, a confirmation of the sense of continuity (caring) and discontinuity (mourning). . . . [It] is more intersubjective and dialogical than exclusively individual."[22]

To better understand this we can return to the earlier descriptions of the primary purpose of the narratives, which I have argued is to allow the current narrator(s) to become ancestors—that is, to be remembered, to be situated in time and place, and to inform another "present." Further, the narrative continuously ties the family to diverse geographies, thus, expanding beyond a geography of shame and humiliation to another geography of rootedness and belonging that connotes a nonslave, nonmarginal context. I do not argue that this is a conscious choice or prepared activity but habit that is ingrained in the culture of the family.

Lambek, in *The Weight of the Past*, explains, "Historicity is located in the spaces prised open between history and memory: between fixed, official, and scholarly accounts and popular or individual versions, fantasies and defense mechanisms . . . spaces and sparks, projects and practices, where the past is conserved and curated, but also crafted, performed, personified; received and addressed, invoked, supplicated, appeased, accepted; authorized and ironized."[23] The practice of the Madagascar family narrative is also the practice of a certain kind of historicity that reminds of a different way to look at the past and a different way to live the past. It involves recalling the ancestor and continuously empowering that ancestor by acknowledging his or her existence and carrying the remembrance forward.

Perhaps the making and sharing of stories about ancestors constitutes a kind of religion. These stories are, in an unconscious way, narratives that allow each generation to respond to the past of the family and to be initiated into another way of looking at the world. They also recount a battle for self-definition in the face of the real and practical need to assimilate in the community, to become homogeneous "blacks" or "Negroes." They suggest resistance to the impersonal and mechanistic white-black definitions that characterized life in nineteenth-century America.

It is intended that this volume open a discussion that motivates new research into the origins and transmission of similar stories. With historical context, African American (and other) family narratives and stories can be seen in a new light, beyond hearsay and family antidote, and become part of a larger story of loss and of human resilience and tenacity. The narratives in this case seem to be messages from the past that continued, in each generational present, to argue Madagascar's differences from continental Africa. It appears that this difference must have mattered to each generation's ancestors since it remains so central to present family stories of people who claim those ancestors. The stories helped configure a vision of the human sensibilities of yesterday's slaves and their immediate descendants. Yes, the narratives of trauma and displacement are stories of people whose ancestors were slaves, but equally important, they are the stories of slave ancestors as *people*. In the same way, the narratives of slave descendants and early immigrants disengage us from the trope of the homogeneous, isolated black community, revealing that the African American community consciously began as a diverse one and has continued as such, often unnoticed, through time.

Appendix

Jeremiah Mahammitt's Malagasy Words

Vocabulary collected from Jeremiah Mahammitt, Baltimore, November 14, 1987; May–June 1988; December 1989.

Word	Meaning from Jeremiah	Identified Malagasy use
taski (TAH-ski)	utensil to hold hair	casqui (hat) (Comoros)
kibuki (ki-BŪKI)	butterfly (?); swimming	
kanaka loa (kanak LOA)	first son	first child (Majunga)
Nyangono nyolo	cry baby	Majunga dialect; Swahili influence, "cry baby"
Thit (Theet)	uncle's name	male name
azib (azEEB)	bird (condor?)	
hassani (hassAHni)	prince (?) high priest (?)	spiritual (Masina)(?)
kalamo (kalAHmo)	book (?)	"to speak" (from Arabic)

These words were collected at interviews during which Jeremiah Mahammitt also described ceremonies and various family practices. The second column contains meanings given by Jeremiah; the third column includes meanings known to exist in northwestern Madagascar. These topics will be covered in forthcoming works on the topic of the Mahammitts of Maryland. The few words that are listed here were from recollections of Jeremiah when he was about sixty-three years old and had had neither reason nor opportunity to speak or refer to this vocabulary for several years. Furthermore, the words, according to him, were in common usage among the adults when he was a child and sat with older men when they were talking.

Glossary

ajami   Basically any language other than Arabic but written in the Arabic alphabet. *Ajami* is a term originating in West Africa that is used to describe texts in a local language that are written in Arabic script. In Madagascar, this Arabic script was known as *Sorabe* when used for sacred writings or royal histories. The term is increasingly used by scholars to refer to all such texts throughout the African continent and its islands.

Antambahoaka An ethnic group from the southeast of Madagascar and related to the Anteimoro. The Antambahoaka are settled in the Mananjary area.

Antanosy   An ethnic group said to have migrated southward from Madagascar's north-central region. They are associated with the Zafiraminia, who arrived on the island sometime in the fourteenth century. Fort Dauphin is historically considered an Antanosy region.

Anteimoro   An ethnic group in Madagascar thought to have formed early in the island's social history with the arrival of Gulf Arab immigrants, perhaps in the eighth century. The Anteimoro served as astrologers, scribes, and advisers in the courts of many of Madagascar's kingdoms. They are credited with developing an *ajami* script, called *Sorabe,* which is the Malagasy language written in Arabic letters.

Betsimisaraka An ethnic group in eastern Madagascar that evolved from several related cultural groups in the northeastern part of the island.

Betsimisaraka A political federation that brought together several
confederation related cultural groups in eastern Madagascar who organized under one leader during the seventeenth

century. This process led by the nineteenth century to the term *Betsimisaraka* as a nomenclature for a shared ethnic community.

endogamous — Marriage allowed only within the social group in question, such as ethnic group, clan, or class.

exogamous — Marriage allowed outside the social group in question. A marriage within an exogamous group is considered incestuous.

maximal lineage — An extended kinship group, including all descendants of the remotest known ancestor within a lineage, traced through the maternal or paternal line.

Menabe kingdom — The older Sakalava dynasty that emerged in southwestern Madagascar and eventually branched to the Sakalava Boina Kingdoms in the northwest.

Merina — An ethnic group that historically settled the central plateaus of Madagascar and formed a kingdom there, based on a hierarchic social structure wherein the royal family was supported by and followed in the hierarchy by the *hova*, people of a free social rank of the Merina state (descended from the original settlers; a middle class). It is thought that the Merina formed sometime in the thirteenth century from groups that migrated from the southeast and settled on the central plateaus of the island. Over time, they developed strict traditions of endogamy that favored the retention of Indonesian physiognomic features within the newly forming society. However, there is still no scholarly agreement on the origins of the Merina. The Merina kingdom, developed by the seventeenth century, was not intensely involved in long-distance slave trading until the nineteenth century, when internal and external slave trading became important features of the Merina economy.[1] The Merina kingdom brought all other states of Madagascar together into a centralized political formation, although some, like the Sakalava, resisted for some time. The Merina were in power throughout most of the island by 1825 and brought the British in as educators and architects during the mid-nineteenth century. The French and British competed for control of the island, and the French eventually took control, dissolving the queen's office in the last years of the nineteenth century.

Saint Mary's Island, Madagascar	An island south of Antongil Bay that was both a slave export center and a holding point for slaves brought over from the Madagascar mainland. It is one of the first areas of significant French and Catholic influence.
Sakalava	An ethnic group in Madagascar thought to have migrated from the southeast to the southwest of the island during the early development of Malagasy society, eventually forming the Menabe kingdom. In the seventeenth century a section of the kingdom, following a son of the king, migrated to what is today the Boina region, in the northwest, while his brother remained in the Menabe kingdom of the south. The Sakalava kingdoms thus evolved two major branches, and a subbranch extended further to the north-central regions to evolve into the Antankarana kingdom. The Sakalava created the first extensive precolonial state in Madagascar and, though not a slave state, the kingdom's merchants were intensively involved in slave trading. Most slave trading was carried out by a subgroup of the Sakalava known as the Antalaotra (people of the sea), thought to be a mixture of Arab, Swahili, Malagasy, and perhaps Indian (Gujarati) elements. The Antalaotra acted as commercial agents for the Sakalava between Madagascar, the Comoros, East Africa, and southern Arabia well before the sixteenth century.[2] The Sakalava Boina state was invaded and then controlled by the Merina at the beginning of the nineteenth century. However, by the mid-eighteenth century, the king of Boina had established his domination over the whole of northern Madagascar, perhaps a third of the island.[3]
Sorabe	Sacred writings held by royal families that are written in the Malagasy language using Arabic script.
Zafiraminy	The Zafiraminy are a subgroup of the Betsileo ethnic group of central Madagascar.

Notes

Foreword

1. W. E. B. DuBois Database, http://www.slavevoyages.org/tast/assessment/estimates.faces. The database does not record any importations at all from the region after 1725. If the 1,450 figure provided by Wilson-Fall is used, that percentage drops to 1 percent.

2. See, for example, Michael A. Gomez, *Black Crescent: The Experience and Legacy of African Muslims in the Americas* (Cambridge: Cambridge University Press, 2005).

Introduction: A Particular Ancestral Place

1. See Virginia Bever Platt, "The East India Company and the Madagascar Slave Trade," *William and Mary Quarterly*, 3rd ser. 26, no. 4 (October 1969): 575–77.

2. This case was first written about, to my knowledge, by Jeffrey R. Brackett, *The Negro in Maryland: A Study of the Institution of Slavery*, Johns Hopkins University Studies in Historical and Political Science, extra vol. 6 (Baltimore, 1889), 27–33, 37.

3. Ibid.

4. For scholars who have written on Indian Ocean slavery, see Edward Alpers (2000, 2003), Richard Allen (1999, 2003, 2009), Robert Shell (1994), Pier Larson (2007, 2009), Gwyn Campbell (1993), and James C. Armstrong (1983), all listed in the bibliography.

5. Slaves from Madagascar arrived in Canada during the seventeenth century, and small numbers also arrived in other ports further south in the American colonies, notably New Netherland (New York) during those years. Many Malagasy slaves were also sent to Barbados.

6. The slave trade, though pronounced illegal in 1808, required successive legal embellishments before it finally came to an end for North Americans. See also Richard B. Allen, "Slavery and the Slave Trades in

the Indian Ocean and Arab Worlds: Global Connections and Disconnections," Proceedings of the 10th Annual Gilder Lehrman Center International Conference at Yale University, November 7–8, 2008, New Haven, http://www.yale.edu/glc/indian-ocean/allen.pdf, pp. 13–14.

7. Pierre Nora perceived a tendency operating to replace scholarly history with popularly generated self-histories, which the nation-state then tends to adopt and popularize. In my view, the narratives covered here are contextually different, though emanating from nonscholarly circumstances. Nora, "Between History and Memory: Les Lieux de Mémoire," in "Memory and Counter-memory," special issue, *Representations*, no. 26 (Spring 1989): 7–24.

8. Early in the slave trade, many Senegambians came to Virginia from Muslim territories, where Arabic was taught to children as part of religious training.

9. James Clifford, "Partial Truths," introduction to *Writing Culture: The Poetics and Politics of Ethnography*, ed. Clifford and George E. Marcus (Los Angeles: University of California Press, 1986), 22.

10. Noteworthy among those sources would be Margaret Brown, "Reclaiming Lost Ancestors and Acknowledging Slave Descent: Insights from Madagascar," *Comparative Studies in Society and History* 46, no. 3 (2004): 616–45; Rosalind Shaw, *Memories of the Slave Trade: Ritual and the Historical Imagination in Sierra Leone* (Chicago: University of Chicago Press, 2002); Michael Lambek, *The Weight of the Past: Living with History in Mahajanga, Madagascar*, Contemporary Anthropology of Religion (New York: Palgrave Macmillan, 1999); Lambek and Andrew Walsh, "The Imagined Community of the Antankaraña: Identity, History, and Ritual in Northern Madagascar," *Journal of Religion in Africa* 27, no. 3 (August 1997): 308–33.

11. For discussion of these new trends and their effect on recent scholarship, see James Sidbury, "Globalization, Creolization and the Not-So-Peculiar Institution," *Journal of Southern History* 73, no. 3 (August 2007): 617–30.

12. Equiano (Gustavus Vassa) has been the subject of many recent essays. For a good discussion of this eighteenth-century abolitionist, see Paul E. Lovejoy, "Olaudah Equiano or Gustavus Vassa—What's in a Name?," *Atlantic Studies* 9, no. 2 (2012): 165–84.

13. It has also recently been reported that Equiano traveled with two Malagasy sailors on a voyage with Horatio Nelson, on the British expedition in 1773 to navigate as close to the North Pole as possible. See Pier Larson, *Ocean of Letters: Language and Creolization in an Indian*

Ocean Diaspora, Critical Perspectives on Empire (New York: Cambridge University Press, 2009), 44.

14. Lovejoy, "Olaudah Equiano or Gustavus Vassa," esp. 167–68. Other well-known scholars in the debate include Vincent Carretta, *Equiano, the African: Biography of a Self-Made Man* (Athens: University of Georgia Press, 2005), and James H.Sweet, "Mistaken Identities? Olaudah Equiano, Domingos Álvarez, and the Methodological Challenges of Studying the African Diaspora," *American Historical Review* 114, no. 2 (2009): 279–306.

15. W. E. B. DuBois, *The Souls of Black Folk: Essays and Sketches* (Boston: Purdy, 1904; Hazelton: Pennsylvania State University, Electronic Classics Series, 2006), 9. DuBois states, "It is a peculiar sensation, this double-consciousness, this sense of always looking at one's self through the eyes of others, of measuring one's soul by the tape of a world that looks on in amused contempt and pity. One ever feels his two-ness—an American, a Negro; two souls, two thoughts, two unreconciled strivings; two warring ideals in one dark body, whose dogged strength alone keeps it from being torn asunder" (1904:9).

16. For more discussion on the concept of cultural legacies in African diaspora communities, see Michael A. Gomez, *Exchanging Our Country Marks: The Transformation of African Identities in the Colonial and Antebellum South* (Chapel Hill: University of North Carolina Press, 1998).

17. Akhil Gupta and James Ferguson, "Ethnography at the End of an Era," in *Culture, Power, Place: Explorations in Critical Anthropology,* ed. Gupta and Ferguson (Durham, NC: Duke University Press, 1997), 12.

18. Pierre Bourdieu, *Practical Reason: On the Theory of Action* (Stanford: Stanford University Press, 1998), 6–7.

19. Maurice Bloch, "Internal and External Memory: Different Ways of Being History," in *Tense Past: Cultural Essays in Trauma and Memory,* ed. Paul Antze and Michael Lambek (New York: Routledge, 1996), 215–33; and Lambek, "The Past Imperfect: Remembering as Moral Practice," also in *Tense Past,* 235–54.

20. Natalie Zemon Davis, "Decentering History: Local Stories and Cultural Crossings in a Global World," *History and Theory* 50, no. 2 (May 2011): 192 .

21. This is well argued in Natalie Zemon Davis and Randolph Starn, introduction to "Memory and Counter-memory," special issue, *Representations,* no. 26 (1989): 1–6; Davis, "Anthropology and History in the 1980s: The Possibilities of the Past," *Journal of Interdisciplinary History* 12, no. 2 (1981): 265–75.

22. Davis, "Anthropology and History," 202. Citing, among other subjects, the case of maroons of Suriname and evidence of the ways in which they exercised judicial prerogatives among themselves, Natalie Zemon Davis, for example, argues that the "direct exchange among scholars across boundaries is one of the best paths to discovery in our globalized latter-day times."

23. See Richard Price and Sally Price, *The Root of Roots; or, How Afro-American Anthropology Got Its Start* (Chicago: Prickly Paradigm Press, 2003); John Thornton, *Africa and Africans in the Making of the Atlantic World, 1400–1680* (New York: Cambridge University Press, 1992).

24. E. Franklin Frazier, *The Negro Family in the United States* (New York: Macmillan, 1949). An exception within the black community was Zora Neal Hurston, who, as an anthropology student of Franz Boas and as an African American from Florida, argued that African-derivative culture was alive and vibrant in her era. She was joined by creative writers of the early and mid-twentieth century such as Jean Toomer and Langston Hughes, who also believed that some unidentifiable African influences provided the foundation of African American culture, in contrast to Frazier's resistance to the idea of any significant African impact on black Americans' lifeways.

25. Melville Herskovits, *The Myth of the Negro Past* (1940; repr., Boston: Beacon Press, 1990).

26. Sidney W. Mintz and Richard Price, *The Birth of African-American Culture: An Anthropological Perspective* (Boston: Beacon Press, 1976). Price's innovative treatment of historical and fieldwork sources in his book *First-Time* in which he concentrated on the maroons of former Dutch Guyana (now Suriname), provides an important point of departure for the way such themes are approached in this book. Price, *First-Time: The Historical Vision of an African American People* (1983; repr., Chicago: University of Chicago Press, 2002).

27. In particular, the publication of the Trans-Atlantic Slave Trade Database through Emory University (Eltis et al.) continues to have an immense impact on American and African diaspora studies.

28. For example, Michael A. Gomez, *Exchanging Our Country Marks: The Transformation of African Identities in the Colonial and Antebellum South* (Chapel Hill: University of North Carolina Press, 1998); J. Lorand Matory, *Black Atlantic Religion: Tradition, Transnationalism, and Matriarchy in the Afro-Brazilian Candomblé* (Princeton: Princeton University Press, 2005).

29. For instance, see Paul Lovejoy, "Transatlantic Transformations: The Origins and Identities of Africans in the Americas," in *Africa, Brazil and the Construction of Transatlantic Black Identities*, ed. Livio Sansone, Elisée Soumonni, and Boubacar Barry (Trenton, NJ: Africa World Press, 2008), 82–111.

30. Ibid.

31. An excellent example is Lorena Walsh's work on the Ibo and other black ethnicities of Virginia, in *From Calabar to Carter's Grove* (Charlottesville: University Press of Virginia, 1997). Walsh has explored the specific conditions of the densely populated colonial communities of Chesapeake Virginia and recently provided revised statistics about specific slave origins.

32. Allan Kulikoff, "The Origins of Afro-American Society in Tidewater Maryland and Virginia, 1700 to 1790," *William and Mary Quarterly*, 3rd ser., 35, no. 2 (April 1978): 228. The term "lot" was used in the nineteenth century to describe groups of slaves, much as one would describe a "lot" of land, a "lot" of tables, or other inanimate objects.

33. See, for example, Gomez, *Exchanging Our Country Marks*; Gomez, *Black Crescent: The Experience and Legacy of African Muslims in the Americas* (Cambridge: Cambridge University Press, 2005).

34. See Mechal Sobel, *The World They Made Together: Black and White Values in Eighteenth-Century Virginia* (Princeton: Princeton University Press, 1987).

35. Research in Brazil and Suriname has begun to explore this question in important ways, in some cases linking cultural movements in the Americas to events and processes in West and Central Africa. For numerous examples of composite New World identities, see essays in Sansone, Soumonni, and Barry, *Africa, Brazil*. Paul Lovejoy's essay in that volume, "Transatlantic Transformations" (81–112), provides in-depth discussion of aggregate African identities in the Americas, and my approach draws on some of his arguments. Allan D. Austin and Gwendolyn Midlo Hall have been able to give documented evidence of people of Senegambian descent, notably in eighteenth-century Louisiana, South Carolina, and Georgia; and Austin finds evidence of a direct relationship between families of the 1940s and their Senegambian predecessors, in spite of the growing minority status of Senegambians relative to other Africans by the middle of the eighteenth century. Austin, *African Muslims in Antebellum America: Transatlantic Stories and Spiritual Struggle* (New York: Routledge, 1997); Hall, *Slavery and African Ethnicities in the Americas: Restoring the Links*

(Chapel Hill: University of North Carolina Press, 2005). For other examples, the volume edited by Ana Lucia Araujo, *Paths of the Atlantic Slave Trade: Interactions, Identities, and Images* (Amherst, NY: Cambria Press, 2011), offers several essays on the subject, including one of mine: Wilson-Fall, "Women Merchants and Slave Depots: Saint Louis, Senegal and St. Mary's, Madagascar," 273–303.

36. Madagascar Ancestry Site, http://freepages.genealogy.rootsweb.com/~malagasy4us/.

37. I have lectured on this subject at meetings of the Afro-American Historical and Genealogical Society, at the Association for the Study of African American Life and History; at a conference on oral history in Frederick County, Maryland; at Catoctin College; in Hanover and Ashland, Virginia; in Washington, DC; and in various places in northeastern Ohio. My interest in the topic began as a response to queries following a presentation I gave with Sheila Thomas at the Historical Society of Washington, DC, in 1989.

38. This is discussed in greater depth in Wendy Wilson-Fall, "Life Stories and Ancestor Debts: 'Creole Malagasy' in Eighteenth-Century Virginia," in *Crossing Memories: Slavery and African Diaspora*, ed. Ana Lucia Araujo, Mariana P. Candido, Paul E. Lovejoy (Trenton, NJ: Africa World Press, 2011), 147–82.

39. In my view, these are the types of issues and questions that must be brought to the fore in African diaspora studies for better understandings of past and contemporary communities.

40. *Shipmates* here refers to slave cohorts who have experienced transfer by boat from one port to another, generally but not always referring to the Middle Passage.

41. Michel-Rolph Trouillot, *Silencing the Past: Power and the Production of History* (Boston: Beacon Press, 1995).

Chapter 1: Madagascar

1. Malagasy slaves were also sent to Brazil and to the Río de la Plata, in Argentina (see note 24, this chapter.

2. Mervyn Brown, *Madagascar Rediscovered, A History from Early Times to Independence* (London: Damien Tunnacliffe, 1978), 1.

3. Mervyn Brown points out that a study of deforestation places the colonization of the island at about one thousand years ago. For more discussion, see ibid., 13–15.

4. Ibid., 24.

5. Ibid., 19–20.

6. Ibid., 20.

7. On taboos in eastern Madagascar and their role in social relationships, see Margaret Brown, "Reclaiming Lost Ancestors and Acknowledging Slave Descent: Insights from Madagascar," *Comparative Studies in Society and History* 46, no. 3 (2004): 616–22.

8. Mervyn Brown, *Madagascar Rediscovered*, 19–21.

9. P. Bradley Nutting, "The Madagascar Connection: Parliament and Piracy, 1690–1701," *American Journal of Legal History* 22, no. 3 (July 1978): 203, 209.

10. Stephen Ellis, "Tom and Toakafo: The Betsimisaraka Kingdom and State Formation in Madagascar, 1715–1750," *Journal of African History* 48, no. 3 (November 2007): 445.

11. James C. Armstrong, "Madagascar and the Slave Trade in the Seventeenth Century," *Omaly sy anio*, no. 17 (1983): 216, and quoted in Ellis, "Tom and Toakafo," 441.

12. Cited in Mervyn Brown, *Madagascar Rediscovered*, 96.

13. Thomas Vernet, "Slave Trade and Slavery on the Swahili Coast, 1500–1750," in *Slavery, Islam and Diaspora*, ed. Behnaz A. Mirzai, Ismael Musah Montana, and Paul E. Lovejoy (Trenton, NJ: Africa World Press, 2009), 37–76. Vernet, however, points out that his figures exclude those slaves shipped by Europeans.

14. Kevin McDonald, "'A Man of Courage and Activity': Thomas Tew and Pirate Settlements of the Indo-Atlantic Trade World, 1645–1730," eScholarship Repository, University of California (October 3, 2005), UC World History Workshop Conference Series, paper 2, http://repositories.cdlib.org/ucwhw/wp/2; citing Representation of the Board of Trade, January 17, 1698, CO 324/6, fols. 222–25, Public Records Office, London (2005).

15. Nutting, "Madagascar Connection," 210.

16. Mervyn Brown, *Madagascar Rediscovered*, 41–45.

17. Ibid., 49. Sieur Pronis traveled to Madagascar as the commander of a monopoly charter to the Société Française de l'Orient.

18. Ibid., 50–53.

19. Armstrong, "Madagascar and the Slave Trade," 211–34.

20. Marcus Rediker, *The Slave Ship: A Human History* (New York: Penguin, 2008). As Rediker points out, pirates were in Madagascar for refuge and respite in a global network of retreat zones that included Africa's western coast, the coastline of North America from Virginia to the Carolinas, and numerous Caribbean islands.

21. Mervyn Brown, *Madagascar Rediscovered*, 97; Margaret Brown, "Reclaiming Lost Ancestors," 622–24.

22. Virginia Bever Platt, "The East India Company and the Madagascar Slave Trade," *William and Mary Quarterly*, 3rd ser., 26, no. 4 (October 1969): 550. Platt gives an earlier example of this sort of conflict with the British state: "in the 1690s, English and colonial slaving vessels going to Madagascar began a practice which soon brought the wrath of the East India Company down on their heads and caused an end to their slaving. They hit upon the idea of carrying supplies to the pirates who had begun to use the island of St. Mary's as a base from which they raided shipping in the Red Sea and the Indian Ocean. In return for food, drink, guns, ammunition and catechisms, . . . the pirates gave gold and silver bullion and East India goods, which were carried to America as part of the cargoes of the slave-bearing ships."

23. Mervyn Brown, *Madagascar Rediscovered*, 93.

24. See ibid., 95–97; Wendy Wilson-Fall, "Women Merchants and Slave Depots: Saint Louis, Senegal and St. Mary's, Madagascar," in *Slaving Paths: Rebuilding and Rethinking the Atlantic Worlds*, ed. Ana Lucia Araujo (Amherst, NY: Cambria Press, 2011), 273–303.

25. Ellis, "Tom and Toakafo," 442.

26. Raymond Kent, *From Madagascar to the Malagasy Republic* (New York: Praeger, 1962), 50.

27. Platt, "East India Company," 548.

28. Ibid.

29. Ibid.

30. McDonald, "Man of Courage," 10. McDonald states "Given the relatively small number of Anglo-American pirates and privateers, Baldridge was probably familiar with some of the former Caribbean pirates then working the Indian Ocean region. By his own admission, he was most interested in trading and raiding for slaves."

31. Platt, "East India Company," 571. As late as 1721, the *Postillon*, registered as the *Crown Galley*, brought a cargo of Malagasy to New York.

32. Noted by scholar Kevin McDonald, "Man of Courage," 10.

33. For example, Rediker, *Slave Ship*.

34. See McDonald, "Man of Courage," 10; Ellis, "Tom and Toakafo," 445.

35. For descriptions of early slave trading from the eastern coast, see Gwyn Campbell, *An Economic History of Imperial Madagascar, 1750–1895: The Rise and Fall of an Island Empire* (New York: Cambridge University Press, 2008); Richard B. Allen, "The Mascarene Slave-Trade and Labour Migration in the Indian Ocean during the Eighteenth and Nineteenth Centuries," *Slavery and Abolition* 24, no. 2 (2003): 33–50.

36. Colonists and their British representatives lobbied intensely to repeal these laws. See Alison G. Olson, "The Virginia Merchants of London: A Study in Eighteenth-Century Interest-Group Politics," *William and Mary Quarterly,* 3rd ser., 40 (1983): 361–87.

37. McDonald, "Man of Courage."

38. Platt, "East India Company," 549, 559.

39. Ibid., 558n22. British Colonial Office Group, class 33, 15, 12, 42, 56, 68.

40. Ibid., 566.

41. Alessandro Portelli, "What Makes Oral History Different?," in *The Death of Luigi Trastulli and Other Stories: Form and Meaning in Oral History* (Albany: SUNY Press, 1991), 51–52.

42. Http://freepages.rootsweb.genealogy/~malagasy4us.

43. Platt, "East India Company," 558, 566, 569.

44. Ibid., 568–69.

45. Portelli, "Oral History," 55.

Chapter 2: Shipmates

1. For more discussion on shipmates, see Sidney W. Mintz and Richard Price, *The Birth of African-American Culture: An Anthropological Perspective* (Boston: Beacon Press, 1976), 43–46.

2. For a discussion of layering, see Babacar M'Baye, Amoaba Gooden, and Wendy Wilson-Fall, "A History of Black Immigration into the United States and Canada with Culture and Policy Implications," in *Africana Cultures and Policy Studies: Scholarship and the Transformation of Public Policy,* ed. Zachery Williams (New York: Palgrave Macmillan, 2009).

3. Examples of the latter have been well described by anthropologists Robert M. Baum, who writes of the Diola peoples of West Africa, and Rosalind Shaw, on the impact of slavery on communities situated in what is now Sierra Leone. Baum, *Shrines of the Slave Trade: Diola Religion and Society in Precolonial Senegambia* (New York: Oxford University Press, 1999); Shaw, *Memories of the Slave Trade: Ritual and the Historical Imagination in Sierra Leone* (Chicago: University of Chicago Press, 2002).

4. See Lorena S. Walsh, "New Findings about the Virginia Slave Trade," Williamsburg: Colonial Williamsburg Foundation, 2010, 2012, http://research.history.org.

5. For example, among the French Huguenots who arrived in Virginia a few years earlier than the Malagasy, only one major family, the Maubreys, eventually married into the Virginia elites and was considered one

of the "great" families. For an excellent discussion on the leading planter families, see Clifford Dowdey, *The Virginia Dynasties: The Emergence of "King" Carter and the Golden Age* (New York: Little, Brown, 1969).

6. Virginia Bever Platt, "The East India Company and the Madagascar Slave Trade," *William and Mary Quarterly*, 3rd ser., 26, no. 4 (October 1969): 549.

7. Ibid., 560. The South Sea Company, founded in 1711, was a British joint-stock company that traded in South America during the eighteenth century; most steady income was from the slave trade. The company assumed the national debt England had incurred during the War of the Spanish Succession. Speculation in the company's stock led to a great economic bubble known as the South Sea Bubble. It crashed in 1720 and caused financial ruin for many. The South Sea debacle was a costly project promoted by the then Secretary of State for the Southern Department, Earl James Stanhope. Amazingly, the same thing was tried with the British East India Company in its second iteration, which was required to loan millions of pounds to the British government for the privilege of reinstating its claims on Indian Ocean trade. Walpole was behind much of the debate and investment planning, though he escaped public censure.

8. Ibid., 568–69.

9. Ibid., 549. "Negroes were construed to be some form of 'Goods Wares Merchandizes and Commoditys'" (553). "As recently as 1708 Attorney General Sir Robert Eyre had confirmed a local ruling of the Leeward Islands certifying that Negroes were merchandise" (555). The debate over the nature of this cruel commodification was settled in favor of slaves from Madagascar as commodities in the broad sense.

10. Journal of Governor Spotswood of Virginia, 1712, manuscript collection, Albert and Shirley Small Special Collections Library, University of Virginia, Charlottesville.

11. Alison Olson, "The Virginia Merchants of London: A Study in Eighteenth-Century Interest Group Politics," *William and Mary Quarterly*, 3rd ser., 40, no. 3 (July 1983): 362–78; Platt, "East India Company," 559–60.

12. The Trans-Atlantic Slave Trade Database puts the figure upward to approximately fourteen hundred, and Lorena Walsh has put the figure at 1,466, including the 466 who arrived at the Rappahannock River; David Eltis et al., *The Trans-Atlantic Slave Trade Database*, http://www.slave-voyages.org/; Lorena S. Walsh, "The Chesapeake Slave Trade: Regional Patterns, African Origins, and Some Implications," *William and Mary Quarterly*, 3rd ser., 58, no. 1, New Perspectives on the Atlantic Slave Trade (January 2001): 139–70.

13. Marcus Rediker, *The Slave Ship: A Human History* (New York: Penguin, 2008), 9.

14. Stephanie Smallwood, *Saltwater Slaves: A Middle Passage from Africa to American Diaspora* (Cambridge, MA: Harvard University Press, 2008), 63.

15. Rediker, *Slave Ship,* 10.

16. Paul Lovejoy, "Transatlantic Transformations: The Origins and Identities of Africans in the Americas," in *Africa, Brazil and the Construction of Transatlantic Black Identities,* ed. Livio Sansone, Elisée Soumonni, and Boubacar Barry (Trenton, NJ: Africa World Press, 2008), 82, 84–85.

17. T. H. Brooke, *A History of the Island of St. Helena, from its Discovery by the Portuguese to the Year* 1806; *to which is added an Appendix* (London: Black, Parry and Kinsbury, 1808), chap. 3, http://www.bweaver .nom.sh/brooke/brooke.htm; Philip Gosse, *St. Helena: 1502–1938* (1938; repr., Shropshire, UK: Anthony Nelson, 1990).

18. Platt, "East India Company," 555–56.

19. Robert "King" Carter, correspondence to Micajah Perry, May 27, 1721, *Letters of Robert Carter, 1720–1727,* ed. Louis B. Wright (San Marino, CA: Huntington Library, 1940).

20. Daniel A. Yon, "Making Place, Making Race: St. Helena and the South Atlantic World," in Sansone, Soumonni, and Barry, *Africa, Brazil,* 116–17.

21. We know that the slaves were Malagasy from the descriptions in Baylor's account books and Carter's letters. See, for example, John Baylor Account Books, 1 and 2 (1719–21); Robert Carter Letterbook, 1719–21, both at Albert and Shirley Small Special Collections Library, University of Virginia, Charlottesville.

22. Platt, "East India Company," 556.

23. Sansone, Soumonni, and Barry, *Africa, Brazil,* 8; Michael A. Gomez, *Exchanging Our Country Marks: The Transformation of African Identities in the Colonial and Antebellum South* (Chapel Hill: University of North Carolina Press, 1998).

24. Madagascar National Archives staff, pers. comm., Antananarivo, 2006.

25. Rediker, *Slave Ship,* 9, 45.

26. Ibid., 17. For a description of the feeling of disorientation experienced at capture, see Olaudah Equiano, *The Interesting Narrative of the Life of Olaudah Equiano, or Gustavus Vassa, the African, Written by Himself,* ed. Werner Sollors (New York: Norton, 2001), 32–43.

27. Platt, "East India Company," 566.

28. Ibid.

29. Ibid., 557.

30. Ibid.

31. Ibid., 567.

32. Ibid., 566, 568.

33. As evidenced by comparing accounting notes in John Baylor's account books and Robert Carter's letters of 1719 and 1721.

34. Both Ira Berlin and Lorena Walsh estimate that the predominant African language in Virginia at that time was Ibo. Berlin, *Generations of Captivity: A History of African-American Slaves* (Cambridge, MA: Belknap Press, 2003), 56; Walsh, "Chesapeake Slave Trade," 145, 149, 150–54.

35. Calabar was a major slave export site in southeastern Nigeria, from where "Ibo," themselves a composite of several ethnic groups in that area, were shipped to Virginia and elsewhere.

36. Walsh, "Chesapeake Slave Trade."

37. Account books of John Baylor, 1719, 1721.

38. The Colonial Williamsburg Foundation supported my research over a summer (2005) in Virginia through a John D. Rockefeller Library grant.

39. Richard B. Allen, "The Mascarene Slave-Trade and Labour Migration in the Indian Ocean during the Eighteenth and Nineteenth Centuries," *Slavery and Abolition* 24, no. 2 (2003): 33–50. Allen writes, "During the first phase (of the Mascarene slave trade), from 1670 to 1769, Madagascar supplied about 70 percent of all slaves reaching the islands" (36).

40. Walsh, "Chesapeake Slave Trade," supplemental materials.

41. Walsh, "Virginia Slave Trade."

42. Walsh, "Chesapeake Slave Trade," 150.

43. Ibid., 139.

44. Ibid.

45. I arrived at this estimate after study of the Robert Carter letter books, John Baylor's account books, and extensive discussions via e-mail with Williamsburg historian Lorena Walsh, whom I wish to thank for her stimulating and helpful comments and observations.

46. Walsh, "Chesapeake Slave Trade."

47. For descriptions of the charges against Captain Stretton of the *Prince Eugene* (described in chap. 1), see Platt, "East India Company," 565, 568–70. Notations in Baylor's account books for food and upkeep costs indicate that some slaves were kept for several weeks.

48. Lorena S. Walsh, *From Calabar to Carter's Grove: The History of a Virginia Slave Community* (Charlottesville: University Press of Virginia, 1997), 35.

49. Richard Price, *First-Time: The Historical Vision of an African American People* (Chicago: University of Chicago Press, 2002), 5.

50. Ibid., xiv.

51. Melvin Wade, "'Shining in Borrowed Plumage': Affirmation of Community in the Black Coronation Festivals of New England, ca. 1750–1850," in *Material Life in America: 1600–1860*, ed. Robert Blair St. George (Boston: Northeastern University Press, 1988), 171–82. By 1790, Wade writes, the practice had reached a peak, appearing in Boston, Providence, Portsmouth, and New Haven.

52. Ibid.

53. Price, *First-Time*, xii.

54. From the oral narrative of Gail Melissa Grant, about her father's family, Washington, DC, circa 1988.

55. Platt, "East India Company," 555, 567.

56. Joseph C. Miller, "Retention, Reinvention, and Remembering: Restoring Identities through Enslavement in Africa and under Slavery in Brazil," in *Enslaving Connections: Changing Cultures of Africa and Brazil during the Era of Slavery*, ed. José Curto and Paul E. Lovejoy (Amherst, NY: Humanity Books, 2004), 81–121.

57. For example, the African American family who remembered the Bundy family as "Malagasy," in T. O. Madden, Jr., *We Were Always Free: The Maddens of Culpeper County, Virginia: A 200-Year Family History*, with the assistance of Ann L. Miller (Charlottesville: University of Virginia Press, 1992).

58. Walsh, *Calabash to Carter's Grove*; Walsh, "Virginia Slave Trade"; Walsh, "Chesapeake Slave Trade," supplemental materials.

59. Walsh, "Virginia Slave Trade."

60. See, for example, Allan Kulikoff, "The Origins of Afro-American Society in Tidewater Maryland and Virginia, 1700–1790," *William and Mary Quarterly*, 3rd ser., 35, no. 2 (April 1978): 226–59; Mechal Sobel, *The World They Made Together: Black and White Values in Eighteenth-Century Virginia* (Princeton: Princeton University Press, 1987); Annette Gordon-Reed, *The Hemingses of Monticello: An American Family* (New York: Norton, 2008).

61. Gomez, *Exchanging Our Country Marks*.

62. The Malagasy scholar Emmanuel Tehindrazanarivelo offers a perspective on the state of enslavement from a local point of view.

A Malagasy ethnohistorian and author, also chair of the Department of Ethics and Systematic Theology at FJKM Ambatonakanga, Faculty of Theology in Antananarivo, Madagascar, Tehindrazanarivelo was extremely helpful in working with U.S. informants' narratives. As a fellow the Library of Congress in 2000–2001, he collaborated in the organization and implementation of the workshop on Malagasy ancestry held at the Library of Congress in early September 2001. See Tehindrazanarivelo, "Fieldwork: The Dance of Power," *Anthropology and Humanities* (American Anthropological Association) 22, no. 1 (1997): 54–60.

63. Wendy Wilson-Fall, "Life Stories and Ancestor Debts: 'Creole Malagasy' in Eighteenth-Century Virginia," in *Crossing Memories: Slavery and African Diaspora,* ed. Ana Lucia Araujo, Mariana P. Candido, and Paul E. Lovejoy (Trenton, NJ: Africa World Press, 2011), 147–82.

64. For more on the documented evidence that enslaved women invested their limited personal lives overwhelmingly into the survival and education of their children, see Gwyn Campbell, introduction to *Women and Slavery,* ed. Campbell, Susan Miers, and Joseph A. Miller (Athens: Ohio University Press, 2008), 6–26.

65. Mintz and Price, *Birth of African-American Culture,* 68.

66. Margaret Brown, "Reclaiming Lost Ancestors and Acknowledging Slave Descent: Insights from Madagascar," *Comparative Studies in Society and History* 46, no. 3 (2004): 623–24.

67. Native Americans were still present at this time, although those encountered were often enslaved. Mary B. Kegley, "From Indian Slavery to Freedom," *Journal of the Afro-American Historical and Genealogical Society* 22, no. 1 (2003): 29–36. I prefer to use the more current term preferred, "Native American."

68. See, for example, Gomez, *Exchanging Our Country Marks,* 8.

69. Ibid., 9.

70. Livio Sansone, Elisée Soumonni, and Boubacar Barry, introduction to *Africa, Brazil,* 10–11; Luis Nicolau Parés, "Ethnic-Religious Modes of Identification among the Gbe-Speaking People in Eighteenth- and Nineteenth-Century Brazil," in Sansone, Soumonni, and Barry, *Africa, Brazil,* 196; Eltis et al., *Slave Trade Database,* www.slavevoyages.org, accessed 2011; Paul E. Lovejoy, "Ethnic Designations of the Slave Trade and the Reconstruction of the History of Trans-Atlantic Slavery," in *Transatlantic Dimensions of Ethnicity in the African Diaspora,* ed. Lovejoy and David V. Trotman (New York: Continuum Press, 2003), 9–42.

71. Eltis et al., *Slave Trade Database*; Lovejoy, "Ethnic Designations."

72. Berlin, *Generations of Captivity*, 29–30. See also Wendy Wilson-Fall, "Women Merchants and Slave Depots: St. Louis, Senegal and St. Mary's, Madagascar," in *Slaving Paths: Rebuilding and Rethinking the Atlantic Worlds*, ed. Ana Lucia Araujo (Amherst, NY: Cambria Press, 2011) 273–303.

73. Lovejoy, "Transatlantic Transformations," 82–84.

74. Platt, East India Company, 576. The text says, "The cessation of the trade is attested in a petition brought before the vestry of William and Mary parish in Maryland in the year 1796. Negro Mary contended that although a female ancestor had been brought to this country from Madagascar many years ago, Madagascar was outside the 'usual course of the trade' in slaves and therefore she should be freed." This was discussed in the opening section of the introduction of this book. Platt, 576n59, quotes from Melville Herskovits, *The Myth of the Negro Past* (1940; repr., Boston: Beacon Press, 1990), 47ff. This is probably in reference to the passages in Jeffrey R. Brackett, *The Negro in Maryland: A Study of the Institution of Slavery*, Johns Hopkins University Studies in Historical and Political Science, extra vol. 6 (Baltimore: n.p., 1889), 27–33, 37, cited above.

75. For example, Sansone, Soumonni, and Barry, *Africa, Brazil*; Linda M. Heywood and John K. Thornton, *Central Africans, Atlantic Creoles, and the Foundation of the Americas*, 1585–1660 (New York: Cambridge University Press, 2007).

76. An online excerpt from David L. Cohn cites transcripts from a criminal trial where a woman reasoned, "My grandma told me not to let nobody call me no nigger," etc., Cohn, "Where I Was Born and Raised," http://www.soc.umn.edu/~samaha/cases/cohn,%20delta%20land.htm, accessed February 7, 2001.
That this woman would be found in Mississippi may be accounted for by the "Second Middle Passage," starting around 1808, when thousands of slaves in the United States were traded from the Upper South to the Lower South, or the illegal transatlantic slave trade (see chap. 4). I first quoted this phrase in Wilson-Fall, "Life Stories."

77. David Streitfeld, review of *The Street*, by Ann Petry, "Petry's Brew: Laughter and Fury: The Author's 1946 Novel Hits Home Once More," *Washington Post*, February 25, 1992, Style Section, E1–E2.

78. In fact, although many of the people I interviewed were not residents of Virginia, they considered their families to be "Virginia families," and most still have relatives who live there.

79. For more discussion on memory, morality, and Malagasy world-views, see Michael Lambek, "The Past Imperfect: Remembering as Moral Practice," in *Tense Past: Cultural Essays in Trauma and Memory*, ed. Paul Antze and Lambek (New York: Routledge, 1996), 235–54.

80. For example, see Robert Farris Thompson and Joseph Cornet, *The Four Moments of the Sun: Kongo Art in Two Worlds* (Washington, DC: National Gallery of Art, 1981).

Chapter 3: History and Narrative

1. There are many known instances of slaves creating lineages that ultimately became free and, in some cases, ruling lineages in their new countries. An outstanding example is the Sidi lineages of southwestern India.

2. We cannot assume that this same phenomenon did not take place in Madagascar. Future research may reveal that slaves in Madagascar also reconstructed their identities, meshing one family story with more recently acquired ones.

3. Ira Berlin, *Generations of Captivity: A History of African-American Slaves* (Cambridge, MA: Belknap Press, 2003), 5; see also Mechal Sobel, *The World They Made Together: Black and White Values in Eighteenth-Century Virginia* (Princeton: Princeton University Press, 1987).

4. Sobel, *World They Made*, 3.

5. In Rhys Isaac, *Landon Carter's Uneasy Kingdom: Revolution and Rebellion on a Virginia Plantation* (New York: Oxford University Press, 2004). A good example would be Carter's relationship to his slave Jack Lubber, as also described by Sobel, *World They Made*, 42.

6. Sobel, *World They Made*, 32.

7. Andrew Levy, *The First Emancipator: The Forgotten Story of Robert Carter, the Founding Father Who Freed His Slaves* (New York: Random House, 2005), xv.

8. Berlin, *Generations of Captivity*, 5.

9. Lorena S. Walsh, *From Calabar to Carter's Grove: The History of a Virginia Slave Community* (Charlottesville: University Press of Virginia, 1997), xvii–xix, 4, 56.

10. I base this supposition on data collected by Walsh and Allan Kulikoff, who provide demographic information on death rates and slave distribution among the Carter households, as well as saltwater slave purchase records.

11. Lorena S. Walsh, "The Chesapeake Slave Trade: Regional Patterns, African Origins, and Some Implications," *William and Mary Quarterly*,

3rd ser., 58, no. 1, New Perspectives on the Transatlantic Slave Trade (January 2001): 139–70; Walsh, "New Findings about the Virginia Slave Trade," Colonial Williamsburg Foundation, 2012.

12. Allan Kulikoff, "The Origins of Afro-American Society in Tidewater Maryland and Virginia, 1700 to 1790," *William and Mary Quarterly*, 3rd ser., 35, no. 2 (April 1978): 242.

13. Ibid., 236; Philip D. Morgan, *Slave Counterpoint: Black Culture in the Eighteenth-Century Chesapeake and Low Country* (Chapel Hill: University of North Carolina Press, 1998), 81. Berlin places the period of stabilization as beginning in the 1720s. Berlin, *Many Thousands Gone: The First Two Centuries of Slavery in North America* (Cambridge, MA: Belknap Press, 1998), 126.

14. Kulikoff, "Afro-American Society," 236.

15. Ibid., 237.

16. Walsh, "Virginia Slave Trade."

17. Levy, *First Emancipator,* 9.

18. Kulikoff, "Afro-American Society," 241.

19. Ibid., 244.

20. I take this phrase, "the weight of the past," from Michael Lambek's work on the Sakalava of northwestern Madagascar, *The Weight of the Past: Living with History in Mahajanga, Madagascar,* Contemporary Anthropology of Religion Series (New York: Palgrave Macmillan, 1999).

21. Walsh, *Calabar to Carter's Grove,* 44.

22. In the second codicil, September 12, 1728, Carter states, "It is my will that my several slaves that are to be annexed according to the intent of my will to the lands and plantations where I live which I hold as tenant in tail under the will of my father & also all the slaves which are to be annexed to all the rest of the lands & plantations which I have given to my said son John in Tail the property in all my said slaves & their increase lent to my said son John as aforesaid I give unto my grandson John." *The Diary, Correspondence, and Papers of Robert "King" Carter of Virginia,* 1701–1732, Wills and Codicils, 1726–1732, carter.lib.virginia.edu.

23. Douglas R. Egerton, *Death or Liberty: African Americans and Revolutionary America* (New York: Oxford University Press, 2009), 176.

24. Kulikoff, "Afro-American Society," 228.

25. Walsh, "Chesapeake Slave Trade," 144.

26. Kulikoff, "Afro-American Society," 229–30.

27. Allan Kulikoff, "A 'Prolifick' People: Black Population Growth in the Chesapeake Colonies, 1700–1790," *Southern Studies* 16, no. 4 (1977): 391–428. Kulikoff points out, "The proportion of recent immigrants

among black slave adults fluctuated with trade cycles: about one-half in 1709, one-third in 1720, one-half in 1728, and one-third in 1740 had left Africa or the West Indies within ten years."

28. Walsh, "Chesapeake Slave Trade," 145.

29. Ibid., 150.

30. Maps by John H. Clark, Data Visualization/GIS Specialist, Skillman Library, Lafayette College, Easton, Pennsylvania.

31. The term Lower James River pertains to the area closer to the bay.

32. Walsh, "Virginia Slave Trade," 5.

33. Ibid., 7.

34. Rhys Isaac, *The Transformation of Virginia, 1740–1790* (Chapel Hill: University of North Carolina Press, for the Omohundro Institute of Early American History and Culture, 1982), 29.

35. During this period, most slaves in Virginia were either Senegambian or from what is today southeastern Nigeria. The latter were commonly called Calabar slaves and referred to as Ibo, although they probably represented several ethnicities living in the Calabar and Cross Rivers regions.

36. Robert Carter, *Letters of Robert "King" Carter*, ed. Edmund Berkeley, Jr., www.monticello.org/library/links/carter.html.

37. Ibid.

38. Walsh, "Chesapeake Slave Trade," 150.

39. Charles Royster, *The Fabulous Story of The Great Dismal Swamp: A Story of George Washington's Life* (New York: Knopf, 1999).

40. Ibid., 29.

41. Ibid., 31–33.

42. Ibid., 38–39.

43. Ibid., 77.

44. Sobel, *World They Made*, 33.

45. Berlin, *Generations of Captivity*, 57.

46. Koulikoff, "Afro-American Society," 248, 250–51.

47. Walsh, "Virginia Slave Trade," 2010.

48. Correspondence of Robert Carter, Robert Carter Letterbook, 1727–28, Colonial Williamsburg microfilm no. M113, October 10, 1727.

49. Madagascar Jack, mentioned in ibid. I have taken this paragraph from my essay "Life Stories and Ancestor Debts: 'Creole Malagasy' in Eighteenth-Century Virginia," in *Crossing Memories: Slavery and African Diaspora*, ed. Ana Lucia Araujo, Mariana P. Candido, and Paul E. Lovejoy (Trenton, NJ: Africa World Press, 2011), 147–82.

50. Michael A. Gomez, *Exchanging Our Country Marks: The Transformation of African Identities in the Colonial and Antebellum South* (Chapel Hill: University of North Carolina Press, 1998), 41.

51. Sobel, *World They Made*, 163.

52. Ibid.

53. Allan Kulikoff, *Tobacco and Slaves: The Development of Southern Cultures in the Chesapeake, 1680–1800* (Chapel Hill: University of North Carolina Press, 1986), 371–80.

54. Morgan, *Slave Counterpoint*, 196–98.

55. Walsh, *Calabar to Carter's Grove*, 45.

56. Isaac, *Transformation of Virginia*, 204.

57. Egerton, *Death or Liberty*, 64.

58. George Washington urged an end to the recruitment of blacks, while John Adams recognized that the issue of race could potentially cripple the patriot cause. See Egerton, *Death or Liberty*, 74–75.

59. Works Progress Administration, Federal Writers' Project in the State of Virginia, *The Negro in Virginia* (New York: Hastings House, 1940; repr., Winston-Salem: John F. Blair, 1994), 25.

60. Robert F. Engs, *Freedom's First Generation: Black Hampton, Virginia, 1861–1890* (New York: Fordham University Press, 1980), 7.

61. Levy, *First Emancipator*, 120.

62. Egerton, *Death or Liberty*, 13.

63. Ted Delaney and Phillip Wayne Rhodes, *Free Blacks of Lynchburg, Virginia, 1805–1865* (Lynchburg: Warwick House, 2001), 2.

64. Engs, *Freedom's First Generation*, 8.

65. Brown family, e-mail correspondence, 2008; interviews, Washington, DC, 2003.

66. Interview by Wendy Wilson-Fall, Boston, autumn 2001.

67. This person is a university professor and biochemist. The story above is about his paternal ancestors.

68. Walsh, *Calabar to Carter's Grove*.

69. Pier Larson, *Ocean of Letters: Language and Creolization in an Indian Ocean Diaspora*, Critical Perspectives on Empire (New York: Cambridge University Press, 2009); on lasting Malagasy identity, see p. 348; on language, see pp. 21–23, 152, 352–55.

70. T. O. Madden, Jr., *We Were Always Free: The Maddens of Culpeper County, Virginia*, with the assistance of Ann L. Miller (Charlottesville: University of Virginia Press, 1992), xx.

71. Ibid., 43.

72. This was the mother of Mr. Melvin McCaw, who at that time was living in Washington, DC, and had facilitated this contact.

73. See a more detailed explanation of this in Wilson-Fall, "Life Stories."

74. Robert Carter III was a rare exception; not only did he acknowledge that slaves were building new identities, he occasionally helped them in the case of conversion to the Baptist persuasion.

75. Michel-Rolph Trouillot, *Silencing the Past: Power and the Production of History* (Boston: Beacon Press, 1995).

76. Levy, *First Emancipator*, 19, 111.

77. Robert "King" Carter Journal, 1719–1734, Albert and Shirley Small Special Collections Library, University of Virginia, Charlottesville.

78. Margaret Brown, "Reclaiming Lost Ancestors and Acknowledging Slave Descent: Insights From Madagascar, *Comparative Studies in Society and History* 46, no. 3 (2004): 616–45: discussions with Emmanuel Tehindrazanariveo, 2002, 2004, and 2006 during my fieldwork in Madagascar.

79. In Senegambia, where many earlier slaves of Virginia originated, *joking relationships* between ethnicities and lineages favored fairly open lateral social relationships. This tradition might have had a role in the development of creole attitudes toward interethnic cooperation and the formation of multiethnic identities.

80. The Letters of Robert "King" Carter, 1719–1721, University of Virginia Manuscript Collection.

81. For discussion of the slave experience as "multilayered and contingent," and agency among slaves, see Stephanie Smallwood, *Saltwater Slaves: A Middle Passage from Africa to American Diaspora* (Cambridge, MA: Harvard University Press, 2008), 61, 119.

82. A useful source on this subject and slavery is *The Devil's Lane: Sex and Race in the Early South,* ed. Catherine Clinton and Michelle Gillespie (New York: Oxford University Press, 1997). See also Catherine M. Lewis and J. Richard Lewis, eds., *Women and Slavery in America: A Documentary History* (Fayetteville: University of Arkansas Press, 2011), esp. 51–53, 64, 88–90, 124–28.

83. Joshua D. Rothman, *Notorious in the Neighborhood: Sex and Families across the Color Line in Virginia, 1787–1861* (Chapel Hill: University of North Carolina Press, 2003); on the sexual use of female slaves, see esp. pp. 130–34, 138–39, 152–54, 210; on hair, esp. 223, 226.

84. E-mail, October 18, 2004.

85. "Malagasy Ancestors Stolen," posted September 27, 2001, http://boards.rootsweb.com/localities.africa.madagascar.general/6/mb.ashx (emphasis in original).

86. I have also collected other queries about African American Ragland families of Louisa County, Virginia. A Genealogy.com posting on October 26, 2000, states, "I have a John Ragland in my family. . . . It seems that some names were extremely popular with them and brothers named sons after brothers and themselves and the names were so repetitive. My black Raglands came from Louisa VA to Ohio @1847 or so. They came with a large number of freed blacks from the will of William Ragland of Louisa. Some of them were his children and some were unrelated."

87. Lisa B. Lee is an example of a person having Malagasy ancestry from two descent lines. She is a genealogist whose great-great-grandfather was George Ragland, but who claims Malagasy descent from another line, through the Lees. She is related to both Randolph and Lee families and hence may unknowingly have more than one line of Malagasy descent. E-mail, August 28, 2003; posting on Genealogy.com, April 21, 2001.

88. I began an e-list sometime in 2001 that became a forum for exchanges on the topic of Malagasy ancestors: freepages.genealogy.rootsweb.com/~malagasy4us.

89. August 2003.

90. E-mail, Dakar, August 28, 2003.

91. Freepages.genealogy.rootsweb.com/~malagasy4us, 2000–2003.

Chapter 4: After the American Revolution

1. Andrew Levy, *The First Emancipator: The Forgotten Story of Robert Carter, the Founding Father Who Freed His Slave* (New York: Random House, 2005), 29.

2. Works Progress Administration, Federal Writers' Project in the State of Virginia, *The Negro in Virginia* (New York: Hastings House, 1940; repr., Winston-Salem: John F. Blair, 1994), 43.

3. Sterling Stuckey and others have shown that in the northern states African-born persons were among the free blacks of this era. Some had been manumitted and others were successful runaways who were swelling the numbers of people in black communities in New York, Philadelphia, and Rhode Island. The family of Rakekata (see chap. 5) moved to Ohio, near Cleveland, and the family of John and Lucy Ann Clark (see "Oral Traditions," this chapter) also moved to Ohio for a few years.

4. Susan Eva O'Donovan, "Traded Babies: Enslaved Children in America's Domestic Migration, 1820–60," in *Children in Slavery through the Ages,* ed. Gwyn Campbell, Suzanne Miers, and Joseph C. Miller (Athens: Ohio University Press, 2009), 88–102.

5. It took about three years for the law to be applied consistently, and throughout this period there was significant resistance.

6. Georgia initially resisted the importation of slaves.

7. Charles Perdue, foreword to Works Progress Administration, *Negro in Virginia*, 10.

8. Levy, *First Emancipator*, 122, 125.

9. Ibid., 136–73.

10. Mechal Sobel, *The World They Made Together: Black and White Values in Eighteenth-Century Virginia* (Princeton: Princeton University Press, 1987), 163.

11. Levy, *First Emancipator*, 150–52.

12. Works Progress Administration, *Negro in Virginia*, 25–26.

13. Suzanne Lebsock, *The Free Women of Petersburg: Status and Culture in a Southern Town, 1784–1860* (New York: Norton, 1984), 6.

14. This transfer occurred at the marriage of John Carter, son of Robert "King" Carter, to Elizabeth Hill, who inherited from her father, Edward Hill, at the death of her brother.

15. National Park Service, "James River Plantations," Discover Our Heritage Series, http://www.nps.gov/nr/travel/jamesriver/.

16. Joshua D. Rothman, *Notorious in the Neighborhood: Sex and Families across the Color Line in Virginia, 1787–1861* (Chapel Hill: University of North Carolina Press, 2003), 21, 38, 44–45, 85, 134, 164.

17. Lebsock, *Free Women*, 7, quoted in Wendy Wilson-Fall, "Life Stories and Ancestor Debts: 'Creole Malagasy' in Eighteenth-Century Virginia," in *Crossing Memories: Slavery and African Diaspora*, ed. Ana Lucia Araujo, Mariana P. Candido, and Paul E. Lovejoy (Trenton, NJ: Africa World Press, 2011), 147–82.

18. Ibid. In that general atmosphere, the Quakers present a particular example. It appears that planters, mostly Anglican and Presbyterian, often freed their slaves and transferred responsibility for their upkeep to Quakers, who were known for successfully overseeing such communities or adopting and sponsoring free blacks.

19. Robert F. Engs, *Freedom's First Generation: Black Hampton, Virginia, 1861–1890* (New York: Fordham University Press, 1980).

20. Rothman, *Notorious in the Neighborhood*, 96.

21. Ibid.

22. Gabriel's Rebellion took place in the Richmond area in the summer of 1800. The leader, Gabriel Posser, was a literate slave and blacksmith who was born in 1776. He and other coconspirators were hanged in 1800

for their unsuccessful uprising, and other results were more restrictions on free blacks and more scrutiny of slaves. See Douglas R. Egerton, *Gabriel's Rebellion: The Virginia Slave Conspiracies of 1800 and 1802* (Chapel Hill: University of North Carolina Press, 1993), 121–22.

23. For more information on the free black population of Petersburg, see Lebsock, *Free Women*.

24. Wendy Wilson-Fall, *Malagasy Free Black Settlement in Hanover County, Virginia, during Slavery: The Intriguing Story of Lucy Andriana Renibe Winston* (Ashland, VA: Hanover County Black Heritage Society and Hanover County Historical Society, 2007).

25. According to family oral tradition, seven churches were established by African American John Clark between Richmond and Hanover and at least five were set up by his relative Dabney Winston.

26. Ted Delaney and Phillip Wayne Rhodes, *Free Blacks of Lynchburg, Virginia, 1805–1865* (Lynchburg: Warwick House, 2001), 15.

27. Works Progress Administration, *Negro in Virginia*, 63. This traditional "Negro song" was reported by Fanny Berry, ex-slave.

28. Ibid., 65.

29. O'Donovan, "Traded Babies," 89, 91.

30. David Eltis et al., *The Trans-Atlantic Slave Trade Database* (Cambridge: Cambridge University Press), http://www.slavevoyages.org/tast/index.faces.

31. James A. McMillin, *The Final Victims: Foreign Slave Trade to North America, 1783–1810* (Columbia: University of South Carolina Press, 2004).

32. Ibid., 31.

33. Ibid., 33.

34. Ibid.

35. Ibid., 47.

36. Ibid., 48.

37. D. R. Murray, "Statistics of the Slave Trade to Cuba, 1790–1867," *Journal of Latin American Studies* 3, no. 2 (November 1971): 131–49.

38. The cedula was an act or bill, passed in Spain in this case to liberalize trade, notably slave trade to the Americas.

39. Murray, "Slave Trade to Cuba," 132. Murray states, "It was not until a treaty was signed between Britain and Spain in 1817 that Spain prohibited the trade in slaves between Africa and her transatlantic colonies, but this prohibition did not become total until 30 May 1820."

40. Ibid., 140; H. T. Kilbee's annual report to the British high commissioners.

41. Frances J. Stafford, "Illegal Importations: Enforcement of the Slave Trade Laws along the Florida Coast, 1810–1828," *Florida Historical Quarterly* 46, no. 2 (October 1967): 124.

42. Ibid., 125.

43. Ibid.

44. Ibid., 126.

45. Members of the Stith family, interviews by author, 2012–13.

46. Posted on an ancestry.com site, February 20, 2000, this post got eight replies. http://boards.ancestry.com/thread.aspx?mv=flat&m=40&p =localities.africa.madagascar.general.

47. Posted on an ancestry.com page by Fountane, May 4, 2000.

48. karomaini, posted August 25, 2002, classification: query, http:// boards.rootsweb.com/localities.africa.madagascar.general/7.1/mb.ashx, emphasis mine.

49. See chap. 2.

50. Michael A. Gomez, *Exchanging Our Country Marks: The Transformation of African Identities in the Colonial and Antebellum South* (Chapel Hill: University of North Carolina Press, 1998), 41; from George P. Rawick, ed., *The American Slave: A Composite Autobiography* (Westport, CT: Greenwood, 1972–77), 4:42.

51. William H. Robinson, *From Log Cabin to the Pulpit; or, Fifteen Years in Slavery*, 3rd ed. (Eau Claire, WI: James H. Tifft, 1973; digital ed., ed. Theresa Church and Natalia Smith, University of North Carolina, Chapel Hill, 1997), 3.

52. Ibid.

53. Isaac Johnson, *Slavery Days in Old Kentucky: A True Story of a Father Who Sold His Wife and Four Children, by One of His Children* (1901; repr., NEH Electronic Publication, Apex Data Services, ed. Ann Morawski and Natalia Smith [Chapel Hill: University of North Carolina Academic Affairs Library, 2000]), 7–8.

54. Discussion about Muhammad Ali online at afrigeneas.org ancestry and history forum, March 20, 2002; John Egerton, "Heritage of a Heavyweight: Ali's Kentucky Roots," *New York Times*, September 28, 1980, SM114.

55. O'Donovan, "Traded Babies," 96.

56. Michael E. Harkin, "Feeling and Thinking in Memory and Forgetting: Toward an Ethnohistory of the Emotions," *Ethnohistory* 50, no. 2 (Spring 2003): 262; the quote by Robert I. Levy is from "Emotion, Knowing, and Culture," in *Culture Theory: Essays on Mind, Self, and Emotion,*

ed. Richard A. Schweder and Robert A. LeVine (Cambridge: Cambridge University Press, 1984), 228.

57. Engs, *Freedom's First Generation*, 12–13. Engs cites an interview with Mrs. Louis Stone, Philadelphia, September 27, 1977; Arthur P. Davis, "William Roscoe Davis and His Descendants," *Negro History Bulletin* 13 (1950): 75–80. Arthur P. Davis, the father of Louise Davis Stone, was co-editor of *The Negro Caravan: Writings by American Negroes,* ed. Sterling A. Brown, Davis, and Ulysses L. Snippet (New York: Citadel Press, 1941); he taught at Howard University from 1944 to 1980. Louise Davis Stone, daughter of Arthur P. Davis, and her husband were close friends of my own parents, and I remember their visits to our house when I was a young girl. These visits often began with my father asking "Chuck" Stone, Louise's husband, how his work as a Chicago journalist was going, and asking Louise, "How is Arthur P.?"

58. Later in his life, Pascal Beverly Randolph made other claims as well, including Persian origins. Whether this was a confused remnant of a Swahili-Malagasy story is unknown.

59. Monica 3025, rootsweb, posted February 27, 2009, accessed November 2009, http://boards.rootsweb.com/localities.africa.madagascar.general/6.3/mb.ashx.

60. The exact date mentioned for this ancestor's birth is dubious, for how would such a person, captured as a slave, know the exact date of his birth? During the late eighteenth century and well into the twentieth, people in Madagascar and continental Africa rarely knew the dates of their birth. Still, it is important to the narrator to situate his birth in the late eighteenth century and to situate the story geographically. The date of birth does correspond to a time when there were French missionaries in northeastern and northwestern Madagascar and when the London Missionary Society was just beginning its work in Madagascar, so it is nevertheless a possibility that this slave knew his date of birth. See Larson, note 72, this chapter.

61. Wilson-Fall, "Life Stories," 147–82.

62. Melva Morgan, interviews by author, Washington, DC, 2009, 2010.

63. Interviews I carried out in Hanover and Ashland, Virginia, 2005, 2007. See my monograph "Malagasy Free Black Settlement."

64. Mildred Eldora Alves Sampson, interview by author, Hanover, VA, July 6, 2007.

65. Willard Raymond Johnson, interview by author and written response, August 6, 2008.

66. Ibid.

67. Ancestry.com, Message Boards > Localities > Africa > Madagascar > General; BKIRBY 6785, March 7, 2001.

68. Ancestry.com; http://boards.rootsweb.com/localities.africa.madagascar.general.

69. Ibid., BKIRBY 6785, posted November 13, 2001, classification: query.

70. See, for example, Wilson-Fall, "Life Histories," 147–82.

71. Gwyn Campbell, introduction to *The Structure of Slavery in Indian Ocean Africa and Asia* (London: Frank Cass, 2004), xv–xxii; Richard B. Allen, "Children and European Slave Trading in the Indian Ocean during the Eighteenth and Early Nineteenth Centuries," in *Children in Slavery through the Ages*, ed. Gwyn Campbell, Suzanne Miers, and Joseph C. Miller (Athens: Ohio University Press, 2009), 35–54.

72. Richard B. Allen, *Slaves, Freedmen, and Indentured Laborers in Colonial Mauritius*, African Studies Series 99 (Cambridge: Cambridge University Press, 1999). Allen describes the slave communities of Mauritius and some aspects of the Malagasy trade; see also Pier M. Larson, *Ocean of Letters: Language and Creolization in an Indian Ocean Diaspora*, Critical Perspectives on Empire (New York: Cambridge University Press, 2009), 62–63, 108, 133–42.

73. "Workshop on Madagascar Ancestry," Library of Congress, Washington, DC, September 2, 2001, with LOC fellow Emmanuel Tehindrazanarivelo. Many of the participants were discussants on the e-list that I managed at the time, on the topic of Malagasy ancestors.

74. I spoke with the granddaughter of Judge Hastie in 2005; the stories of Catlett and Terrell were told to me by an elderly African American woman whose family had been neighbors with the Catletts in Essex County, Virginia.

Chapter 5: Free, Undocumented Immigrants

1. For more information, see Gwyn Campbell, "The State and Pre-colonial Demographic History: The Case of Nineteenth-Century Madagascar," *Journal of African History* 32, no. 3 (October 1991): 415–45; Pier M. Larson, *History and Memory in the Age of Enslavement: Becoming Merina in Highland Madagascar, 1770–1822* (Portsmouth, NH: Heinemann, 2000).

2. Campbell, "Demographic History."

3. "An Account of Outward Bound Ships arrived at the Isle of France [Mauritius] from different Ports of Europe, America & India during the period of Ten Years with the particulars of their Cargoes &c," app. 7, Port

Louis, February 8, 1811; Administrator General, Chanvaloa, Kew Gardens, National Archives of Britain (formerly Public Record Office), Colonial Office, ser. 167, vol. 5, PRO/CO/167/5.

4. Pier M. Larson, *Ocean of Letters: Language and Creolization in an Indian Ocean Diaspora*, Critical Perspectives on Empire (New York: Cambridge University Press, 2009), 103.

5. Ibid., 105.

6. Richard B. Allen, *Freedmen and Indentured Laborers in Colonial Mauritius*, African Studies Series 99 (Cambridge: Cambridge University Press, 1999), 13–16.

7. Larson, *Ocean of Letters*, 42.

8. Christopher Saunders, "Liberated Africans in Cape Colony in the First Half of the Nineteenth Century," *International Journal of African Historical Studies* 18, no. 2 (1985): 223.

9. Ibid., 224.

10. Ibid.

11. Ibid., 225.

12. Ibid., 226.

13. Ibid., 229–30.

14. Ibid., 232–33.

15. Ibid., 234.

16. Ibid., 237.

17. Pier M. Larson, "Enslaved Malagasy and 'le Travail de la Parole' in the Pre-revolutionary Mascarenes," *Journal of African History* 48, no. 3 (November 2007): 459–61.

18. Larson, *Ocean of Letters*, 38.

19. Ibid., 222–52.

20. Elyria, Ohio, 1880 census, roll T9-1042, Family History Film 1255042, p. 462C, Enumeration District 171, image 0273, Church of Jesus Christ of Latter Day Saints, 1999, Intellectual reserve, Inc.

21. Saunders, "Liberated Africans," 238.

22. This informant was Peggy Peterman, a former journalist for the *Louisville Times* and the *Saint Petersburg Times*. Ms. Peterman died in 2004. I had interviewed her uncle, Dr. Townshend, chief of internal medicine at Howard University, on several occasions and knew him for ten years before being introduced to Ms. Peterman. At the time of our first encounter, I was unaware that her story was the story of Dr. Townshend's family and that Townshend was her uncle.

23. As I have stated elsewhere, this also raises questions about naming in general, as well as "nonsense songs" among certain families in

the African American community, and how nonsensical meanings are assumed for names and words that may in reality merely be mispronunciations of words understood more clearly by preceding generations. Wilson-Fall, "Life Stories and Ancestor Debts: 'Creole Malagasy' in Eighteenth-Century Virginia," in *Crossing Memories: Slavery and African Diaspora*, ed. Ana Lucia Araujo, Mariana P. Candido, and Paul E. Lovejoy (Trenton, NJ: Africa World Press, 2011), 147–82; Wilson-Fall and Charles Sow, "Kimoh, Dar You Are!" *Journal of Pan African Studies* 1, no. 10 (2007): 19–40.

24. Very relevant here is Janet Ewald, "Crossers of the Sea: Slaves, Freedmen, and Other Migrants in the Northwestern Indian Ocean, c. 1750–1914," *American Historical Review* 105, no. 1 (February 2000): 69–91.

25. Larson, *Ocean of Letters*, 225.

26. Wendy Wilson-Fall, field notes, Baltimore, 1988–90. The speaker was my mother's second cousin.

27. For example, in that census Edward, Jerry, Julia, Margaret, Margaret A., Martha, Rosetta, and Sarah are listed in one household as free blacks. The elder Jerry Mahammitt, perhaps the person also known as Ali Salaha, is listed as a free black of fifty years of age, and his daughter Margaret, also listed as black in this census (elsewhere as mulatto), is twenty-five years old. Free inhabitants in Frederick election district, County of Frederick, State of Maryland, Schedule 1, reproduced in Edward S. Delaplaine, *The Origin of Frederick County, Maryland: A Bicentennial Address* (Washington, DC: Judd and Detweiler, 1949), 76.

28. The only documentation that might refer to Jeremiah (alias Ali Salaha Mahomet) is a record of entry of a ship originating in Sumatra that arrived at Baltimore in 1822. This record refers to "Po Mahomet" on the ship *Johannes*, in *Passenger Arrivals at the Port of Baltimore, 1820–1834: From Customs Passenger Lists*, ed. Michael H. Tepper (Baltimore: Genealogical Publishing Company, 1979), 405.

29. *Williamsport Gazette*, 1890.

30. *The Colored American*, an African American newspaper published in Washington, DC, January 13, 1900, page 4. Walter Mahamitt's obituary appeared in the *Washington Times*, February 4, 1913.

31. Assistance with translating this vocabulary was provided by a staff member of the Embassy of Madagascar who was a native of Diego Suarez (present-day Antsiranana), in the north of Madagascar. Ethnically Sakalava, Suzanne Tsiranana (now deceased) was very helpful and was at that time cultural attaché at the embassy.

32. According to Jeremiah Mahammitt, the family was joined by relatives from Newport News, the men donned multicolored sashes and the women undid their braids in order to perform a slow circular dance, during which time a sword "from home" and "a flag" were displayed as part of the ceremony. The men, he said, wore their hair in braids as well.

33. Wilson-Fall, "Life Stories," 147–82.

34. Larson, *Ocean of Letters*, 19.

35. Ibid., 21.

36. Ibid., 26.

Chapter 6: The Problem of the Metanarrative

1. Michel-Rolph Trouillot, *Global Transformations: Anthropology and the Modern World* (New York: Palgrave Macmillan, 2003), 22.

2. For these and other documented stories of Muslim Africans in the eighteenth and nineteenth centuries, see Allan D. Austin, *African Muslims in Antebellum America: Transatlantic Stories and Spiritual Struggle* (New York: Routledge, 1997).

3. *Star* (Reynoldsville, PA), February 27, 1895, Library of Congress, http://chroniclingamerica.loc.gov/lccn/sn87078321/1895-02-27/ed-1/seq-3/.

4. For example, *Washington (DC) Bee*, June 22, 1901, Library of Congress, http://chroniclingamerica.loc.gov/lccn/sn84025891/1901-06-22/ed-1/seq-7/; *Hopkinsville Kentuckian*, November 19, 1895, Library of Congress, http://chroniclingamerica.loc.gov/lccn/sn86069395/1895-11-19/ed-1/seq-6/; *Manning (SC) Times*, December 18, 1918, Library of Congress, http://chroniclingamerica.loc.gov/lccn/sn86063760/1918-12-18/ed-1/seq-9/.

5. Waller served as counsel from 1891 to 1894. Suspected by the French of passing privileged information to the Malagasy, he was sentenced to twenty years in prison in Marseilles. He was saved from imprisonment by the French colonial government by President Grover Cleveland, who brought him back to the United States. This event, known as the Waller Affair, was also closely followed by the U.S. press. See Randall Bennett Woods, *A Black Odyssey: John Lewis Waller and the Promise of American Life, 1878–1900* (Lawrence: Regents Press of Kansas, 1981). American commercial houses were active in various Malagasy ports as early as 1824; see G. Michael Razi, *Malgaches et Américains: Relations commerciales et diplomatiques au XXième siècle* ([Antananarivo]: Agence d'Information des États Unis, n.d.).

6. Barry Singer, *Black and Blue: The Life and Lyrics of Andy Razaf* (New York: Schirmer Books, 1992).

7. Ruth Behar, *The Vulnerable Observer: Anthropology That Breaks Your Heart* (Boston: Beacon Press, 1996), 7, 20.

8. Ibid., 9, 20.

9. Natalie Zemon Davis, "History's Two Bodies," *American Historical Review* 93, no. 1 (February 1988): 1–30; Jeffrey M. Perl, introduction to "Fuzzy Studies: A Symposium on the Consequences of Blur," *Common Knowledge* 17, no. 3 (2011): 441–49.

10. Paul Stoller, *The Power of the Between: An Anthropological Odyssey* (Chicago: University of Chicago Press, 2009), 31.

11. See J. L. Austin, "Performative Utterances," in *Philosophical Papers*, ed. J. O. Urmson and G. J. Warnock, 3rd ed. (Oxford: Oxford University Press, 1979), 233–52.

12. Stoller, *Power of the Between*, 35.

13. "Cammie," now deceased. Data collected by author in 2001, through telephone conversations and e-mail correspondence. Her family has been described elsewhere, notably in Wendy Wilson-Fall, "Life Stories and Ancestor Debts: 'Creole Malagasy' in Eighteenth-Century Virginia," in *Crossing Memories: Slavery and African Diaspora*, ed. Ana Lucia Araujo, Mariana P. Candido, and Paul E. Lovejoy (Trenton, NJ: Africa World Press, 2011), 147–82.

14. See Babacar M'Baye, Amoaba Gooden, and Wendy Wilson-Fall, "The Impact of Immigration Policies on African Diaspora Communities," in *Africana Cultures and Policy Studies: How African American History, Culture, and Studies Can Transform Africana Public Policy* (New York: Palgrave Macmillan, 2009).

15. The reader is referred to chapters 2 and 3, where memory is discussed relative to the family narrative of the slave descendants.

16. Paul Antze and Michael Lambek, eds., *Tense Past: Cultural Essays in Trauma and Memory* (New York: Routledge, 1996), xxi.

17. Ibid.

18. Laurence J. Kirmayer, "Landscapes of Memory," in Antze and Lambek, *Tense Past*, 175.

19. Ibid. (emphasis added).

20. Ibid.

21. Michael J. Lambek, *The Weight of the Past: Living with History in Mahajanga, Madagascar* (New York: Palgrave Macmillan, 2002).

22. Michael J. Lambek, "The Past Imperfect: Remembering as Moral Practice," in Antze and Lambek, *Tense Past*, 239, emphasis Lambek's.

23. Lambek, *Weight of the Past*, 13.

Glossary

1. Gwyn Campbell, "Madagascar and the Slave Trade (1810–1895)," *Omaly sy anio,* nos. 17–20 (1983–84): 279–310.

2. Stephen Ellis, "Tom and Toakafo: The Betsimisaraka Kingdom and State Formation in Madagascar, 1715–1750," *Journal of African History* 48, no. 3 (November 2007): 443.

3. Ibid., 444.

Bibliography

Allen, Richard B. "Children and European Slave Trading in the Indian Ocean during the Eighteenth and Early Nineteenth Centuries." In Campbell, Miers, and Miller, *Children in Slavery*, 35–54.

———. "The Mascarene Slave-Trade and Labour Migration in the Indian Ocean during the Eighteenth and Nineteenth Centuries." *Slavery and Abolition* 24, no. 2 (2003): 33–50.

———. *Slaves, Freedmen, and Indentured Laborers in Colonial Mauritius.* African Studies Series 99. Cambridge: Cambridge University Press, 1999.

Alpers, Edward A. "The African Diaspora in the Indian Ocean: A Comparative Perspective." In *The African Diaspora in the Indian Ocean*, edited by Shihan de S Jayasuriya and Richard Pankhurst, 19–50. Trenton, NJ: Africa World Press, 2003.

———. "Flight to Freedom: Escape from Slavery among Bonded Africans in the Indian Ocean World, c. 1750–1962." In Campbell, *Structure of Slavery*, 51–68.

———. "'Moçambiques' in Brazil: Another Dimension of the African Diaspora in the Atlantic World." Paper presented at the conference Enslaving Connections: Africa and Brazil during the Era of the Slave Trade, York University, Toronto, October 12–15, 2000.

———. "Recollecting Africa: Diasporic Memory in the Indian Ocean World." *African Studies Review* 43, no. 1 (2000): 83–99.

Antze, Paul, and Michael Lambek, eds. *Tense Past: Cultural Essays in Trauma and Memory.* New York: Routledge, 1996.

Armstrong, James C. "Madagascar and the Slave Trade in the Seventeenth Century." *Omaly sy anio* (Antananarivo: University of Madagascar), no. 17 (1983): 211–34.

Assman, Jan, and John C. Czaplicka. "Collective Memory and Social Identity." *New German Critique* 65 (1995): 125–33.

Austin, Allen. *African Muslims in Antebellum America: Transatlantic Stories and Spiritual Struggle.* New York: Routledge, 1997.

Austin, J. L. "Performative Utterances." In *Philosophical Papers,* edited by J. O. Urmson and G. J. Warnock, 233–52. 3rd ed. Oxford: Oxford University Press, 1979.

Axel, Brian Keith. *From the Margins: Historical Anthropology and Its Futures.* Durham: Duke University Press, 2002.

Baker, Lee D. *From Savage to Negro: Anthropology and the Construction of Race, 1896–1954.* Berkeley: University of California Press, 1998.

Ballarin, Marie-Pierre. *Les reliques royales à Madagascar: Source de légitimation et enjeu de pouvoir (XVIIIe – XXe siècles).* Paris: Karthala, 2000.

Baylor, John. The John Baylor Account Books, 1 and 2 (1719–21). Albert and Shirley Small Special Collections Library, University of Virginia, Charlottesville.

———. Ledger of Account Books of 1719. M763. John D. Rockefeller Library, Williamsburg, VA.

Behar, Ruth. *The Vulnerable Observer: Anthropology That Breaks Your Heart.* Boston: Beacon Press, 1996.

Bennett, Norman R., and George E. Brooks, Jr., eds. *New England Merchants in Africa: A History through Documents, 1802 to 1865.* African Research Studies, 7. Boston: Boston University Press, 1965.

Berkin, Carol. "Clio's Daughters: Southern Colonial Women and Their Historians." In *The Devil's Lane: Sex and Race in the Early South,* edited by Catherine Clinton and Michele Gillespie, 15–23. New York: Oxford University Press, 1997.

Berlin, Ira. *Generations of Captivity: A History of African-American Slaves.* Cambridge, MA: Belknap Press, 2003.

———. *Many Thousands Gone: The First Two Centuries of Slavery in North America.* Cambridge, MA: Belknap Press, 1998.

———. *Slaves without Masters: The Free Negro in the Antebellum South.* New York: New Press, 1974.

———. "The Structure of the Free Negro Caste in the Antebellum United States." *Journal of Social History* 9, no. 3 (1976): 309–10.

Bethal, Elizabeth Rauh. *The Roots of African American Identity: Memory and History in Antebellum Free Communities.* New York: St. Martin's, 1997.

Bialuschewski, Arne. "Pirates, Slavers, and the Indigenous Population in Madagascar, c. 1690–1715." *International Journal of African Historical Studies* 38, no. 3 (2005): 401–25.

Blight, David W. "W. E. B. DuBois and the Struggle for American Historical Memory." In Fabre and O'Meally, *History and Memory,* 45–71.

Bloch, Maurice. "Internal and External Memory: Different Ways of Being History." In Antze and Lambek, *Tense Past*, 215–33.

Booth, W. James. "Communities of Memory: On Identity, Memory, and Debt." *American Political Science Review* 93, no. 2 (1999): 249–63.

Bourdieu, Pierre. *Practical Reason: On the Theory of Action*. Stanford: Stanford University Press, 1998.

———. "Structures, Habitus, Power: Basis for a Theory of Symbolic Power." In Dirks, Eley, and Ortner, *Culture/Power/History*, 155–99.

Brackett, Jeffrey R. *The Negro in Maryland: A Study of the Institution of Slavery*. Johns Hopkins University Studies in Historical and Political Science, extra vol. 6. Baltimore: n.p., 1889.

Brady, Cyrus Townsend. *Commerce and Conquest in East Africa*. Salem, MA: Essex Institute, 1950.

Brooke, T. H. *A History of the Island of St. Helena, from its Discovery by the Portuguese to the Year 1806; to which is added an Appendix*. London: Black, Parry and Kinsbury, 1808. http://www.bweaver.nom.sh/brooke/brooke.htm.

Brown, Margaret L. "Reclaiming Lost Ancestors and Acknowledging Slave Descent: Insights from Madagascar." *Comparative Studies in Society and History* 46, no. 3 (2004): 616–45.

Brown, Mervyn. *Madagascar Rediscovered: A History from Early Times to Independence*. London: Damien Tunnacliffe, 1978.

Butler, Sana. *Sugar of the Crop: My Journey to Find the Children of Slaves*. Guilford, CT: Lyons Press, 2009.

Campbell, Gwyn. *An Economic History of Imperial Madagascar, 1750–1895: The Rise and Fall of an Island Empire*. New York: Cambridge University Press, 2008.

———. Introduction to Campbell, Miers, and Miller, *Women and Slavery*, 6–26.

———. "Madagascar and the Slave Trade (1810–1895)." *Omaly sy anio*, nos. 17–20 (1983–84): 279–310.

———, ed. *The Structure of Slavery in Indian Ocean Africa and Asia*. London: Frank Cass, 2004.

———. "The Structure of Trade in Madagascar, 1750–1810." *International Journal of African Historical Studies* 26, no. 1 (1993): 111–48.

Campbell, Gwyn, Suzanne Miers, and Joseph C. Miller, eds. *Children in Slavery through the Ages*. Athens: Ohio University Press, 2009.

———, eds. *Women and Slavery*. 2 vols. Athens: Ohio University Press, 2008.

Carretta, Vincent. *Equiano, the African: Biography of a Self-Made Man*. Athens: University of Georgia Press, 2005.

Carter Family Papers, 1651–1861. Part 5.

Carter, Charles, John Carter, and Landon Carter. Letterbook, 1732–82. Albert and Shirley Small Special Collections Library, University of Virginia, Charlottesville.

Carter, Robert. *Letters of Robert Carter: The Commercial Interests of a Virginia Gentleman, 1720–1727.* Edited by Louis B. Wright. San Marino, CA: Huntington Library, 1940. http://carter.lib.virginia.edu/.

Carter, Robert "King." Robert Carter Journal, 1719–1734. Albert and Shirley Smalls Special Collections Library, University of Virginia, Charlottesville.

———. Letterbook, 1719–21. Albert and Shirley Smalls Special Collections Library, University of Virginia, Charlottesville.

———. Robert Carter Letterbook, 1727–28. Microfilm M113. Colonial Williamsburg Rockefeller Library of Williamsburg, Virginia.

Chase, Jeanne. "New York Slave Trade, 1698–1741: The Geographical Origins of a Displaced People." *Histoire et mesure* (Paris) 18, nos. 1–2 (2003): 95–112.

Clifford, James, and George E. Marcus, eds. *Writing Culture: The Poetics and Politics of Culture.* Los Angeles: University of California Press, 1986.

Clinton, Catherine, and Michele Gillespie. *The Devil's Lane: Sex and Race in the Early South.* New York: Oxford University Press, 1997.

Cole, Jennifer. *Forget Colonialism? Sacrifice and the Art of Memory in Madagascar. Ethnographic Studies in Subjectivity.* Berkeley: University of California Press, 2001.

———. "The Work of Memory in Madagascar." *American Ethnologist* 25, no. 4 (1998): 610–33.

Davis, Arthur P. "William Roscoe Davis and His Descendants." *Negro History Bulletin* 13 (1950): 75–80.

Davis, Natalie Zemon. "Anthropology and History in the 1980s: The Possibilities of the Past." *Journal of Interdisciplinary History* 12, no. 2 (1981): 265–75.

———. "Decentering History: Local Stories and Cultural Crossings in a Global World." *History and Theory* 50, no. 2 (May 2011): 188–202.

———. "History's Two Bodies." *American Historical Review* 93, no. 1 (February 1988): 1–30.

Davis, Natalie Zemon, and Randolph Starn. Introduction to "Memory and Counter-memory," edited by Davis and Starn. Special issue, *Representations* 26 (Spring 1989): 1–6.

Dayal, Samir. "Diaspora and Double Consciousness." *Journal of the Midwest Modern Language Association* 29, no. 1 (Spring 1996): 46–62.

Delaney, Ted, and Phillip Wayne Rhodes. *Free Blacks of Lynchburg, Virginia, 1805–1865*. Lynchburg: Warwick House, 2001.

Dening, Greg. *The Death of William Gooch: A History's Anthropology*. Honolulu: University of Hawai'i Press, 1995.

Diouf, Sylviane A. *Dreams of Africa in Alabama: The Slave Ship Clotilda and the Story of the Last Africans Brought to America*. New York: Oxford University Press, 2007.

Dirks, Nicholas B., Geoff Eley, and Sherry B. Ortner, eds. *Culture/Power/History: A Reader in Contemporary Social Theory*. Princeton: Princeton University Press, 1994.

Domenichini-Ramiaramanana, Bakoly, and Jean-Pierre Domenichini. "Aspects de l'esclavage sous la monarchie merina." *Omaly sy anio*, no. 15 (January–June 1982): 53–98.

Dowdey, Clifford. *The Virginia Dynasties: The Emergence of "King" Carter and the Golden Age*. New York: Little, Brown, 1969.

DuBois, W. E. B. *The Souls of Black Folk: Essays and Sketches*. Boston: Purdy, 1904; Hazelton: Pennsylvania State University, Electronic Classics Series, 2006.

Dyson, Michael Eric. "Essentialism and the Complexities of Racial Identity." In *Multiculturalism: A Critical Reader*, edited by David Theo Goldberg, 218–29. Cambridge, MA: Blackwell, 1994.

Egerton, Douglas R. *Death or Liberty: African Americans and Revolutionary America*. New York: Oxford University Press, 2009.

Ellis, Stephen. "Tom and Toakafo: The Betsimisaraka Kingdom and State Formation in Madagascar, 1715–1750." *Journal of African History* 48, no. 3 (November 2007): 439–55.

Eltis, David, et al. *The Trans-Atlantic Slave Trade Database*. Cambridge: Cambridge University Press. http://www.slavevoyages.org/.

Ely, Melvin Patrick. *Israel on the Appomattox: A Southern Experiment in Black Freedom from the 1790s through the Civil War*. New York: Vintage Books, 2004.

Engs, Robert F. *Freedom's First Generation: Black Hampton, Virginia, 1861–1890*. New York: Fordham University Press, 1980.

Ewald, Janet. "Crossers of the Sea: Slaves, Freedmen, and Other Migrants in the Northwestern Indian Ocean, c. 1750–1914." *American Historical Review* 105, no. 1 (February 2000): 69–91.

Fabre, Geneviève, and Robert O'Meally, eds. *History and Memory in African-American Culture*. New York: Oxford University Press, 1994.

Fields, Karen. "What One Cannot Remember Mistakenly." In Fabre and O'Meally, *History and Memory*, 150–63.

Fischer, Michael M. J. "Ethnicity and the Post-modern Arts of Memory." In Clifford and Marcus, *Writing Culture*, 194–233.

Foster, Vonita White. "Personal Account of Mrs. Ida Dandridge Bates." In *Black Hanoverians: An Enlightened Past*, 35. Rockville, VA: ITS, 1999.

Frazier, E. Franklin. *The Negro Family in the United States*. New York: Macmillan, 1949.

Gatewood, Willard B. *Aristocrats of Color: The Black Elite, 1880–1920*. Bloomington: Indiana University Press, 1990.

Geertz, Clifford. *Local Knowledge: Further Essays in Interpretive Anthropology*, New York: Basic Books, 1983.

———. "Religion as a Cultural System." In *The Interpretation of Cultures: Selected Essays*, edited by Geertz, 87–125. 1966. Reprint, New York: Basic Books, 1973.

Geggus, David. "The French Slave Trade: An Overview." *William and Mary Quarterly*, 3rd ser., 58, no. 3 (January 2001): 119–38.

Genovese, Eugene D. *Roll, Jordan, Roll: The World the Slaves Made*. New York: Vintage Books, 1972.

Gomez, Michael A. *Black Crescent: The Experience and Legacy of African Muslims in the Americas*. Cambridge: Cambridge University Press, 2005.

———. *Exchanging Our Country Marks: The Transformation of African Identities in the Colonial and Antebellum South*. Chapel Hill: University of North Carolina Press, 1998.

Gordon-Reed, Annette. The Hemingses of Monticello: An American Family. *New York: Norton, 2008*.

Gosse, Philip. *St. Helena: 1502–1938*. 1938. Reprint, Shropshire, UK: Anthony Nelson, 1990.

Gupta, Akhil, and James Ferguson. "Ethnography at the End of an Era." In *Culture, Power, Place: Explorations in Critical Anthropology*, edited by Gupta and Ferguson, 1–32. Durham, NC: Duke University Press, 1997.

Gutman, Herbert G. *The Black Family in Slavery and Freedom, 1750–1925*. New York: Pantheon, 1976.

Gwaltney, John Langston. *Drylongso: A Self-Portrait of Black America*. New York: Random House, 1980.

Hall, Gwendolyn Midlo. *Slavery and African Ethnicities in the Americas: Restoring the Links*. Chapel Hill: University of North Carolina Press, 2005.

Hamilton, Carolyn, et al., eds. *Refiguring the Archives*. Boston: Kluwer Academic Publishers, 2002.

Harkin, Michael E. "Feeling and Thinking in Memory and Forgetting: Toward an Ethnohistory of the Emotions." *Ethnohistory* 50, no. 2 (2003): 261–84.

Harris, Leslie M. *In the Shadow of Slavery: African Americans in New York City, 1626–1863.* Chicago: University of Chicago Press, 2003.

Harris, Malcolm H. M. D. "The Ports of the Pamunkey." *William and Mary Quarterly*, 2nd ser., 23, no. 4 (October 1943): 493–516.

Harrison, Simon. "Cultural Difference as Denied Resemblance: Reconsidering Nationalism and Ethnicity." *Comparative Studies in Society and History* 45, no. 2 (2003): 343–61.

Herskovits, Melville. *The Myth of the Negro Past.* 1940. Reprint, Boston: Beacon Press, 1990.

"Histoire et civilisation du Nord-Ouest malgache: Actes de colloque de Majunga (13–18 avril 1981)." *Omaly sy anio* (Unité d'enseignement et de recherche d'histoire, l'Université de Madagascar), nos. 17–20 (1983–84).

Hoelscher, Steven, and Derek H. Alderman. "Memory and Place: Geographics of a Critical Relationship." *Social and Cultural Geography* 5, no. 3 (2004): 347–55.

Isaac, Rhys. "*Ethnographic Method in History: An Action Approach.*" In St. George, *Material Life, 39–62.*

———. *Landon Carter's Uneasy Kingdom: Revolution and Rebellion on a Virginia Plantation.* New York: Oxford University Press, 2004.

———. *The Transformation of Virginia, 1740–1790.* Chapel Hill: University of North Carolina Press, for the Omohundro Institute of Early American History and Culture, 1982.

Johnson, Isaac. *Slavery Days in Old Kentucky: A True Story of a Father Who Sold His Wife and Four Children, by One of His Children.* 1901. Reprint, NEH Electronic Publication, Apex Data Services, edited by Ann Morawski and Natalia Smith. 1st ed. Chapel Hill: University of North Carolina Academic Affairs Library, 2000.

Jones, Delmos J. "Toward a Native Anthropology." *Human Organization* 29, no. 4 (1970): 251–59.

Jordan, Winthrop D. *White over Black: American Attitudes toward the Negro: 1550–1812.* Chapel Hill: University of North Carolina Press for the Institute of Early American History and Culture, 1968.

Judd, Jacob. "Frederick Philipse and the Madagascar Trade." *New York Historical Society Quarterly* 55, no. 4 (October 1971): 354–74.

Kapchan, Debora A., and Pauline Turner Strong. "Theorizing the Hybrid." *Journal of American Folklore* 112, no. 445 (Summer 1999): 239–53.

Kent, Raymond. *Early Kingdoms in Madagascar, 1500–1700.* New York: Holt, Rinehart and Winston, 1970.

——. *From Madagascar to the Malagasy Republic.* New York: Praeger, 1962.

Kirmayer, Laurence J. "Landscapes of Memory: Trauma, Narrative, and Dissociation." In Antze and Lambek, *Tense Past,* 173–98.

Koss-Chionino, Joan. Introduction to "Do Spirits Exist? Ways to Know." *Anthropology and Humanism* 35, no. 2 (2010): 131–41.

Kulikoff, Allan. "The Origins of Afro-American Society in Tidewater Maryland and Virginia, 1700 to 1790." *William and Mary Quarterly,* 3rd ser., 35, no. 2 (April 1978): 226–59.

——. "A 'Prolifick' People: Black Population Growth in the Chesapeake Colonies, 1700–1790." *Southern Studies* 16, no. 4 (1977): 391–428.

——. *Tobacco and Slaves: The Development of Southern Cultures in the Chesapeake, 1680–1800.* Chapel Hill: University of North Carolina Press, 1986.

Lambek, Michael J. "The Past Imperfect: Remembering as Moral Practice." In Antze and Lambek, *Tense Past,* 235–54.

——. *The Weight of the Past: Living with History in Mahajanga, Madagascar.* Contemporary Anthropology of Religion. New York: Palgrave Macmillan, 1999.

Lambek, Michael, and Andrew Walsh. "The Imagined Community of the Antankaraña: Identity, History, and Ritual in Northern Madagascar." *Journal of Religion in Africa* 27, no. 3 (August 1997): 308–33.

Larson, Pier M. "Enslaved Malagasy and 'le Travail de la Parole' in the Pre-revolutionary Mascarenes." *Journal of African History* 48, no. 3 (November 2007): 457–79.

——. *History and Memory in the Age of Enslavement: Becoming Merina in Highland Madagascar, 1770–1822.* Social History of Africa. Portsmouth, NH: Heinemann, 2000.

——. *Ocean of Letters: Language and Creolization in an Indian Ocean Diaspora.* Critical Perspectives on Empire. New York: Cambridge University Press, 2009.

Lavie, Smadar, and Ted Swedenburg. Introduction to *Displacement, Diaspora, and Geographies of Identity.* Durham: Duke University Press, 1996, 1–27.

Lebsock, Suzanne. *The Free Women of Petersburg: Status and Culture in a Southern Town, 1784–1860.* New York: Norton, 1984.

Levy, Andrew. *The First Emancipator: The Forgotten Story of Robert Carter, the Founding Father Who Freed His Slaves.* New York: Random House, 2005.

Lewis, Catherine M., and J. Richard Lewis, eds. *Women and Slavery in America: A Documentary History*. Fayetteville: University of Arkansas Press, 2011.

Louis, Brett. "The Difference Sameness Makes: Racial Recognition and the 'Narcissism of Minor Differences.'" *Ethnicities* 5, no. 3 (September 2005): 344–63.

Lovejoy, Paul E. "Ethnic Designations of the Slave Trade and the Reconstruction of the History of Trans-Atlantic Slavery." In *Transatlantic Dimensions of Ethnicity in the African Diaspora*, edited by Lovejoy and David V. Trotman, 9–42. New York: Continuum Press, 2003.

———. "Olaudah Equiano or Gustavus Vassa?—What's in a Name?" *Atlantic Studies* 9, no. 2 (2012): 165–84.

———. "Transatlantic Transformations: The Origins and Identities of Africans in the Americas." In Sansone, Soumonni, and Barry, *Africa, Brazil*, 82–111.

Madden, T. O., Jr. *We Were Always Free: The Maddens of Culpeper County, Virginia*. With the assistance of Ann L. Miller. Charlottesville: University of Virginia Press, 1992.

Marcus, George E., and Michael M. J. Fischer. *Anthropology as Cultural Critique: An Experimental Moment in the Human Sciences*. 2nd ed. Chicago: University of Chicago Press, 1999.

Matory, J. Lorand. "The English Professors of Brazil: On the Diasporic Roots of the Yorùbá Nation." *Comparative Studies in Society and History* 41, no. 1 (1999): 72–103.

M'baye, Babacar. *The Trickster Comes West: Pan-African Influence in Early Black Diasporan Narratives*. Jackson: University Press of Mississippi, 2009.

McDonald, Kevin. "'A Man of Courage and Activity': Thomas Tew and Pirate Settlements of the Indo-Atlantic Trade World, 1645–1730." eScholarship Repository, University of California. (October 3, 2005). UC World History Workshop Conference Series. Paper 2. http://repositories.cdlib.org/ucwhw/wp/2.

McMillin, James A. *The Final Victims: Foreign Slave Trade to North America, 1783–1810*. Columbia: University of South Carolina Press, 2004.

Merleau-Ponty, Maurice. *The Phenomenology of Perception*. London: Routledge, 1962.

Miller, Joseph C. "Retention, Reinvention, and Remembering: Restoring Identities through Enslavement in Africa and under Slavery in Brazil." In *Enslaving Connections: Changing Cultures of Africa and Brazil during the Era of Slavery*, edited by José Curto and Paul E. Lovejoy, 81–121. Amherst, NY: Humanity Books, 2004.

Mintz, Sidney W., and Richard Price. *The Birth of African-American Culture: An Anthropological Perspective.* Boston: Beacon Press, 1976.

"More Missionaries to the Heathen." *American Baptist Magazine* 7, no. 11 (November 1827): 331.

Morgan, Philip D. *Slave Counterpoint: Black Culture in the Eighteenth-Century Chesapeake and Low Country.* Chapel Hill: University of North Carolina Press, 1998.

Morton, Fred. "Small Change: Children in the Nineteenth-Century East African Slave Trade." In Campbell, Miers, and Miller, *Children in Slavery,* 55–70.

Murray, D. R. "Statistics of the Slave Trade to Cuba, 1790–1867." *Journal of Latin American Studies* 3, no. 2 (November 1971): 131–49.

Narayan, Kirin. "How Native Is a 'Native' Anthropologist?" *American Anthropologist,* n.s., 95, no. 3 (September 1993): 671–85.

Nora, Pierre. "Between History and Memory: Les Lieux de Mémoire." In "Memory and Counter-memory," edited by Natalie Zemon Davis and Randolph Starn. Special issue, *Representations,* no. 26 (Spring 1989): 7–24.

Nutting, P. Bradley. "The Madagascar Connection: Parliament and Piracy, 1690–1701." *American Journal of Legal History* 22, no. 3 (July 1978): 202–15.

Obadele-Starks, Ernest. *Freebooters and Smugglers: The Foreign Slave Trade in the United States after 1808.* Fayetteville: University of Arkansas Press, 2007.

O'Donovan, Susan Eva. "Traded Babies: Enslaved Children in America's Domestic Migrations, 1820–60." In Campbell, Miers, and Miller, *Children in Slavery,* 88–102.

Olson, Alison G. "The Virginia Merchants of London: A Study in Eighteenth-Century Interest-Group Politics." *William and Mary Quarterly,* 3rd ser., 40 (July 1983): 361–87.

Ortner, Sherry. "Theory in Anthropology since the Sixties." In Dirks, Eley, and Ortner, *Culture/Power/History,* 372–411.

Patterson, Orlando. *Slavery and Social Death: A Comparative Study.* Cambridge, MA: Harvard University Press, 1982.

Perdue, Charles L., Jr., Thomas E. Barden, and Robert K. Phillips, eds. *Weevils in the Wheat: Interviews with Virginia Ex-slaves.* Charlottesville: University Press of Virginia, 1976.

Platt, Virginia Bever. "The East India Company and the Madagascar Slave Trade." *William and Mary Quarterly,* 3rd ser., 26, no. 4 (October 1969): 548–77.

Portelli, Alessandro. "What Makes Oral History Different?" In *The Death of Luigi Trastulli and Other Stories: Form and Meaning in Oral History*, 45–58. Albany: SUNY Press, 1991.

Pouwels, Randall L. "Eastern Africa and the Indian Ocean to 1800: Reviewing Relations in Historical Perspective. *International Journal of African Historical Studies* 35, nos. 2–3 (2002): 385–425.

Price, Richard. *First-Time: The Historical Vision of an African American People.* 1983. Reprint, Chicago: University of Chicago Press, 2002.

Price, Richard, and Sally Price. *The Root of Roots; or, How Afro-American Anthropology Got Its Start.* Chicago: Prickly Paradigm Press, 2003.

Raboteau, Albert J. *Slave Religion: The "Invisible Institution" in the Antebellum South.* New York: Oxford University Press, 1978.

Rantoandro, Gabriel. "Une communauté mercantile du Nord-Ouest: Les Antalaotra." *Omaly sy anio*, no. 15 (1983–84): 195–211.

Razi, G. Michael. *Malgaches et Américains: Rélations commerciales et diplomatiques au XIXème siècle.* [Antananarivo]: Agence d'information des États-Unis, 1981.

Rediker, Marcus. *The Slave Ship: A Human History.* New York: Penguin, 2008.

Robinson, William H. *From Log Cabin to the Pulpit; or, Fifteen Years in Slavery.* Eau Claire, WI: James H. Tifft, 1913. Electronic ed., http://docsouth.unc.edu/fpn/robinson/robinson.html. In Loren Schweninger, Race and Slavery Petitions Project. *library.uncg.edu/slavery/petitions/.*

Rothman, Joshua D. *Notorious in the Neighborhood: Sex and Families across the Color Line in Virginia, 1787–1861.* Chapel Hill: University of North Carolina Press, 2007.

Royster, Charles. *The Fabulous Story of the Great Dismal Swamp: A Story of George Washington's Life.* New York: Knopf, 1999.

Sansone, Livio, Elisée Soumonni, and Boubacar Barry, eds. *Africa, Brazil and the Construction of Trans-Atlantic Black Identities.* Trenton, NJ: Africa World Press, 2008.

Saunders, Christopher. "Liberated Africans in Cape Colony in the First Half of the Nineteenth Century." *International Journal of African Historical Studies* 18, no. 2 (1985): 223–39.

Shaw, Rosalind. *Memories of the Slave Trade: Ritual and the Historical Imagination in Sierra Leone.* Chicago: University of Chicago Press, 2002.

Shell, Robert Carl. *Children of Bondage: A Social History of the Slave Society at the Cape of Good Hope, 1652–1838.* Hanover, NH: Wesleyan University Press, 1994.

Shifflett, Crandall A. *Patronage and Poverty in the Tobacco South: Louisa County, Virginia, 1860–1900.* Knoxville: University of Tennessee Press, 1982.

Sieminski , Mary L. "Margaret Mahammitt Hagan: 19th-Century Williamsport Mixed-Race Female Electro-therapist and Owner of the 'Electric Baths.'" *Williamsport Sun Gazette,* December 21, 2010. NorthcentralPA .com, http://www.northcentralpa.com/article/margaret-mahammitt -hagan-19th-century-williamsport-mixed-race-female-electrotherapist -and-ow.

Singer, Barry. *Black and Blue: The Life and Lyrics of Andy Razaf.* New York: Schirmer Books, 1992.

Smallwood, Stephanie. *Saltwater Slaves: A Middle Passage from Africa to American Diaspora.* Cambridge, MA: Harvard University Press, 2008.

Smedley, Audrey. "'Race' and the Construction of Human Identity." *American Anthropologist* 100, no. 3 (September 1998): 690–702.

Smolenski, John. "Hearing Voices: Microhistory, Dialogicality and the Recovery of Popular Culture on an Eighteenth-Century Virginia Plantation." *Slavery and Abolition* 24, no. 1 (April 2003): 1–23.

Sobel, Mechal. *The World They Made Together: Black and White Values in Eighteenth-Century Virginia.* Princeton: Princeton University Press, 1987.

Stafford, Frances J. "Illegal Importations: Enforcement of the Slave Trade Laws along the Florida Coast, 1810–1828." *Florida Historical Quarterly* 46, no. 2 (October 1967): 124–33.

Stewart, Pamela J., and Andrew Strathern. *Landscape, Memory and History: Anthropological Perspectives.* London: Pluto Press, 2003.

Stevenson, Brenda E. *Life in Black and White: Family and Community in the Slave South.* New York: Oxford University Press, 1996.

St. George, Robert Blair, ed. *Material Life in America, 1600–1860.* Boston: Northeastern University Press, 1988.

Stoller, Paul. *The Power of the Between: An Anthropological Odyssey.* Chicago: University of Chicago Press, 2009.

Stråth, Bo, ed. *Myth and Memory in the Construction of Community: Historical Patterns in Europe and Beyond.* Brussels: Peter Lang, 1999.

Stuckey, Sterling. *Slave Culture: Nationalist Theory and the Foundations of Black America.* New York: Oxford University Press, 1987.

Swann-Wright, Dianne, *A Way out of No Way: Claiming Family and Freedom in the New South.* Charlottesville: University of Virginia Press, 2002.

Sweet, James H. "Mistaken Identities? Olaudah Equiano, Domingos Álvarez, and the Methodological Challenges of Studying the African Diaspora." *American Historical Review* 114, no. 2 (2009): 279–306.

Teelock, Vijaya. "The Influence of Slavery in the Formation of Creole Identity." *Comparative Studies of South Asia, Africa and the Middle East* 19, no. 2 (1999): 3–8.

Tehindrazanarivelo, Emmanuel. "Fieldwork: The Dance of Power." *Anthropology and Humanities* 22, no. 1 (1997): 54–60.

Thelen, David. "Memory and American History." *Journal of American History* 75, no. 4 (March 1989): 1117–29.

Thomas, Sheila Gregory, and Wendy Wilson. "A Nineteenth-Century Immigrant from Madagascar: Prince Ali Mahomet." Paper presented at the Africans in Washington Project Panel, Washington Historical Society, 18th Annual Conference, February 1991.

Thornton, John. *Africa and Africans in the Making of the Atlantic World, 1400–1680.* New York: Cambridge University Press, 1992.

Trouillot, Michel-Rolph. *Global Transformations: Anthropology and the Modern World.* New York: Palgrave Macmillan, 2003.

———. *Silencing the Past: Power and the Production of History.* Boston: Beacon Press, 1995.

Van Horne, John C., editor. *Religious Philanthropy and Colonial Slavery: The American Correspondence of the Associates of Dr. Bray, 1717–1777.* Urbana: University of Illinois Press, 1985.

Vansina, Jan. *Oral Tradition as History.* Madison: University of Wisconsin Press, 1985.

Vernet, Thomas. "Slave Trade and Slavery on the Swahili Coast, 1500–1750." In *Slavery, Islam and Diaspora,* edited by Behnaz A. Mirzai, Ismael Musah Montana, and Paul E. Lovejoy, 37–76. Trenton, NJ: Africa World Press, 2009.

Vincent, Joan. "Engaging Historicism." In *Recapturing Anthropology: Working in the Present,* edited by Richard G. Fox, 45–58. Santa Fe: School of American Research Press, 1991.

Wade, Melvin. "'Shining in Borrowed Plumage': Affirmation of Community in the Black Coronation Festivals of New England, ca. 1750–1850." In St. George, *Material Life,* 171–82.

Walsh, Lorena S. *From Calabar to Carter's Grove: The History of a Virginia Slave Community.* Charlottesville: University Press of Virginia, 1997.

———. "The Chesapeake Slave Trade: Regional Patterns, African Origins, and Some Implications." *William and Mary Quarterly,* 3rd ser., 58, no. 1, New Perspectives on the Transatlantic Slave Trade (January 2001): 139–70.

———. *Motives of Honor, Pleasure, and Profit: Plantation Management in the Colonial Chesapeake, 1607–1763.* Chapel Hill: University of North Carolina Press, 2010.

———. "New Findings about the Virginia Slave Trade." Williamsburg: Colonial Williamsburg Foundation, 2012. http://research.history.org /Historical_Research/Research_Themes/ThemeEnslave/SlaveTrade .cfm.

Wilson-Fall, Wendy. "Life Stories and Ancestor Debts: 'Creole Malagasy' in Eighteenth-Century Virginia." In *Crossing Memories: Slavery and African Diaspora,* edited by Ana Lucia Araujo, Mariana P. Candido, and Paul E. Lovejoy, 147–82. Trenton, NJ: Africa World Press, 2011.

———. *Malagasy Free Black Settlement in Hanover County, Virginia, during Slavery: The Intriguing Story of Lucy Andriana Renibe Winston.* Ashland, VA: Hanover County Black Heritage Society and Hanover County Historical Society, 2007.

———. "Women Merchants and Slave Depots: Saint Louis, Senegal and St. Mary's, Madagascar." In *Paths of the Atlantic Slave Trade: Interactions, Identities, and Images,* edited by Ana Lucia Araujo, 273–303. Amherst, NY: Cambria Press, 2011.

Woods, Randall Bennett. "Black America's Challenge to European Colonialism: The Waller Affair, 1891–1895." *Journal of Black Studies* 7, no. 1 (September 1976): 57–75.

Works Progress Administration. Federal Writers' Project in the State of Virginia. *The Negro in Virginia.* New York: Hastings House, 1940. Reprint, Winston-Salem: John F. Blair, 1994.

Yon, Daniel A. "Making Place, Making Race: St. Helena and the South Atlantic World." In Sansone, Soumonni, and Barry, *Africa, Brazil,* 113–26.

Index

Abdul Rahman, 148
abolition of slavery and slave trade, 129
Acts of Trade and Navigation (British), classification of slaves in, 29
Adams, John, 185n58
African Americans. *See* black people in America, as homogeneous unit; free blacks; free immigration; Malagasy in America; mixed white/black ancestry
African Muslims in the Americas, xii–xiii, 148, 168n8
age at capture, 19, 54
ajami, 163
Alabama, 101, 124, 125, 126, 136, 154
Alexander family, 125
Ali, Muhammad (Cassius Clay), 117
Ali ben Ali "Butcherknife" (Eddie Puckett), 137–38
Ali Salaha Mahomet (Jeremiah Mahomet), 138–39, 194nn27–28
Allen, Richard B., 126, 131, 178n39, 192n72
Amelia Island (Florida), 112
American Indians. *See* Native Americans and Native American ancestry
American Revolution, 85–87, 102, 185n58
Anabaptists, 102, 106
ancestors: family narratives as means of signifying presence of, 157–59; revering and communicating with, 63–64, 135–36; slaves as, 65–66, 152
andevo (nonbeing), 57
Angola, 48, 68, 72
Antalaotra, 140, 165

Antambahoaka, 25, 163
Antananarivo (Madagascar), 3, 149
Antanosy, 25, 163
Anteimoro, 25, 163
Antongil Bay (Madagascar), 29, 165
Antze, Paul, 155
Arabic language and script, 5, 25, 138, 163, 165, 168n8
Arabs, in Madagascar, 24–25
Argentina, Rio de la Plata in, 27, 172n1
Ashland (Virginia), 106, 122
Austin, Allan D., 171n35
Austin, J. L., 152

Bafil (runaway slave), 82
Baldridge, Adam, 30, 174n30
Baltimore (Maryland), 91, 100, 106, 138–40, 142, 161
Bambara, 9, 77
Baptists, 85, 102, 107, 123, 186n74
Barbados, 26, 27, 37, 38, 42, 167n5
Barker, John, 115
Bass, William, 50
Bates, Austin, 49
Baum, Robert M., 175n3
Baylor, John, 46, 47, 49, 54, 75–77, 79, 177n21, 179n47
Bayly, Thomas, 50
Beckinridge family, 96
Behar, Ruth, 151
Belsches family, 96
Benin, Bight of, 55
Berkeley family and plantations, 75, 81
Berlin, Ira, 47, 55, 59, 60, 178n34
Berry, Fanny, 189n27
betel nuts, 61, 115
Betsimisaraka, 28–29, 31, 42, 58, 163–64

Betty (slave near Vicksburg, Mississippi), 124
Biafra, 48, 68, 72, 93. *See also* Calabar
"big house" slaves, 83, 90
birth dates, knowledge of, 191n60
black people in America, as homogeneous unit: construction of, 8–9, 52, 56, 77, 146–47; creolization/hybridization process, 2, 4, 14–16, 21, 56, 60, 67, 142; newly enslaved arrivals not seeing themselves as, 7, 9; planters' attitudes and, 80, 85; race, slave ships producing, 41; recognition of diversity within, 145
Bland, Richard, 99
Bloch, Maurice, 12
Boas, Franz, 170n24
Boina, Bay of (Madagascar), 42, 131
Boina, Sakalava kingdom of, 27, 29, 164, 165
Bourdieu, Pierre, 11, 62, 97
Brandon (plantation), 73
Brazil, slavery and slave trade in, 21, 37, 45, 53, 101, 109–13, 171n45, 172n1
British East India Company, 31, 41–42, 174n22, 176n7
Brooke, Robert, 41
Brooks, Richard, 50
Brown, Mervyn, 172n3
Brown, Robert, 138
Brown family, 96
Buckingham (Virginia), 95
Bundy family, 55, 89–90, 179n57
Burnette family, 114, 125
Burwell, Nathaniel, 79
Burwell, Robert, 79
Burwell family and plantations, 71, 73–75, 74, 76, 85, 96
Butler family, 123
Byrd, William, II, 66, 79

Calabar, 47, 48, 50, 55, 64, 72, 78, 88, 92, 178n35, 184n35. *See also* Biafra
Calhoun (free immigrant), 137
Cammie (descendant of Rakekata), 135–36, 194n13
Campbell, Gwyn, 126, 130

Canada, Malagasy in, 95–96, 121, 167n5
cargo/commodity, slaves as, 29, 66, 110, 179n9
Carter, Anne, 106
Carter, Charles, 73, 79, 85, 104, 106
Carter, Elizabeth, 79
Carter, George, 73
Carter, John, 73, 79, 183n22, 188n14
Carter, Judith, 75, 79
Carter, Landon, 66, 67, 73, 83, 85
Carter, Lucy, 81
Carter, Robert "King," 20, 46; cultural clusters of slaves owned by, 15, 68; distemper of the eyes affecting slaves imported by, 42; on Hopewell area, 103; inheritors of slaves of, 73, 106, 107; land properties, slaves classified as, 71, 183n22; Malagasy slaves of, 66, 77, 81, 99, 177n21; mortality of slaves of, 69; organization and management of slaves by, 70, 80, 90; relationship with Jack Lubber, 182n5; on sex ratios in Malagasy shipments, 50; as slave investor, 38–39, 46, 47, 76; South Sea bubble losses of, 38–39
Carter, Robert, II, 66, 73, 85
Carter, Robert, III, 67, 85, 91, 102–3, 186n74
Carter family and plantations, 73–75, 74, 76, 77, 81, 88, 96, 99, 103–4
Carter's Grove (plantation), 68, 85
Carver, George Washington, 137
Catlett, Elizabeth, 127, 192n74
Catlett family, 96
Cedar Creek (Virginia), 123
cedula of 1789 (Spain), 112, 189n38
Central African ethnicities, 9, 48, 54, 64, 68, 146, 147, 171n35
Charleston (South Carolina), 110–11, 117, 133
charter generations, 55, 59, 60
Cherry, Ethel Johnson, 124
Chesley, Robert, 82
children and child slaves: age at capture, determining, 19, 54; in domestic slave trade, 108–9; with

European fathers, xii, 59; in illegal slave trade, 19, 118, 126; from Madagascar, xii, 19, 46–47, 51, 54, 77–78, 84, 92; Malagasy women and, 92; mortality rates and population levels, 69; settlement and distribution of, 68, 70–71, 92; slave women investing personal lives in, 180n64
China, Doctor, 50
Chinese, in Madagascar, 25
Christian Malagasy refugees, 3, 127, 130, 134
Christian missionaries on Madagascar, 134, 150, 191n60
Church of England, 85
Claibourne, Butler, 87
Claibourne, Sterling, 86–87
Clark, Flora, 120
Clark, John, 122–23, 189n25
Clark, Lucy, 122–23
Clark, Mariah, 122, 123
Clark, William "Buck," 122–23
Clark family, 120, 122
Clay, Cassius (Muhammad Ali), 117
Clay, Edith Greathouse, 117
Clay, Herman, 117
Cleveland, Grover, 195n5
Clotilda (slave ship), 126
Cohn, David L., 181n76
Coker Snow (slave ship), 44
Coleman, Robert, 49
Coleman, Thomas, 50
Colored American, 140, 194n30
commodity/cargo, slaves as, 29, 66, 110, 179n9
Comoros Islands, 25, 130, 138, 165
concubinage, xii, 33–34, 93–94, 104, 116, 124
Congo, 48, 61, 68
Corbin, Joanna, 79
Coromantee (Kromanti), xiii
Corotoman plantation, 81
country-born slaves. See creole/ country-born slaves
Courtney family, 122, 123
Crenshaw, Nathaniel, 106, 122–23
creole communities of Madagascar, 28–29, 59, 60, 93

creole/country-born slaves: family oral tradition and, 90–91; relationship of saltwater slaves with, 56, 58–59, 67–68, 77–78, 80
creolization/hybridization process, 2, 4, 14–16, 21, 56, 60, 67, 142
Crisis magazine, 141
Croom, Daniel, 50
Cuba, slavery and slave trade in, 21, 53, 101, 109–12
Culpeper (Virginia), 55, 89, 96, 107
cultural clusters: as anthropological theory, 15, 55; settlement and distribution of slaves and, 68, 71, 77–78, 80–81; of slave cohorts of 1719–21 in Virginia, 37, 45, 48–49, 53–56, 62; of slaves owned by Robert "King" Carter, 15, 68

Dandridge family, 75, 96
dates of birth, knowledge of, 191n60
Davis, Arthur P., 119, 141, 191n57
Davis, John, 115
Davis, Lewis, 136
Davis, Martha, 136, 141
Davis, William Roscoe, 119, 120, 135
Dawkins, William, 77
Delaney, Ted, 87, 107
Dickerson, Joi, 94–95
difference or exceptionality trope, xii–xiii, 2, 54, 61, 90, 145
Digges, Cole, 75, 95
Diola, 9, 175n3
Diouf, Sylviane, Dreams of Africa in Alabama, 126, 154
discipline of slaves, 67, 90
Dismal Swamp project, 78–79
"Dis Time Tomorrer Night" (spiritual), 108, 189n27
domestic slave market, 101; in family oral tradition, 113; in historical record, 108–9; planter interrelationships and, 47, 49
double consciousness, 9, 169n15
DuBois, W. E. B., 9, 169n15
Duckinfield (slave ship), 33
Duckinfield, John, 32–34
Duke family, 90
Dunham, Albert Millard, 127

Galveston (Texas), 133
Gascoigne Galley (slave ship), 44, 45
Geertz, Clifford, 151
gender: children, slave women
   investing personal lives in, 180n64;
   in illegal slave trade, 118; on large
   versus small plantations, 68–69;
   Malagasy lineage and, xii, 92–93;
   separation of slave captives by,
   46–47; settlement and distribution
   by, 68–69, 77–78; sex ratios in
   slave population, 47, 50–51, 77–78;
   transmission of culture and, 92–94
Georgia, 101, 111, 112, 152, 171n35, 188n6
Gladman, Claibourne, 86–87
Glocester (runaway slave), 82
Gloucester Billy (sailor), 103
Gomez, Michael A., xvi, 56
Gordon family, 122
grammar, sociocultural, 62, 63, 147
Grant, Gail Melissa, 179n54
Gregory, T. M., 141
Gregory and Mahomet/Mahammitt
   families, 138–41, 142
Grimes, James, 124
Gruff (runaway slave), 76, 82, 84

habitus, 19, 62, 97
Haiti, 27, 129
Halifax County (Virginia), 79
Hall, Gwendolyn Midlo, 171n35
Hamilton Galley (slave ship), 42
Hampton (Virginia), 86, 87, 103, 105,
   115, 117, 119
Hampton Roads (Virginia), 91, 105, 135
Hanover/Hanover County (Virginia),
   77, 79, 95, 96, 106–7, 122, 123, 189n25
Harkin, Michael, 118
Harrison family, 75
Hastie, William Henry, 127, 192n74
Hausa, xiii
health, illnesses, and mortality:
   discipline of slaves, 67;
   management to stabilize slave
   population, 69–70; of slave cohorts
   of 1719–21 in Virginia, 42, 45, 49, 51
Hemings, Betsy "Critta," 104
Hemings, Sally, 104
Henrietta (slave ship), 45

Herskovits, Melville, 14, 16
Heysham and Company, 42
Hickory Hill plantation, 106
Hill, Edward, 188n14
Hill, Elizabeth, 188n14
Hopewell (Virginia), xi, 103–4, 108
Hopkins, Johns, sister of, 106, 122
House of Burgesses, Virginia, 80, 99, 102
House of Delegates, Virginia, 102
households. *See* families/households;
   marriage
Howard University, 141
Hughes, Langston, 170n24
Hurston, Zora Neal, 170n24
hybridization/creolization process, 2,
   4, 14–16, 21, 56, 60, 67, 142
hyperhistoricity of Virginia planter
   families, 37
hypocognition, 118

Ibo: African American descent from,
   9; on Carter plantations, 68, 71, 78,
   85, 88; enlargement and expansion
   of African sensibilities and, 77;
   Equiano as, 7; lineage, transmitting,
   93; manumission of, 99; in maroon
   ethno-cultural enclaves, 88; origins
   of, 178n35; in Virginia, 47–48,
   171n31, 178n34, 184n35
identity: authenticity of, 5–10, 97;
   formation and maintenance of,
   ix–x, 5–10, 171n35; with multiple
   lineages, 57–58, 92, 137; new
   cultural self, construction of,
   62–64, 146–47; reasons for specific
   survival of Malagasy identity,
   59–61; settlement and distribution
   of slaves and retention of Malagasy
   identity, 81–84, 87–98; slaves
   reclaiming, 40, 55–61
Igbo, xii, 64
illegal slave trade, 20–21, 100–101;
   children in, 19, 118, 126; in family
   oral tradition, xi, 113–27; gender
   ratios, 118; in historical record,
   109–12; in lower South, 110–13,
   123–26, 128; Madagascar trade
   illegal between 1698 and 1712, 32;
   numbers of slaves in, 110;

illegal slave trade (*cont.*)
  shipmates, absence of, 118–19;
  shipment of captives, 32–33;
  transatlantic slave trade made
  illegal in 1808, 31, 100, 109; in
  Virginia, 119–23
illness. *See* health, illnesses, and
  mortality
Imerina (Merina state; Madagascar
  highlands), 129–30, 164–65
Indian Ocean spice trade, 3, 31, 130
Indian Ocean trade window for North
  Americans, 38–39
Indians. *See* Native Americans and
  Native American ancestry
Indonesians in Madagascar, 24, 121, 164
"ink spitters," 61, 114–15
Isaac, Rhys, 76
Islam, xii–xiii, 148, 168n8

Jamaica, xiii, 26, 32–34, 37, 47
James City (Virginia), 81
James River (Virginia), slaves on, 44,
  49, 73, *74*, 75–76, 79, 82, 103, 104–6
Jefferson, Maria, 104
Jefferson, Martha Wayles, 104
Jefferson, Thomas, 83, 99, 102, 104, 107
Jefferson family, 104
Job Ayuba ben Solomon, 148
Johannes (passenger ship), 194n28
Johnson, George, 124
Johnson, Isaac, 116
joking relationships among
  Senegambian ethnicities, 186n79
Jones, Robert, 81
junkanoo festivals, 52, 63

Kentucky, 101, 115, 116–17, 121, 150, 152
kidnapping, slavery due to, 53–54, 90
kinship, situationally created, 54–55, 87
Kirmayer, Lawrence, 155–56
Kline, Charles, 140
Knipe, Sir Randolph, 42
Kongo, 9, 60, 64
Kromanti (Coromantee), xiii
Kulikoff, Alan, 69–70, 71, 72, 83

Lambek, Michael, 12; *The Weight of the
  Past,* 157, 158, 183n20

Lamu, 138
land, entailment or annexation of
  slaves to, 71–72, 183n22
Larson, Pier, 131, 133, 138, 142–43;
  Ocean of Letters, 88
Lebsock, Susan, 105
Lee, Lisa B., 187n87
Lee, Robert E., 96
Lee, William (former slave of George
  Washington), 103
Lee family, 95–96, 187n87
Leeward Islands, 176n9
Leo (Carter plantation), 103
Levy, Robert, 118
Lewis family, 75, 96
"Little England" estate, Hampton, 119
Louisiana, 53, 171n35
Lovejoy, Paul, 7–8, 59, 171n35
Luanda, 68
Luber, Jack, 182n5
luso-African or lusophone
  populations, 55, 59
Lynchburg (Virginia), 95, 103, 105–8

Madagascar, 23–35; creole communities
  of, 28–29, 59, 60, 93; exile of
  Ranavalona III, 149–50; family oral
  traditions and Anglo-American
  networks in, 33–35; geography
  of, 24; in global context, 31–32;
  historical background, 24–29; legal
  North American slave trading in,
  29–31; map with central ports, *23*;
  merchant activity in, 130–31; Merina
  state (Imerina), 129–30, 164–65;
  number of slaves brought from,
  xi, 37, 40, 45, 48, 51, 72–73, 167n1,
  176n12; pirates and piracy in, 3, 26–
  30, 173n20, 174n22, 174n30; shipment
  of captives to Virginia from, xi, 3,
  30–33, 39–43; slaves in, 57, 65–66,
  127, 182n2; slave trade in, ix–x, 1–4,
  25–31, 38–39
Madagascar Jack (slave of Robert
  "King" Carter), 81
Madden, T. O., and Madden family,
  55, 89–90, 179n57
Mahajanga (Majunga; Madagascar), 3,
  23, 42, 131, 133, 161

Mahammitt, Jeremiah, 139–41, 142, 161–62, 195n32
Mahammitt, Jerry, 140, 194n27
Mahammitt, John, 139
Mahammitt, Joshua, 140
Mahammitt, Josiah, 140
Mahammitt, Thomas, 140
Mahammitt, Walter, 140, 194n30
Mahavelona (Foulpointe; Madagascar), 28, 29
Mahomet, Hannah, 140
Mahomet, Jeremiah (Ali Salaha Mahomet), 138–39, 194nn27–28
Mahomet, John, 139
Mahomet, Margaret, 139, 140, 141, 194n27
Mahomet/Mahammitt and Gregory families, 138–41, 142
Maintirano (Madagascar), 133
Majunga (Mahajanga; Madagascar), 3, 23, 42, 131, 133, 161
Malagasy in North America, ix–xvi, 1–22; domestic slave market, 101 (*see also* domestic slave market); exceptionality or difference trope, xii–xiii, 2, 54, 61, 90, 145; in family oral tradition, ix–x, 5–7, 10–12 (*see also* family oral tradition); as free blacks, 102–8 (*see also* free blacks); free immigration, xiii–xiv, 3, 21, 129–43 (*see also* free immigration); gender, lineage, and descent, xii; geographical and chronological focus, xi, 3; in history and ethnography, 12–16; illegal slave trade, 20–21, 100–101 (*see also* illegal slave trade); as metanarrative, 21–22, 144–59 (*see also* metanarrative); methodological approach, xiv–xvi, 3–4, 17–19; physiognomic distinction of, xii, 54, 82, 93, 121–22, 145; reasons for specific survival of identity of, 59–61; settlement and distribution of, 20, 65–98 (*see also* settlement and distribution); slave cohorts of 1719–21, 19–20, 36–64 (*see also* slave cohorts of 1719–21). *See also* identity; Madagascar; slavery and slave trade

Malagasy language, 24–25, 62, 88, 133, 140–41, 142, 161–62
Malay descent, claims of, 136
Mananjary (Madagascar), 29, 163
Mande, 9
manumission, 85–87, 99–100, 102–3
Manumission Act (Virginia, 1782), xi, 86, 99, 102
maritime workers. *See* sailors and seamen
maroons and maroon communities, 51, 53, 88, 170n22, 170n26
marriage: ability of slave couples to live together, 83–84; away from home plantation, 80; endogamous and exogamous, 57, 164; to Malagasy partners, 87–89, 91–92
Maubrey family, 175–76n4
Mauritius, 27, 48, 115, 126, 130–33, 142, 192n72
maximal lineage, 25, 164
McCaw, Melvin, 186n72
McCaw family, 90
McDonald, Kevin, 174n30
McKizzic, Oscar, 113–14
McMillin, James, *The Final Victims*, 110–11
Meade, David, 79
memory, 12, 155–57
men. *See* gender
Menabe Sakalava, 27, 164, 165
merchants, as free immigrants, 130–31, 134, 136
Mercury (slave ship), 42, 43, 95
Merina state (Imerina; Madagascar highlands), 129–30, 164–65
Meriweather family, 96
meta-ethnicity, 59, 60
metamemory, 156
metanarrative, 21–22, 144–59; ancestors, signifying presence of, 157–59; defined, 21–22, 144; exile of Ranavalona III and, 149–50; in family oral tradition, 151–55; memory and, 12, 155–57; noble savage, idea of, 147–51, 154; purpose of, 144–47
Methodists, 85, 102
Mexico, slavery and slave trade in, 101, 108

physiognomic distinction of Malagasy, xii, 54, 82, 93, 121–22, 145
pirates and piracy: in Madagascar, 3, 26–30, 93, 173n20, 174n22, 174n30; the noble savage and, 147; slave cohorts of 1719–21 in Virginia and, 38, 39–40, 44, 45, 49
planters and planter families, 73, 74; American Revolution and, 85–87; freeing of slaves by, 85; hyperhistoricity of, 37; inheritance practices, 71, 73, 76, 78, 84–85; investment in slave trade by, 47; large versus small plantations, 68–69, 72; naming of slaves by, 66; origins of, 37, 175–76n4; relationships with slaves, 66–68; sales of slaves between, 47, 49; settlement and distribution of slaves and interrelationships of, 73–81, 74, 89; surname of master, slaves using, 72, 96, 125; westward spread of, 89, 100, 108. See also specific families and individuals
Platt, Virginia Bever, 32, 45, 46, 174n22, 181b74
Polks, 140
Port Louis (Mauritius), 131
Portelli, Alessandro, 33, 34, 96, 115
Potomac River (Virginia), slaves on, 75, 76
Price, Richard, 14–15, 16, 55, 57, 58, 62, 63, 147; First Time, 51, 170n26
Prince Eugene (slave ship), 32–33, 39, 42, 43, 44–45, 50, 95, 178n47
Prince George County (Virginia), 103
Prince William County (Virginia), 82
"Prize Negroes" of Cape Town, 132–33, 136
Pronis, Sieur (Huguenot slave trader), 27, 173n17
Prosser, Gabriel, 106, 188–89n22
Puckett, Eddie (Ali ben Ali "Butcherknife"), 137–38
Puckett, John, 137

Quakers (Society of Friends), 85, 102, 106, 112, 121, 122, 123, 188n18
Quarles, Moses, 50

race: hair as marker of, 93; physiognomy and, 121–22; slave ships producing, 41. See also black people in America, as homogeneous unit; mixed white/black ancestry
Radama I (Merina ruler), 130
Ragland, George, 187n87
Ragland, John D., 94
Ragland family, 94–96, 187n86
Ragsdale family, 96
Rahena (Betsimisaraka princess), 28
Rakekata and descendants, 135–36, 141, 153, 187n3
Ranavalona I (Merina ruler), 130
Ranavalona III (queen of Madagascar), 149–50
Randolph, Sir John, 46, 47, 76, 99, 120
Randolph, John, of Roanoke, 120
Randolph, Pascal Beverly, 115, 119–20, 191n58
Randolph, Thomas, 50
Randolph family and plantations, 73, 74, 77, 81, 95–96, 99, 104, 187n87
Rappahannock River (Virginia), slaves on, xi, 30, 36, 44, 48–49, 65, 72, 74, 75, 79, 176n12
Ratsimilaho (Betsimisaraka leader), 28–29
Razaf, Andy, 150
Rebecca Snow (slave ship), 33, 44, 45
Rediker, Marcus, 40–41, 44, 173n20
reenslavement of free blacks, 103
religion and religious groups, 85, 102, 103, 106, 107, 135–36, 159, 186n74. See also specific religions and denominations by name
Réunion, 48, 130, 149
Revolutionary War, 85–87, 102, 185n58
Rhodes, Phillip Wayne, 107
Richmond (Virginia), 81, 94, 95, 96, 103, 105–7, 117, 120, 123, 133, 188n22, 189n25
Rippon Hall (plantation), 73
ritual, retention of, 52, 63, 141, 195n32
Robin (runaway slave), 82
Robinson, William H., 115–16
Rosewell (plantation), 73
Rosicrucian movement, 119

Rothman, Joshua, 93, 107
runaway slaves, 76, 81–82, 86, 87, 105, 187n3

sailors and seamen, 134–43; with British navy and merchant ships, 129, 132, 138; in family oral traditions, 87–88, 115–16, 134, 138; freed Malagasy slaves as, 132–33; marriage partner from Madagascar, seeking, 87–88
Saint Helena (island), 41–43, 44, 45, 57
Saint Mary's County (Maryland), 60, 61, 82–83
Saint Mary's Island (Madagascar), 23, 27, 28, 30, 32, 46, 59, 165
Sakalava, 25, 27, 29, 58, 130, 164, 165
Sallee, Abraham, 50
saltwater slaves: creole/country-born slaves, relationship with, 56, 58–59, 67–68, 77–78, 80; as runaways, 81; as term for emigrating generation, 56. See also illegal slave trade; slave cohorts of 1719–21 in Virginia
Sam (runaway slave), 76, 82
Saramaka, 51, 52, 53
Saunders, Christopher, 133, 136
Savannah (Georgia), 133
Scott family, 114
seamen. See sailors and seamen
"Second Middle Passage," 181n76
Senegambian ethnicities: African American descent from, 9; Arabic, knowledge of, 168n8; Carter's preference for, 78; on Carter plantations, 71; European interactions of, 60; identity formation and maintenance, 171n35; joking relationships, 186n79; Malagasy, interaction with, 68; in Virginia, 48, 55, 76, 184n35, 186n79
servants, as free immigrants, 94, 141
settlement and distribution, 20, 65–98; American Revolution, planter and slave responses to, 85–87; of child slaves, 68, 70–71, 92; division of slaves into units, 69–71, 80–81; ethnic and cultural groups, 68, 71, 77–78, 80–81; family oral

tradition and, 87–98; gender and transmission of culture, 92–94; gender distribution of slaves, 68–69, 77–78; in historical record, 66–73; inheritance practices and, 71, 73, 76, 78, 84–85; land, entailment or annexation of slaves to, 71–72, 183n22; large versus small plantations, 68–69, 72; Malagasy identity, retention of, 81–84, 87–98; manumission, 85–87, 91–92; planter families and, 73–81, 74, 89; population stabilization, 69–70; traveling of slaves with masters, 86–87. See also families/households
sex. See gender
Shaw, Rosalind, 175n3
Sheppard, Elizabeth, 49
Shields, Mrs., 119
shipmates: arrival in Virginia, 43–44, 46; concept of, xiv, 172n40; continued existence of networks of, 20; illegal slave trade's absence of, 118–19; plantation culture and communication of, 76–77; shared experience of Middle Passage by, 40; situationally created kinship of, 54–55, 87
Shirley plantation, 103, 104, 106
Shrubbery Hill (Crenshaw house, Virginia), 122–23
Sidis and Sidi lineages, 138, 182n1
Sierra Leone, 175n3
situationally created kinship, 54–55, 87
slave cohorts of 1719–21, 19–20, 36–64; arrival in Virginia, 43–47; construction of new cultural self, 62–64; ethnic and cultural cohesiveness of, 37, 45, 48–49, 53–56, 62; family and oral traditions reflecting, 51–55; health, illnesses, and mortality of, 42, 45, 49, 51; historical record on, 38–39; loss and trauma experienced by, 37–38, 43–44, 48, 56–57; Middle Passage from Madagascar, 39–43; North American slave trade in Madagascar and, 30–31; numbers of, 37, 40, 45, 48, 51, 176n12;

www.ingramcontent.com/pod-product-compliance
Lightning Source LLC
Chambersburg PA
CBHW072103020426
42334CB00017B/1609